W9-AZJ-098

UNDERSTANDING, MAINTAINING, AND RIDING THE TEN-SPEED BICYCLE

UNDERSTANDING, MAINTAINING, AND RIDING

THE TEN-SPEED BICYCLE

BY
DENISE M. de la ROSA &
MICHAEL J. KOLIN

Illustrated by Joseph R. Horvath

Photography by Sally Ann Shenk

 Rodale Press, Emmaus, Pennsylvania

Copyright © 1979 by Denise M. de la Rosa
and Michael J. Kolin

All rights reserved. No part of this
publication may be reproduced or
transmitted in any form or by any means,
electronic or mechanical, including
photocopy, recording, or any information
storage and retrieval system without the
written permission of the publisher.

Printed in the United States of America on
recycled paper, containing a high percentage
of de-inked fiber.

**Library of Congress Cataloging in
Publication Data**

De la Rosa, Denise M
     Understanding, maintaining, and riding
the ten-speed bicycle.

     Bibliography: p.
     Includes index.
     1. Bicycles and tricycles.   2. Bicycles
and tricycles—Maintenance and repair.
3. Cycling.   I. Kolin, Michael J., joint
author.   II. Title.   III. Title: The ten-speed
bicycle.
TL410.D43   629.22′72   79-17619
ISBN 0-87857-268-6   hardcover
ISBN 0-87857-281-3   paperback

     4   6   8   10   9   7   5   3   hardcover
     4   6   8   10   9   7   5   3   paperback

Photo 2–5, page 30, courtesy of
     TI Raleigh Limited.
Photo 11–3, page 243, courtesy of
     Eclipse.
Photo 11–4B, page 245, courtesy of
     Kirtland.

This book is dedicated to our parents.

CONTENTS

Contents

ACKNOWLEDGMENTS

We would like to thank the many individuals, all authorities in their respective fields, who provided invaluable aid: Mike Walden; Greg Hine, Kirtland Tour Pak; Bob Williams, Frostline Kits; Jean Alley, Touring Cyclist Shop; Jerry Keefe, Velocipac/Sojourn Designs; Patti Prestidge, Bell Helmets; Gene Smith, Cycle Components; Sven Yelusid, Zeus Cyclery Corp.; James T. Howell, Jr., National Cotton Council of America; Lynn Parker Smith, Redwood Cycling Clothing; Emily K; Oliver Martin, Jr., Protogs; Alfred Todrys, Todson, Inc.; Fran Mattera, Izumi Chain Co.; Alain Breuil, TA; Amos York and Michele Chiarella, Campagnolo/USA; A. Raimond, Ateliers de Champirol; Zane Seely, Grab-On Products; D. L. Ward, Dahltron Corp.; Steve Jasik, Jasik Designs; M. De Vivie, Cibie Projecteurs; B. de Lattre, Soubitez; Raymond N. Seakan, Bike Security Systems; Margie Foley, KBL Corp.; Russell A. Bauer, Master Lock Co.; E. J. Healy, Bluemels; J. Gordon Dixon, Halt!; Rip H. S. Rippey, Jr., RVW; David Chaney, Safety Sport Mirror; H. C. Stebbins, Stewart Warner; Patricia Vail, Falcon Safety Products; Al Edge, DEMCO; R. J. Bakewell, Sturmey-Archer; R. P. O'Donovan, TI Raleigh; Alan Goldsmith, Bikecology; Mel Pinto; Bert Matissen, Beconta; F. Van Donselaar, Wolber; M. A. Mai and D. Setton, Hutchinson; F. Beker, Canetti; H. L. Adamczyk, Michelin Tire Co.; Howard C. Hawkins, Park Tool Co.; Alain and Roger Huret; Harlan Meyer, Hi-E; John Dykstra, Dri-Slide; George De Moss, LPS Research Laboratories, Inc.; Harold Graham, Paket Corp.; Robert Johnson, R.W.J., Inc.; Edward Borysewicz, USCF cycling coach; Rick Schwinn; Cino and Andrea Cinelli; Jerry Baker; and many others too numerous to mention. We would also like to extend a very special thanks to James C. McCullagh, editor of *Bicycling* magazine; Susan Weiner, copy editor; and the staff at Rodale Press.

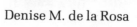

Denise M. de la Rosa   Michael J. Kolin

INTRODUCTION

This book was written in response to the countless, unanswered questions about how to equip, maintain, and ride the 10-speed bicycle. Furthermore, we hoped to dispel many "myths" surrounding bicycle equipment. Although several good books describing bicycle repairs are available, we've never come across a book that explains the advantages or disadvantages among bicycle and component designs. For instance, which is "better":

- Sidepull or centerpull brakes?
- Clincher or tubular tires?
- Cottered or cotterless cranks?
- Alloy or steel handlebars?
- Leather or plastic saddles?
- Quick-release or nutted hubs?

Of course, there are no simple answers to these questions. "Better" is a relative term which is meaningless unless we match the actual use of a component with its design intentions. For example, a five-ounce silk tire might be better for a speed record than a heavier, wired-on tire, but it would be totally impractical for normal day-to-day commuting. Most cyclists have little trouble in making decisions between two products with intended uses that are as obviously different as our tire example. It isn't quite so simple to evaluate the good points or the bad points of two pairs of hand brakes—sidepull vs. centerpull, for instance.

The bicycle is a highly refined tool that is designed to meet one or more needs. To get the most from the bicycle, the rider should make every effort to match the design intentions of the bicycle (and its components) to his or her riding requirements.

How does the cyclist evaluate a bicycle, its components, and accessories? The first place to start is your local bicycle shop. Sometimes the mechanics are untrained in the subtleties of the advantages or disadvantages of all of their products, but who else has more interest in the product or in satisfying you as a customer? If nothing else, we hope that after reading this book, the reader will be able to make a logical evaluation of the good and bad features on the majority of cycling components and accessories. Combine the information in this book with the opinions expressed at your bicycle shop. Most important, physically examine the bicycle or components to complete your own evaluations. The cycling requirements of the racer who rides 500 miles per week on a lightweight bicycle that is maintained daily by a team mechanic will be very different from the requirements of the recreational cyclist who wants a light bike for pleasure use.

Before we go any further, we must clarify our position. We are not experts in all areas of cycling. Our many years of racing and touring plus the benefits of owning and operating a bicycle store (which specialized in quality lightweight bicycles) taught us that we *don't* know all the answers. We did discover that the best way to learn is to ask questions. And we learned *who* to question.

Accordingly, *The Ten-Speed Bicycle* is not a compilation of our "pet" cycling theories. Instead, it is a review of the answers to our many questions. In every case, we approached the world's cycling experts and repeatedly asked, "why?" We went to the technical experts such as Clement, D'Allessandro, and Cannetti for the answers to tire questions; to Campagnolo, Shimano, and Sun Tour for answers to questions about brakes and derailleurs; and to the wool and cotton industries (as well as the jersey manufacturers) to prove or disprove widespread beliefs and opinions. In short, unless we indicate that a statement is our opinion, the information we present is based on the results of our thorough research on every available type of bicycle equipment. This research consists of our personal riding and repair experiences, the advice and design theories of the equipment manufacturers, and interviews with actual users of the equipment.

For your convenience, we have separated the book into chapters that deal with individual components or related groups of components. In each chapter, we attempt to describe the intent of each product; the variations that occur (sidepull vs. centerpull vs. cantilever brakes, for instance); the advantages and disadvantages of each; and basic repair or maintenance information. Individual brand names are used only if we believe a product stands out as truly superior or unique.

Each component chapter also includes charts that are designed to summarize information for easy reference. Essentially, there are two different kinds of charts. In a component-by-component summary, one group of charts lists the characteristics, advantages, and disadvantages of sidepull, centerpull, cantilever, and disc brakes, reviewed in one handy reference. Similarly, another chart covering problem diagnosis and repair tips can be found in each component chapter.

CHAPTER ONE

FRAMES

The frame is the largest single part of the bicycle. It is the skeleton onto which all of the components attach. In terms of frame *design*, selecting a bicycle for a child is easy. A boy gets a "boy's" bicycle and a girl gets a "girl's" bicycle. The only real difference is the "cross bar," or its proper term, the top tube. There is no real reason for the distinction, since the top tube is removed solely to accommodate wearing a dress.

Since children's bicycles are made for strength and durability rather than performance, the frame is constructed with heavy pipe or seamed tubing. Because performance is considered more important in adult bicycles, tubing of lighter weight is used and the standard ladies frame isn't strong enough. Most women ride 10-speed bicycles with the diamond (the correct term for men's) frame. The top tube provides additional strength for cornering, braking, accelerating, and hill climbing.

Riders who desire a lightweight bicycle without a top tube usually ride a mixte frame. At first glance it looks like a ladies frame, but closer examination reveals that instead of two down tubes that attach to the head and seat tubes, it has two small tubes that run from the head to the sides of the seat tube and to the back where they join the rearstays at the fork ends. This frame configuration provides similar handling to the diamond frame but still permits riding with a skirt.

Unlike other bicycle components that are fairly easy to evaluate (it's easy to determine which derailleur shifts best and which brakes stop the best), the bicycle frame is difficult to judge since small design variations can alter the characteristics of, and recommended use of, the bicycle.

To better understand why some frames cost $600 while similar-looking frames cost $125, let's take a look at the parts that go together to complete a frame; the varying assembly techniques; and the design philosophies of transportation, sports, and racing bicycles.

A

B

C

Photo 1–1: **Basic Frame Styles.** The ladies-style frame (A) is usually found on only utility and children's bicycles, since the absence of the top tube affects the overall strength of the frame.

The mixte frame (B) allows the cyclist to ride with a skirt. However, its twin down tubes running from the head tube to the rearstays provide more strength than the standard ladies frames.

The standard frame style for 10-speeds is the diamond frame (C). It is unexcelled for overall lightness and strength.

MAIN TRIANGLE

There are two basic methods for building a frame: with or without lugs. In general, lugless frames are found on inexpensive bicycles since it is the lesser complicated of the two methods of construction. Inexpensive lugless frames are usually made of pipe and are welded together. Unlike a tube which is seamless, a pipe (also called a welded tube) has a seam. This method of manufacture is wholly satisfactory when light weight is not important; strength of the joint is accomplished by heavy, thick-gauge pipe. But remember that such construction is intended for utility use rather than performance. In some rare instances, high-quality super-light bicycles *are* built without lugs. These are generally special-purpose bicycles

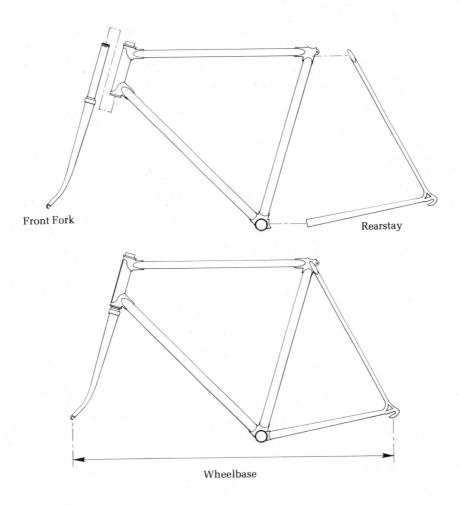

Front Fork

Rearstay

Wheelbase

Figures 1–1A and 1–1B:
Main triangles, including front fork, rearstays, and wheelbase.

that receive special assembly and treatment. The vast majority of quality 10-speed bicycles are built with lugs, and for good reason. The lug provides a greatly increased brazing area and the benefit of additional strength without a large weight penalty.

There are two basic types of lugs: cast and pressed steel. The cast lug is rarely used because its strength is not required under most riding conditions. Moreover, the nature of the cast lug tends to make it less convenient for normal frame building. The pressed lug is basically a steel pressing which has been formed, welded at the joint, and machined to perfect roundness. The quality of the pressed lug has increased to the point where it is almost always the manufacturing norm because of adequate strength, reasonable cost, and ease of use.

The bottom bracket is also available in cast or pressed steel. Many custom frame builders believe that the cast bottom bracket is required in a racing bicycle because of the enormous stresses that occur when pedaling. The cast bottom bracket is considerably more expensive and takes much more work to produce an aesthetically pleasing finished product.

Although the frame tubing can be joined in the lugs using CO_2 welding with oxygen–acetylene, bronze brazing is recommended by the tubing manufacturers and is the method used by most quality builders. Bronze has the advantage of being relatively easy to use, is readily available, and flows at a fairly low temperature with a wide dispersion of heat. Excessive heat during the building process is the number one enemy of the lightweight tube, too much heat makes the tube brittle and prone to early failure. A popular alternative to bronze is a mixture of silver solder. However, the high material

THE FRAME

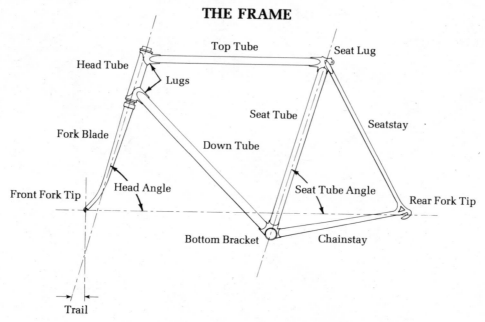

Figure 1–2:
Detail of bicycle frame and fork-rake angle.

TRAIL

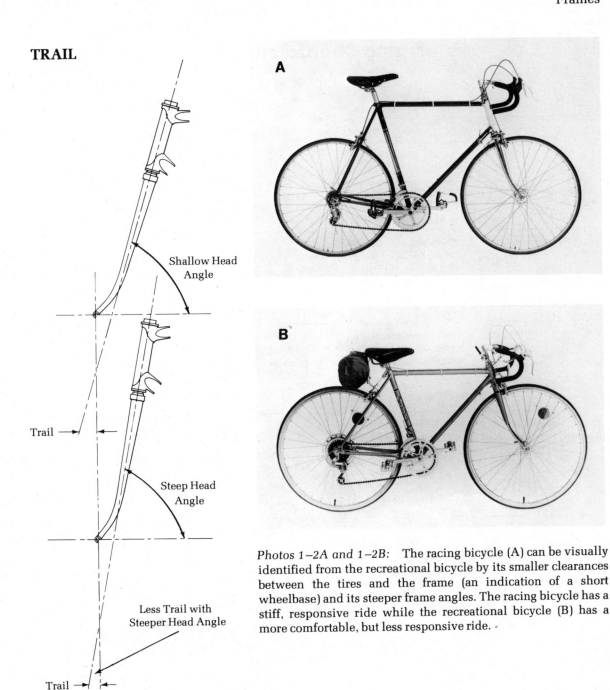

Shallow Head Angle

Steep Head Angle

Trail

Less Trail with Steeper Head Angle

Trail

A

B

Photos 1–2A and 1–2B: The racing bicycle (A) can be visually identified from the recreational bicycle by its smaller clearances between the tires and the frame (an indication of a short wheelbase) and its steeper frame angles. The racing bicycle has a stiff, responsive ride while the recreational bicycle (B) has a more comfortable, but less responsive ride.

Figure 1–3:
Stability increases as the amount of trail increases.

Frame Characteristics

	Frame Construction	Wheelbase/Frame Angles	Design Intent
Transportation Bicycle	Pipe (welded tubing) might or might not have lugs	Very long wheelbase; shallow angles	General transportation; reliability and sturdiness over performance
Inexpensive Sports Bicycle	Low-carbon pipe (welded tubing) might or might not have lugs	Long wheelbase; shallow angles	General transportation and recreational
Basic Sports Bicycle	High-carbon, seamless-tubing frame with lugs and stamped fork ends	Fairly short wheelbase with sports angles: 72- to 73-degree parallel angles	Recreational
Serious Sports Bicycle	Lugged frame with double-butted tubes; forged fork ends	Wheelbase reflects design intent of bicycles—specialization begins here	Sports or touring depending on special design
Professional Sports Bicycle	Lugged frame with double-butted tubes; forged fork ends	Wheelbase reflects design intent of bicycles—specialization begins here	Sports or touring depending on special design
Racing Bicycle	Lugged frame with double-butted tubes; forged fork ends	Very short wheelbase; steep frame angles. Custom designed to rider's needs	Performance more important than comfort

cost and increased need of assembly accuracy normally limits its use to only light-gauge tubing.

The strength of a joint is dependent upon the fit of the components and the proficiency of the person who brazes them together. If the gap between the tube and the lug is too large, too much braze will be required. If the gap is too small, too little braze will be able to enter and insure the strength of the joint. The quality of the lug and builder's preparation to insure proper tolerances will have a measurable effect on the strength of the joint. The importance of the fit can be best demonstrated when silver braze is used. The properties of silver require that the gap between tubes and lug not exceed 0.003 inch to insure a strong joint!

Bicycle Characteristics	Weight	Price	Comments
Nonresponsive upright riding position	Heavy (over 35 lbs.)	Inexpensive (under $100)	Ideal for short-distance commuting in all kinds of weather
Fairly responsive drop-handlebar position	Moderate (30–35 lbs.)	Inexpensive ($100–135)	The bicycle for the performance-oriented rider with a strict budget
Fairly responsive drop-handlebar position	Fairly light (28–32 lbs.)	Moderate ($135–200)	The bicycle for the sports rider. It includes many inexpensive alloy components; quick-release hubs; more alloy components.
Responsive drop-handlebar position	Light (24–28 lbs.)	Expensive ($200–400)	For the serious rider who can tell the difference in quality and whose long-distance use demands reliability and ease of repair.
Fairly responsive drop-handlebar position	Light (21–24 lbs.)	Very expensive ($400–1,000)	Frame is basically the same as found in the serious sports bicycle. The difference in price reflects the quality of finish and the quality of components used.
Very responsive; very stiff	Very light (18–23 lbs.)	Very, very expensive ($700–1,500)	The bicycle and its components are designed with performance as the primary objective. Cost considerations are secondary.

One prime difference between most production and quality frames is the practice of mitering all the tubes on a quality frame. A mitered tube is shaped to fit around the tube it butts against. The unmitered tube leaves room for movement inside the lug under extreme stress. The tube that has been mitered cannot move. Careful mitering can be time consuming, but its importance is recognized by all manufacturers.

After the tubes and lugs have been properly sized and prepared, the pieces are ready to be brazed. How does the builder hold all the pieces and, at the same time, braze them in perfect alignment? Most builders use a jig to guarantee that the various parts fit properly and maintain perfect alignment during the brazing process.

(continued on page 13)

LUGS

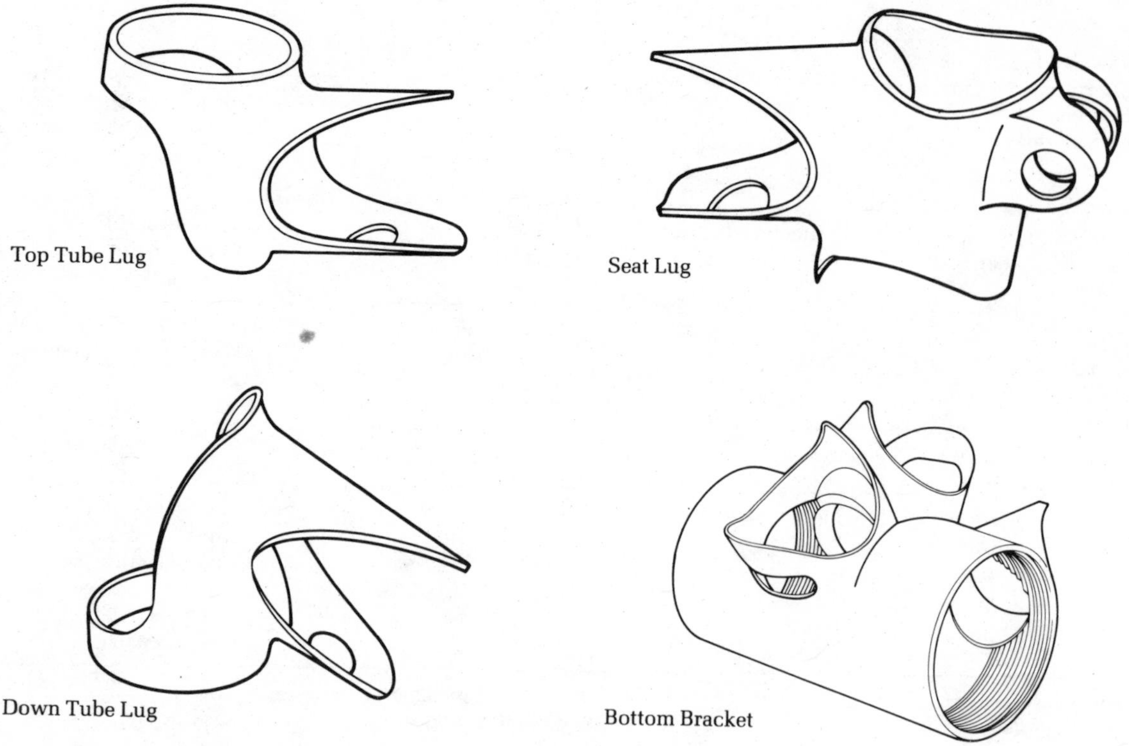

Top Tube Lug

Seat Lug

Down Tube Lug

Bottom Bracket

Figure 1–4: Four bicycle lugs.

Photo 1–3: A simple test for evaluating frame flex is performed as follows:

• Hold the bicycle by the saddle and the handlebars;

• Lean the top of the bicycle away from you;

• Step on the pedal nearest you (with the pedal at the bottom of its stroke).

This approximates the effect of each pedal stroke on the frame. By performing this test on several bicycles, you will be able to see obvious strength differences that are unnoticeable by visual inspection.

Photos 1–4A and 1–4B: Estimating the frame size is easiest by looking at the intersection of the frame tubes at the head tube. The amount of distance between the top tube and the down tube at the head tube is an indicator of the size of the frame. (A) This is a 21-inch frame and B is a 19½-inch frame.

Sports Bicycle Characteristics

	Frames	Handlebars and Stems	Handlebar Tapes
Inexpensive Sports Bicycle	Lugged frame usually with seamed tubing (pipe) Low-carbon steel Stamped fork ends Little time spent on final detailing	Steel Exposed expander and binder bolts	Plastic
Basic Sports Bicycle	Lugged frame with seamless tubing High-carbon steel Stamped fork ends Little time spent on final detailing	Dull-finish alloy Exposed (nutted) expander and binder bolts	Plastic or cloth
Serious Sports Bicycle	Lugged frame with good-quality double-butted frame tubes Forged fork ends Moderate attention to final detailing	Polished alloy May be engraved Recessed allen-key binder and expander bolts	Cloth
Professional Sports/Racing Bicycle	Lugged frame with top-quality double-butted tubing Forged fork ends Great deal of attention to final detailing	Polished alloy Engraved Recessed allen-key binder and expander bolts	Cloth

Seatposts	Saddles	Brakes	Cranksets
Steel seat pillar with seat clamp	Plastic	Inexpensive steel side-pull or alloy centerpull brakes May have "safety" levers Will not have rubber brake-lever hoods or quick-release	Inexpensive steel with cotter-pin mounting
Steel or alloy seat pillar with seat clamp	Plastic	Good-quality alloy centerpull brakes Probably will have "safety" levers, rubber brake-lever hoods, and quick-release	Inexpensive, three-pin alloy cotterless cranks with stamped-alloy chainwheels; or a good-quality, steel cottered crank
Inexpensive micro-adjusting seatpost	Good-quality leather-top plastic saddle or good-quality leather saddle	Good-quality alloy side-pull or centerpull brakes Will not have "safety" levers Will have rubber brake-lever hoods and quick-release	Good-quality, five-pin cotterless alloy cranks Machined chainwheels
Top-quality alloy micro-adjusting seatpost	Top-quality leather-top plastic saddle or top-quality leather saddle	Top-quality sidepull brakes Will not have "safety" levers Will have rubber brake-lever hoods and quick-release	Top-quality, five-pin cotterless alloy cranks with machined chainwheels

Sports Bicycle Characteristics

(continued)

Pedals	Derailleurs	Hubs	Rims	Tires
Inexpensive steel Nonadjustable cones Very wide design for use with street shoes	Inexpensive steel derailleurs Slow, unresponsive shifting	Steel Three piece Low flange Nutted	Steel	Wired-on (clincher) Low pressure (55 lbs.)
Inexpensive steel Nonadjustable cones	Good-quality steel or plastic derailleurs (may also be partially alloy) Good, smooth shifting under most conditions	Alloy cast hub High flange Quick-release, nutted; or a combination with the quick-release on the front and the nutted on the rear	Steel	Wired-on (clincher) High-pressure gumwall (70 lbs. plus)
Steel or alloy Adjustable cones Narrow pedals designed for use with sports shoes	Good-quality alloy derailleurs Good, smooth shifting under most conditions	Alloy cast hub High or low flange Quick-release	Alloy	Wired-on (clincher) or sew-up cotton High pressure (70–90 lbs.)
Top-quality steel axle with alloy cage Accurate, adjustable cones Narrow pedal for use with bicycle shoes	Top-quality alloy derailleurs Very smooth shifting under all conditions— even uphill	Alloy cast hub High or low flange Quick-release	Alloy	Sew-up Top-quality cotton or silk

FORKS

Since it is the prime contributor to how the bicycle will handle, the fork is an interesting and complex part of the bicycle. The shape of the fork (which consists of tips, blades, crown, and steering column) can significantly increase or decrease responsiveness, comfort, and safety.

There are three types of construction for fork crowns: pressed steel (stamped), forged, and cast. Pressed crowns are usually found on inexpensive production bicycles. They are the weakest of the three types of fork crowns. Generally, high-quality frames include forged or cast crowns according to the use of the bicycle. Like a forged hand tool, the forged crown is produced with the grain of the steel "in line." It is very strong, but it requires a great deal of filing to properly clean the pitted finish. Like cast lugs, the cast crown is extremely expensive, very strong, and usually comes with the greatest degree of accuracy in tolerances.

All of the three types of fork crowns are stronger than the fork blades that are attached. Most fork failures occur immediately below the fork crown and are a direct result of the effects of extended use of tubes that have become brittle from overheating or damaged in a crash.

Fork blades vary in design according to their use. Since a road bicycle is fitted with brakes, the fork blade must be oval to eliminate the shuddering that would otherwise result under hard braking. Track bicycles, which have no brakes, have round fork blades due to the greatly increased stresses caused by centrifugal force and side-loading, the result of the banking of a track. In addition, since tracks are smooth surfaces, the necessity for a fork to act as a shock absorber is reduced.

Fork design has changed with the improvement in roads. Years ago, forks had a great deal of bend at the bottom which was necessary for adequate shock absorption. Racing bicycles of the fifties had more bend (rake) than the touring bicycles today. Current thinking in fork design is that as the radius of the bend in the fork is increased, the strength of the fork is increased.

CHAINSTAYS AND SEATSTAYS

Of all the parts of the frame, the chainstays seem to generate the least controversy. Some frame builders prefer round chainstays, some prefer oval, and some prefer round with indentations for tires and chainwheels. Yet paradoxically, most builders do not believe that there is a significant difference in actual use. While there are differences in the method of attaching the seatstays to the seat lug, methods tend to follow the current style trend.

As we indicated earlier, fairly subtle design variations can alter the handling characteristics, design intentions, and "feel" of a bicycle. For the purposes of this book, we will review only basic design theory and its effects.

Generally, there are three basic design areas in a frame: (1) long vs. short wheelbase, (2) steep vs. shallow angles, and (3) the size of the frame.

WHEELBASE

The wheelbase of a frame is the measurement between the front axle and the rear axle of the bicycle. This measurement can be estimated by simply looking sideways at the bicycle. Clearance of less than 2 inches between the *front tire* and *down tube* (and *rear tire* and the *seat tube*) indicate a short wheelbase (38–39 inches). Several additional inches of clearance at the same two points indicate a long wheelbase (greater than 40 inches).

If the bicycle is intended to include fenders, a long wheelbase is essential to provide enough clearance for the tire inside the fender and space to anchor the fender itself. Adequate clearance is particularly important for the front wheel as the wheel must turn freely without contact between the fender and the down tube. Long-wheelbase bicycles tend to provide a more comfortable ride and, therefore, are very popular with tourists.

On the other hand, short-wheelbase bicycles tend to ride harder but they are more responsive. They seem to magnify the effects of riding over a bump, but since bikes with a shorter wheelbase do not absorb as much of the rider's pedal stroke as those with a longer wheelbase, they are more popular with racers. Most noticeable is the difference between the long vs. the short wheelbase in terms of acceleration. Overall, the short-wheelbase bicycle is faster, but not more comfortable.

FRAME ANGLES

The complexity of a frame can probably be best illustrated by analyzing the difference in frame angles. Generally, the ultra-steep-angled racing bicycle will have 74-degree angles while the shallow touring bicycle will have 71-degree angles. The total difference is only 3 degrees, yet the handling of the bicycles is completely different!

In most cases, the head and seat angles

will be the same on any given bicycle. If they are the same, the bicycle is usually referred to as having "parallel angles." A bicycle with shallow parallel angles will "feel" very solid since it will tend to be very stable. This is true because, technically, the stability of a bicycle increases with a shallow head angle because the trail of the fork is increased (figure 1-3). Although there are other factors which will affect stability, the frame angles are most important.

Bicycles with shallow angles generally have fairly long wheelbases and are primarily designed for comfort and stability. The degree of comfort and stability will, of course, vary with the geometry of the bicycle. If the rider is interested in a bicycle that can be ridden without holding the handlebars on very rough (gravel) roads or with heavy packs and camping equipment, a bicycle with very shallow parallel angles should be selected (possibly 72 degrees). For all-around use with good stability but with increased responsiveness, slightly steeper parallel angles might be preferred (possibly 73 degrees). The racer who is interested in responsiveness over comfort might select even steeper angles (74-degree head and 73-degree seat angles). Specific applications require the careful analysis of an expert; however, the basic rule involving trail and its effect on stability remains true.

FRAME SIZES

Proper matching of the rider's individual physique to the bicycle is one of the most misunderstood areas of cycling. Proper sizing techniques have been closely guarded secrets by the cycling coaches. Little has been passed on to the consumer. Here are the most popular misconceptions about frame size.

INCORRECT

The bicycle frame is the correct size if the rider can stand over the top tube with 1½-inch clearance between crotch and top tube. Although this rule may make sense when sizing a child on a bicycle (to keep children from injuring themselves on the top tube), it has no relation to the proper position of the adult cyclist when riding the bicycle. This method of measurement does not take bottom bracket height into consideration. The rule would be appropriate only if the cyclist operated the bicycle by pushing with his or her feet on the ground instead of placing the feet on the pedals.

INCORRECT

Proper frame size is determined by dividing the height of the rider by 3. Example: Rider is 5 feet, 6 inches; therefore, frame size is 22 inches (66 ÷ 3 = 22). This method of determining frame size is inexact at best. Unfortunately, not everyone in the world is equally proportioned. While one person might have very short legs and a very long torso, another might have long legs and a very short torso. Although the two riders might be the same height, they could require different size frames.

INCORRECT

Proper frame size is determined by subtracting nine or ten inches from the measurement of the rider from the crotch to the floor in bare feet. Again, a "formula" rule does not take individual variation into consideration. This method of sizing, however, comes closer to approximating the true size of the frame than the previous two methods.

CORRECT

Determination of frame size takes a few minutes. But, isn't it worth a few minutes to guarantee a proper fit? The following photographs explain each step of the sizing process. It is important to understand that each of the steps should be taken in sequence, since each step will affect the outcome of each subsequent adjustment.

(continued on page 22)

Photo 1–5: **Step 1.**
Measure the distance from the head of the femur to the floor (in bare feet). Subtract 13¾ inches (35 centimeters) from that measurement to determine the correct frame size.

15

Photo 1–6: **Step 2.**
Adjust the tilt of the saddle using a yardstick as a guide. The tip of the
saddle should be *slightly higher* than the back of the saddle.

Photo 1–7: **Step 3.**
Adjust saddle height by placing both heels on the pedals. The saddle
is properly adjusted when there is a slight bend in the knees.

Photo 1–8: **Step 4.**
Adjust front-to-rear saddle position with both feet in the toe clips and the cranks parallel to the ground. Adjust the front-to-rear saddle position so that a plumb line dropped from the center of the knee falls through the pedal axis.

Photo 1—9: **Step 5.**
Handlebar position is determined by checking the set-up handlebar
positions outlined in chapter fourteen. In handlebar Position 1, the
rider's weight should be evenly balanced with the back in an angle
greater than 45 degrees.

Photo 1–10: **Step 6.**
In handlebar Position 2, the rider's back should drop slightly below 45 degrees and a plumb line dropped from the rider's nose will be slightly over one inch behind the handlebars.

Photo 1–11: **Step 7.**
In handlebar Position 3, a plumb line dropped from the rider's nose
should fall directly over the handlebars.

Rules of Thumb

- Always protect the frame from damage by the handlebar by wrapping the top tube with tape at the point where the handlebars touch when the front wheel is turned sideways.

- Apply a coat of wax to the frame and chrome components (not the sides of wheel rims) to preserve and protect the finish. Always put a small piece of tape under any type of frame-mounted accessory (derailleur control levers, water-bottle holders, and lights) to protect the paint from scratches.

- Whenever you lay your bicycle on its side, remember to put its left side *down*. Lying the bicycle on its right side can bend the derailleur.

- Generally, a frame can be straightened after a crash if the tubing is bent but not "kinked." If a tube has been kinked, the tube or the entire frame should be replaced.

- Do not plug the small holes that have been drilled in the fork blades, chainstays, and seatstays. They allow water trapped inside to evaporate. Never drill holes (to reduce weight) in the frame or any components. Most bicycle components are designed to withstand specific pressures or uses. Structural strength can be dangerously reduced by owner modification.

- Periodically check the adjustment of the headset bearings. This can be easily done by picking up the front end of the bicycle six inches from the ground, and dropping it. If it goes "clunk," the bearings are loose. Another check: actuate the front brake and, standing next to the bicycle, rock it forward and back. Loose headset bearings will be immediately obvious as the front fork "slops" back and forth.

CHAPTER TWO

BRAKES

The purpose of any braking system is to stop or decelerate a moving vehicle. Although the concept is simple, the design requirements are complex since the factors that affect brake design involve much more than how well the brakes slow the vehicle.

For instance, bicycle brakes must be light weight; they must not affect the performance of the vehicle when the brakes are not in use. Brakes must also be durable, long lasting, aerodynamic, and capable of exerting strong braking pressures without the benefit of hydraulics; and, at the same time, inexpensive.

The bicycle rider is inherently limited in the horsepower he or she can generate. Therefore, he or she requires the use of lightweight components that will perform a necessary function without failure. The importance of light weight can be illustrated by the automobile manufacturers who have realized recently that the easiest way to achieve good gas mileage is to reduce the gross weight of the automobile. Although steel is a relatively

inexpensive material to use for components, its production-cost advantages are overshadowed by the weight-reduction advantage inherent in the aluminum alloys. Consequently, quality lightweight bicycle components can be disproportionately expensive; however, the overall weight difference between steel and alloy may be slight.

The most important factor in determining the effect of weight on a bicycle is *where* the weight is located. Revolving weight (the mass that must be moved under normal operation: rims, tires, spokes) affects performance far more than stationary weight (saddle, handlebars, water bottle). This can be easily demonstrated by using your own bicycle. First, ride your bicycle with a two-pound weight firmly attached to the frame. Now, remove the two-pound weight and instead of using your wheels, use a set of wheels that are two pounds heavier. The most noticeable difference is the increased difficulty in accelerating the heavier revolving components. By attaching an external caliper-type brake on the bicycle frame, the overall feel of the bicycle is lighter than it would be if motorcycle-type drum brakes were used. In other words, the brakes should not affect the handling or performance of the bicycle as a result of increased weight or friction.

Since wind resistance is another important performance factor, the brakes must be small enough to minimize the disruption of air flow. This is a particularly difficult design requirement because considerable force is required to slow a fast-moving bicycle. Since cost and weight problems eliminate the use of hydraulics (which can multiply the amount of force applied by the brake pads against the rim), bicycle brakes make use of the principles of leverage. Bicycle hand brakes can translate moderate hand pressure into the extremely strong pressure of the brake pads against the rim. Simply stated, hand pressure is increased by:

- The brake lever
    and
- The pivot arm of the brake itself.

Now that we have reviewed the basic design theory, let's look at the types of brakes that are found on today's lightweight bicycles.

Photo 2–1:   Closeup view of sidepull brake.

SIDEPULL BRAKES

How does the sidepull brake work? The braking action begins as the rider squeezes the brake lever that pulls the brake cable. The other end of the brake cable is attached to one of the brake arms (calipers). When the rider pulls the cable, one of the arms is raised by the inner cable, one arm is lowered by the outer cable housing, and the brake pads are forced against the rim. The tolerances of the moving parts are critical since the two arms (which are shaped differently) can cause uneven pressure against the rim. Moreover, sloppy manufacturing tolerances can make minor adjustments more difficult. A frequent problem is the tendency for one brake pad to contact the rim before the other pad.

Paradoxically, the sidepull brake can be found on both the least and most expensive bicycles! Nonetheless, even though the less-expensive bikes may include sidepull brakes, the two types are very different in construction and operation.

The inexpensive sidepull brake is made

out of steel and is chromed to prevent rust. Although this brake will adequately stop all but the fastest moving bicycles, its technically unsophisticated design does not optimally multiply the force applied at the brake lever. As a rule, the cheaper sidepull brake is found on a bicycle with "upright" handlebars; consequently, the brake lever is shaped differently than the brake lever that is designed for use with "drop" bars. Reduced brake leverage (a result of the long calipers made necessary by the larger rim-to-frame clearance on less-expensive bikes) causes the brake to feel spongy and unresponsive. On the other hand, the racing-type sidepull brake is manufactured to exacting standards calling for extremely short caliper arms which make up a brake that is reliable and responsive.

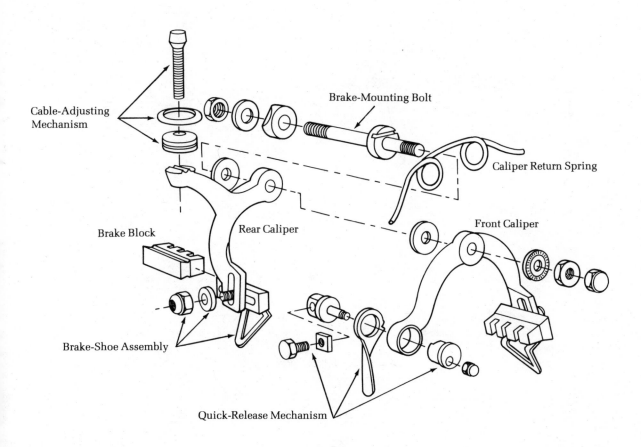

Figure 2–1:   **Sidepull Brake (Exploded View).**

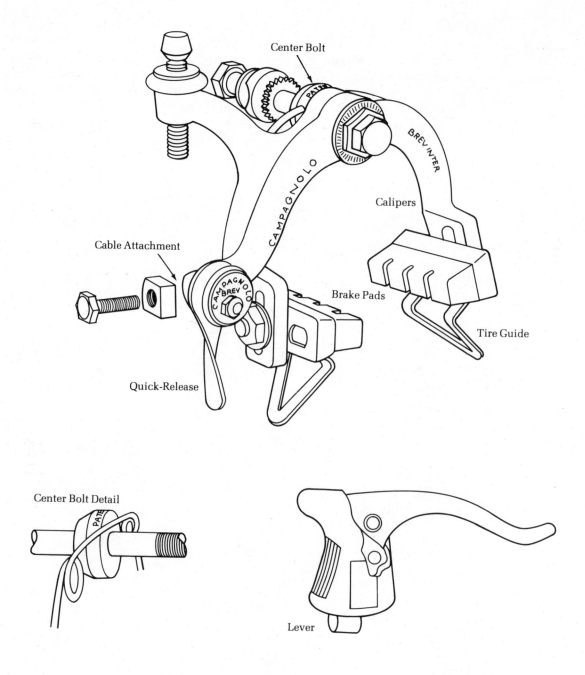

Figure 2–2: **Campagnolo Sidepull Brake.** All other brakes are measured against the standards set by the engineering and manufacturing quality of the Campagnolo brake.

CENTERPULL BRAKES

Because of the smooth action and efficient stopping power of the centerpull brake, it has become the most popular brake on middle-quality 10-speed bicycles. The similarity between the sidepull and the centerpull brake ends at the brake lever.

The two calipers on the centerpull brake are virtually identical, except that one caliper is placed behind the other. Unlike the sidepull brake that pivots from the center bolt, the centerpull brake has two separate pivot points—one for each arm. The pivot points are located at the ends of a fixed plate that utilizes a center bolt for attachment to the frame. Since the brake is actuated by a cable that stretches between the two arms, brake action is smooth and equally distributed through each caliper. It is quite easy to adjust a centerpull brake (and they tend to stay in adjustment longer), because slight movement of the backing plate moves *both* arms proportionately.

The cantilever brake, another type of centerpull brake, is rarely seen on production bicycles. This brake is the lightest of the bicycle brakes because it has no backing plate and has extremely short arms. Installation of the cantilever requires braze-on fittings on the front fork blades and rearstays, as the fittings are the sole means of attaching the brake to the frame. If sturdy cables are used, the braking action is very good due to the short brake arms (which limit caliper flex). Cantilever brakes are most frequently used on tandems and cyclo-cross frames. These brakes are particularly effective if the tire-to-fork clearance is large; "regular" brakes would require very long brake arms. Large clearances are required on cyclo-cross bicycles to permit mud that collects on the tires to pass through the fork openings.

Photo 2–2: Since the centerpull brake has two pivot points, it has two bolts that adjust free play in the caliper arms.

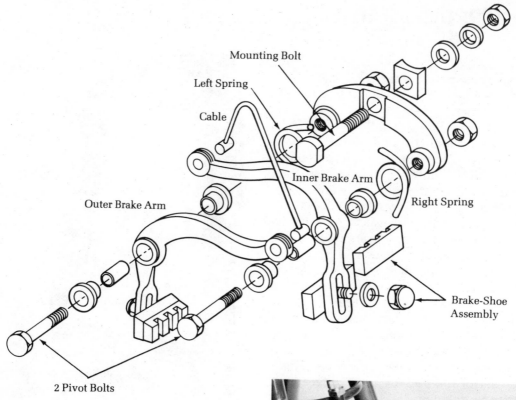

Figure 2–3: **Centerpull Brake (Exploded View).**
The complexity of a centerpull brake becomes
obvious in the exploded view. Unlike the sidepull
brake that has one return spring and one pivot
point, the centerpull has two pivot points, two
free-play adjustments, and two return springs
attached to the mounting plate.

Photo 2–3: The cantilever brake is a type of
centerpull brake; however, it is not mounted with
a backing plate. Instead, it utilizes braze-on frame
fittings for each caliper.

DRUM AND DISC BRAKES

Drum and disc brakes can also be used on lightweight bicycles. Both types are similar to those used on motorcycles and cars. Very simply, a drum brake relies on internal brake shoes which are expanded by the control cable. The advantage of a drum brake over a caliper brake is the large area of contact between the brake shoes and the drum. The disadvantage is the large weight penalty that is further magnified by the revolving mass of the brake itself. Most experts agree that existing caliper brakes can effectively stop the bicycle under most conditions. The effectiveness of bicycle-type caliper brakes is attested to by their use on the 100-mph, road-racing Honda Grand Prix motorcycles of the 1960s.

The disc brake utilizes a revolving disc that is mounted to the hub of the wheel. The calipers are located on opposite sides of the disc and are actuated by a control cable. Although the disc brake is the preferred high-performance stopping device for automobiles and motorcycles, it has several disadvantages for bicycles. It is heavy, very expensive to manufacture, and its high degree of stopping power is unnecessary on a lightweight bicycle under normal circumstances. There is one clear advantage to the drum and disc brake, however, and that is the superior stopping ability in wet conditions. But this advantage should not be overemphasized as proper adjustment and selection of hand-brake components will result in satisfactory stopping power. This has been demonstrated by professional bicycle racers who have unanimously selected sidepull and centerpull brakes.

Photo 2–4: The disc brake requires a hub-mounted disc with a frame-mounted caliper assembly. Although the unit is heavy and expensive, strong braking power is possible.

Photo 2—5: The drum brake is an integral part of the hub. Although its wet-weather braking is good, its heavy weight usually limits its popularity with sport riders. Some manufacturers provide steel rods instead of cables to actuate their brakes.

Photo 2—6: **Properly Adjusted Brake Shoe.** The brake shoe is parallel to the rim, and it is adjusted so that the entire face of the block will squarely contact the rim.

BRAKE SHOES

Brake shoes consist of a metal holder that fixes the rubber brake block (or pad) to the calipers. Brake blocks are available in a bewildering number of shapes, sizes, and colors. How do these factors affect the braking action?

Generally, the least expensive (and least effective) shoe is made of hard black rubber. This type of shoe is usually long wearing but not as effective in stopping power as some of the other designs.

Most popular of the centerpull brakes is the red brake block with "nodules." The block is constructed with a slightly softer rubber than is found on the inexpensive black brake blocks and the surface usually has a varying quantity of nodules. The intention of the nodules is twofold: (1) the rapid dispersion of heat reduces brake "fade" and (2) the first nodule tends to remove any water on the rim so that the remaining nodules can more effectively grip the rim. As a rule, you should not mix different types of brake blocks. Always match replacement brake blocks with the original blocks unless the manufacturer of the replacement brake blocks specifically recommends their use with a particular brand of hand brakes.

Recently, several manufacturers have developed special brake-pad compounds that improve braking under both wet and dry braking conditions.

(continued on page 35)

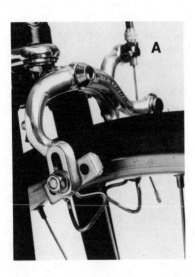 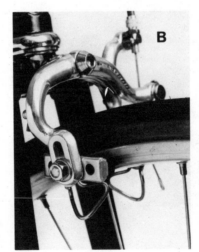 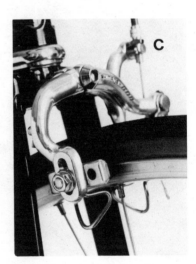

Photos 2–7A, 2–7B, and 2–7C:
Improperly Adjusted Brake Shoes.

(A) The brake shoe is not parallel to the rim. When the brake is actuated, part of the brake block will hit the tire resulting in reduced braking power, tire damage, and a potential blowout.

(B) The brake shoe is not parallel and will result in reduced braking efficiency since only a portion of the brake block will actually contact the rim.

(C) Although the brake shoe is parallel to the rim, the shoe is adjusted too high and will result in reduced braking efficiency since a portion of the brake block will not contact the rim.

Photo 2–8: The brake block holder is designed for use in one direction only—the end plate should be toward the front of the bicycle. This allows the brake block to be installed from the opposite end. As long as the brake block holder is installed properly, normal braking action will keep the brake block in place. If the brake block holder is inserted backwards, normal braking action will push the brake block out of its holder.

Photo 2–9: If one brake block touches the rim before the other, assuming the wheel is properly dished (see chapter eight), the brake should be recentered. The Campagnolo brake provides a surface so a cone wrench can be held on the pivot (mounting) bolt as the bolt is tightened. For sidepull brakes that do not have the machined slots, the brake centering is easily performed using a punch and hammer. The mounting bolt should be tightened prior to using the punch and hammer. Examine the brake calipers to determine which side should be moved closer to the rim. Place the punch on the return spring (coiled position) on the side that needs to be moved in. Tap the punch with a hammer until the calipers are equidistant from the rim.

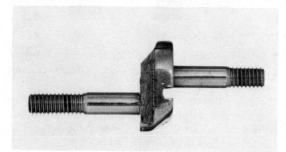

Photo 2–10: If your sidepull brake does not have calipers that are long enough to allow the brake blocks to reach the rim, a drop bolt may provide the necessary repositioning. This bolt is designed to replace the normally straight, pivot (mounting) bolt.

Photo 2–11: Although all brake blocks are designed for the sole purpose of stopping the bicycle, manufacturers have chosen many different designs to improve braking effectiveness.

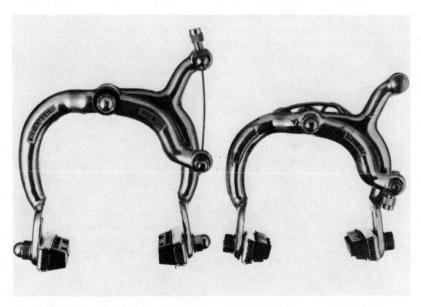

Photo 2–12: **Long-Reach vs. Short-Reach Brakes.** Brake calipers are available in several reaches to accommodate design variations on rim-to-frame dimensions that occur among different manufacturers.

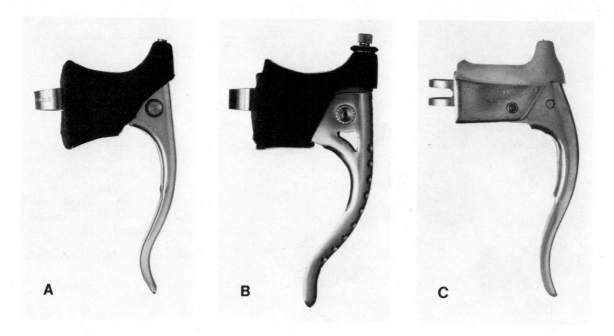

A   B   C

Photos 2–13A, 2–13B, and 2–13C: Brake levers are available in many different styles. (A) Campagnolo lever without weight-reducing holes in the brake arm. This brake lever includes a wraparound rubber hood. (B) Zeus lever with rubber hood and weight-reducing holes. (C) Mafac lever with partial rubber hood.

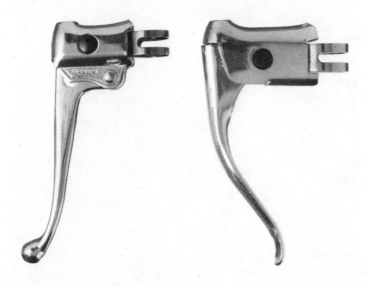

Photo 2–14: Brake levers are designed differently for upright or drop handlebars. The brake lever on the right is designed for drop handlebars—the curve in the lever allows maximum leverage for the average hand. The brake lever on the left is designed for upright handlebars; it is relatively straight to allow for adequate movement to actuate the brake. A drop-bar brake lever should not be used on upright bars and an upright-bar brake lever should not be used on drop bars.

BRAKE LEVERS

The variance in quality between brake levers is relatively slight if the least and most expensive levers are eliminated. The least expensive are steel and their chief appeal is low cost. The most expensive brake lever pictured in photo 2-13A is unique. Most other brake levers are made of aluminum alloy and are attached to the handlebars by adjustable steel bands. For all practical purposes, they are equal in ease of operation and efficiency.

A popular addition to the brake lever is a rubber hood. This hood does not affect the operation of the brake; it is designed to provide a comfortable resting place for the rider's hands.

(continued on page 41)

Photo 2–15: Properly placed brake levers can assist the rider in climbing hills. The brake levers allow the rider to pull against the force of each pedal stroke without reducing steering stability. The tops of the handlebars should be used because of the extra need for free breathing that is required when climbing.

Photo 2–16: **Proper Use of the Hand Brake.** When riding with the hands on the bottom of the handlebars, the brake should be actuated with two or three fingers. This insures adequate control of the bicycle while decelerating. This position provides the maximum stopping power.

Photo 2—17: The brake can be actuated from the comfortable "top" position on the handlebars. To maximize stopping power, the rider should hook the thumb around the top of the brake handle to increase leverage. Although this position does not offer as much braking power as when the hand is at the bottom of the bars, it is usually sufficient for all but emergency braking requirements.

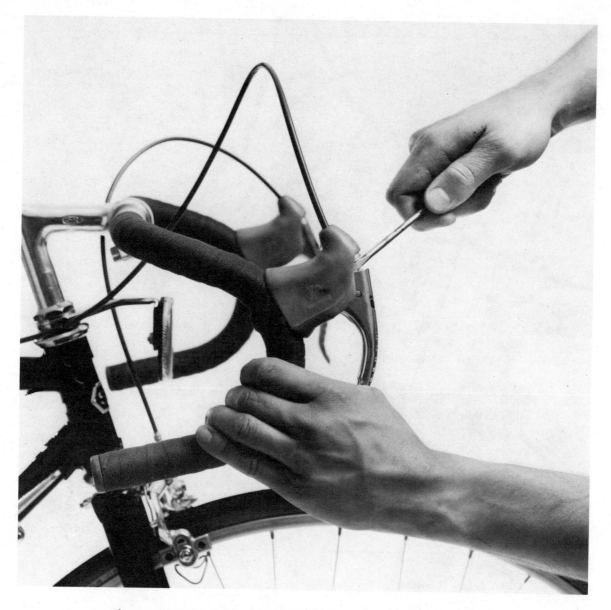

Photo 2–18: **Mounting or Removing the Brake Handle.** The brake handle is held onto the handlebar by a steel strap, which is tensioned by an adjusting bolt. The brake lever must be actuated to expose the bolt. In some cases, the brake cable limits access to the bolt and removal of the cable is required before the bolt can be reached.

Photo 2–19: When bending the brake caliper, use a small wrench and do not apply too much pressure. Excessive force will result in a broken or weakened caliper. The brake block should be bent to a position where the pad edge touches the rim *slightly* before the trailing edge.

Brake Characteristics

	Sidepull Steel	Sidepull Alloy	Centerpull	Cantilever	Disc or Drum
Weight	Heavy	Light	Light	Very light	Very heavy
Cost	Inexpensive	Moderate to very expensive	Moderate	Moderate	Expensive
Feel	Sloppy; imprecise	Very precise	Precise	Precise	Precise
Ease of Adjustment	Difficult	Easy	Moderately easy	Moderately difficult	Difficult initially
Effectiveness (stopping power)	Poor	Excellent	Good	Good	Excellent
Strong Points	Low cost	Quick, positive action Light weight Excellent stopping power Easy to adjust	Reasonably priced Light brake lever pressure required to actuate Good stopping power	Extremely light Reasonably priced Efficient stopping power in spite of large frame clearances Unaffected by mud and snow	No maintenance or adjustments required after installation Consistent stopping power wet or dry Very effective stopping power
Weak Points	Sloppy action Uncomfortable hoods No quick-release	Tend to go out of adjustment easily Cannot be used on frames with large clearances	Cable stretching requires frequent adjustment and feels fairly soft	Severe cable stretching requires more frequent adjustment and soft feel Awkward to adjust Difficult to insure proper brake-block-to-rim relationship	Very few drum and disc brakes are manufactured Very expensive Increased complexity of wheel removal High stopping power only required for tandem and mountain riding

BRAKE CABLES

At one time, a brake cable, was a brake cable, was a brake cable . . . now, there are several choices. The basic replacement cable (made of wrapped wire strands) is perfectly adequate in virtually every situation. Manufacturers of specialty cables are aiming at extraordinary situations. For instance, some racers prefer the feel of extra-thick cables which stretch less under heavy braking. Some riders insist on stainless steel cable because of its increased reliability. Another alternative offers smoother brake action because the cable housing has a Teflon insert that reduces friction between the cable and the housing.

BRAKE FEATURES

The most important parts of brake mechanisms include the following.

Quick-Release

To insure quick brake action, the brake blocks must be adjusted to run close to the rims. If the brake blocks are too close to the rim, it can be difficult to remove the bicycle wheel since the tire is wider than the rim. To remedy this inconvenience, engineers designed a release mechanism. The mechanism is usually found in one of three basic locations: at the lever (least common), at the brake

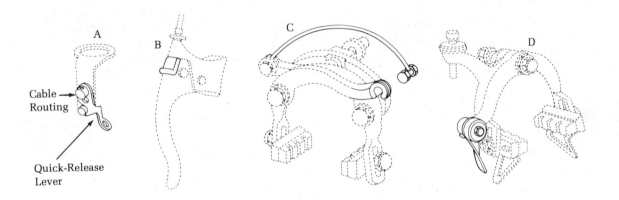

Figure 2–4: **Quick-Release Mechanisms.** Centerpull brakes generally have two basic types of quick-release mechanisms. The most common is depicted in A. This particular model is fitted at the headset and the brake cable is routed through a cam-action lever. Moving the quick-release lever will adjust the amount of tensioned brake cable and will, in turn, spread the brake calipers. Another type of quick-release is located in the brake lever. Pushing in the lever results in de-creased cable tension and opens the brake calipers. Quick-release B varies from A in that the lever-mounted quick-release (B) disconnects the quick-release by pulling the brake lever. Quick-release A must be reset with the quick-release lever. The Mafac centerpull (C) utilizes a different type of quick-release. In this case, the cable end is merely removed to spread the calipers. Sidepull brakes mount the quick-release mechanism on the front brake caliper (D).

caliper (most common with sidepull brakes), or at the cable-positioning bracket (most common on centerpull brakes). All three operate similarly—actuating the lever increases the amount of cable to the brake caliper. Consequently, the distance from the rim to the brake pad increases.

Although most quick-release actions are fairly simple on–off levers, some are very sophisticated. The Campagnolo quick-release is unique, since its lever is infinitely adjustable. It was designed to meet the needs of the bicycle racer and its complex design and exact tolerances contribute to its high cost.

Cable Adjusters

Regardless of the quality of a brake cable, it will stretch with use. As the cable stretches, the distance from the brake blocks to the rim will increase and braking effi-

ciency will be reduced. To eliminate the need for tools to remove minor slack in the cable, cable adjusters are often provided. Usually, they are nothing more than fixtures that can be turned by hand to effectively increase the tension in the brake cable.

Safety Levers

Most bicycle experts oppose the use of safety levers because they severely limit overall braking effectiveness, due to the greater degree of movement required to actuate the brake calipers. Safety levers do provide easy access to the brake levers when the rider's hands are on the "tops" of the handlebars. In addition, some riders with very small hands have difficulty in effectively reaching standard brake levers and find the safety levers more convenient. Generally speaking, the rider should attempt to learn the proper use of standard brake levers before relying on safety levers.

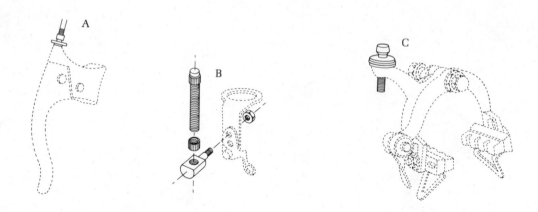

Figure 2–5: **Cable-Tension Adjusters.** Like quick-release brake levers, the cable-tension adjusters are usually found in one of three basic positions: (A) on the brake lever, (B) at the cable routing bracket (this unit is combined with the quick-release lever), and (C) on one of the brake calipers on sidepull brakes.

THIRD HAND TOOL

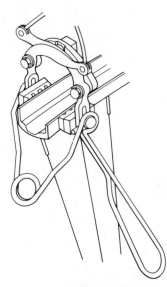

Figure 2–6: Although cable tension can be adjusted without the use of any special tools, the third hand is an inexpensive tool that makes the task easier. Simply, the tool pushes both brake calipers toward the rim so that the cable-tension bolt can be loosened, the brake cable pulled snug, and the bolt tightened.

Photo 2–20: Cut the cable at an angle to eliminate fraying. There are two methods of permanently reducing fraying: (1) Heat the end of the cable with a soldering iron (or gun) and cover the end with solder; or (2) place a plastic cap over the cable end.

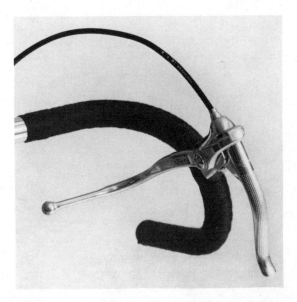

Photo 2–21: The safety lever is designed for operation with the rider's hands at the top, center position on the handlebars.

Troubleshooting Guide: Brakes

Problem	Probable Cause	How to Repair
Squealing brakes	Improper brake-pad alignment to rim	Bend brake caliper to insure that front part of brake shoe contacts the rim before the back part (photo 2-19).
	Dirty rims/brake block	Remove any rim cement, dirt, and old brake block remains from rim with a solvent. *Do not allow solvent to touch tire.*
		If squealing persists, replace brake blocks with new blocks of softer composition.
Excessive brake-lever travel before brakes are effective	Improper cable adjustment	By hand, tighten the cable-tension adjuster. If the adjuster is near its maximum position, return adjuster to its minimum position. Loosen the cable-tension bolt and using a third hand, retighten the bolt (figure 2-6).
	Worn brake blocks	Replace brake blocks.
Brakes shudder when applied	Loose calipers	Check to insure that the pivot bolts are tight. The bolts should be adjusted to a point where the caliper operates smoothly without any front-to-back looseness.
	Loose headset	Tighten headset.
	Bent or damaged rim	Check wheel for trueness (see chapter eight).
	Misaligned brake blocks	Check to see that brake blocks are properly aligned. One-hundred percent of the face of the brake block should touch the rim when the brake is applied. The brake block should never touch the tire.
Brake lever action is not smooth	Bent or kinked cable(s)	The outer brake cable housing must be kept free of acute bends or kinks will result. If the cable has been kinked, it must be replaced.
	Inadequate cable lubrication	Remove the inner brake cable from the outer housing. Apply a dry lubricant (or oil) to the inner cable and insert the inner cable into its housing. Check for smooth action prior to attaching the cable to the brake lever and caliper.
	Inadequate caliper lubrication	Lubricate pivot points on brake caliper.
	Bent brake lever	In the unlikely event that the problem persists after the above-mentioned steps, check the operation of the brake lever without the cable attached. Any bent or misaligned parts should be replaced.

Problem	Probable Cause	How to Repair
One brake block touches the rim before the other	Frayed brake cable	Replace cable.
	Misaligned mounting plate (centerpull brake)	Loosen rear mounting nut and reposition mounting plate so that both shoes are equidistant from the rim.
	Misaligned return spring (sidepull brake)	Loosen mounting bolt and roughly approximate correct position. Using a hammer and punch (photo 2-9), bend spring.
	Wheel improperly dished	The problem could be caused by a new wheel that has been installed on the bicycle. To determine if the front wheel has been improperly dished (without special tools):

- Insure that the hub is properly affixed in the fork.
- Check the relationship of the brake blocks to the rim.
- Remove the wheel and reverse the hub position.
- The relationship of the brake block to the rim will be the same as in photo 2-6, if the wheel is properly dished.

(If the wheel is improperly dished, see chapter eight.)

Rules of Thumb

- Brake levers must be adjusted so that the braking action occurs in the first one to two inches of travel in the brake lever. Too much "slack" in the cable may reduce emergency stopping power because the hand-brake lever may contact the handlebar before reaching optimum braking force.

- Do not throw away frayed rear brake cables. The frayed end can be cut off and the cable can be used on the front brake.

- Always cut brake cables and cable housings so the front wheel can be turned from side to side freely. On the other hand, cables that are too long can flap around, causing a potential safety problem and reduced braking efficiency.

- Do not work on your bicycle while it is lying upside down on the saddle and brake levers. The brake cables will become kinked and stiff to operate.

CHAPTER THREE

HANDLEBARS AND STEMS

Most 10-speed bicycles are equipped with drop handlebars. Why has this handlebar become standard, when it appears to be uncomfortable due to the rider's "bent-over" position? It's simple. If carefully selected and adjusted, the drop bar increases cycling efficiency and comfort.

The primary advantage of drop bars is the reduced wind resistance that results from the bent-over position. Furthermore, another advantage is that the unique shape of the handlebars provides improved leverage for the cyclist.

The modern drop handlebar is the result of years of experimentation and modification aimed at one goal—improved cycling efficiency. The practical benefit of the drop bar can be best illustrated (without the use of a bicycle) as follows: Place one foot on a bathroom scale and press down as hard as you can. Make note of the total weight registered on the scale. Normally, the weight registered will not exceed 50 to 75 percent of your body weight.

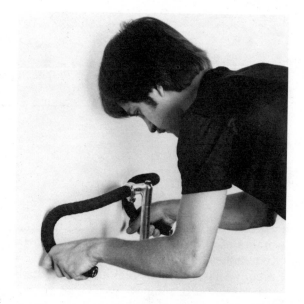

Photo 3–1: Test to prove the benefits of the bent-over handlebar position.

Now try the same experiment with the scale adjacent to a wall. Attach a pair of handlebars to the wall, three feet above the ground. Grab the handlebars with your hands and, once again, press down on the scale with one foot. This time you should use the handlebars to increase your leverage against the scale. The increased leverage gained by using the combined strength of your hands, arms, back, and shoulder muscles will cause the scale to read in excess of your body weight. Since brute strength is not the only factor governing efficiency, handlebar designs have been modified over the years to consider the importance of metal fatigue, comfort, and wind resistance.

HANDLEBAR STYLES

There are three basic types of bicycle handlebar styles: road (maes), track (pista), and touring bar (randonneur).

Road or **Maes**

The road handlebar is designed to fulfill the needs of most cyclists under normal riding conditions. The bar is relatively "square"; that is, when viewed from the top, the bars contain two short 90-degree bends. The lower part of the bars is nearly parallel to the tops of the bars and the total drop is usually about 6 inches (150 mm.). The handlebar is designed for comfortable riding in the three basic handlebar positions (photos 3-4A, 3-4B, 3-4C).

Road bars are usually manufactured using an aluminum alloy to reduce weight. Some of the most popular road bars have a reinforced sleeve in the center of the bar to reduce the danger of breakage and to insure adequate stiffness. Although the sleeve is not a guarantee of adequate strength, it is a good indication. Many manufacturers choose to identify and decorate their handlebars using the front face of the reinforcement.

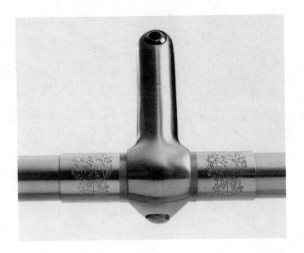

Photo 3-2: Top-quality road handlebars include a reinforcement to increase stiffness and minimize breakage. The reinforcement is frequently engraved.

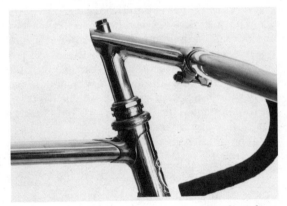

Photo 3-3: Sprint racers prefer ultralow handlebars and some utilize a handlebar stem that includes a sharply angled drop to provide the low handlebar position.

Track or **Pista**

Although the overall measurement of the track bar does not appear to be significantly different from the road bar, the track bar is completely different in design and composition.

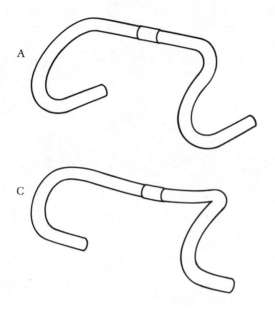

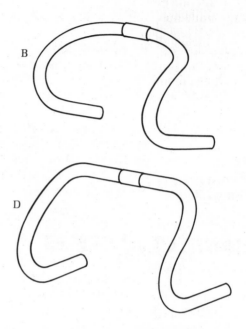

Figure 3–1: **Types of Handlebars.**

The road or *maes* handlebar (A) is the best choice for all-around use. It has medium drop and reach, and permits varied hand positions.

The track or *pista* handlebar (B) is used primarily for short-distance track races. It has fairly short reach with a large drop. The bar offers few comfortable hand positions; its chief design criterion is performance.

The touring or *randonneur* handlebar (C) offers a long reach and a very shallow drop. The tops of the bars are upswept, offering several comfortable riding positions. This bar is designed to fit the needs of the long-distance tourist.

The inexpensive drop handlebar (D) should be avoided unless price is the only consideration. Its design does not permit proper placement of the hands and its sloping reach limits the number of comfortable hand positions.

Track bars contain very little straight areas. Some track bars are even curved at the point where they attach to the handlebar stem. Since the track racer does not require a comfortable upright (touring) position, the tops of the bars are not parallel to the bottoms and the reach is shallow. Unlike the relatively shallow drop of the road bar, the track bar can have a drop of 7 or 8 inches (175 to 200 mm.). The track bar is designed to satisfy the requirements of the track racer who positions his hands at the bottoms of the bars.

Track bars are usually made of steel to insure adequate stiffness under the heavy stresses caused by the rider who uses the bars to increase force to the pedals. The art of sprinting involves the simultaneous use of legs, back, shoulder, and arm muscles working together to reach top speed in the shortest possible time. Sprinters soon realize that strengthened back, shoulder, and arm muscles can radically improve sprint times so they work to improve upper body strength. As the upper body strength increases, lightweight-alloy track handlebars become less desirable because they tend to flex and, on occasion, break.

(continued on page 53)

Photo 3—4A: **Handlebar Position 1.** The hands are on the tops of the handlebars near the stem. This position provides the least amount of bend in the rider's back.

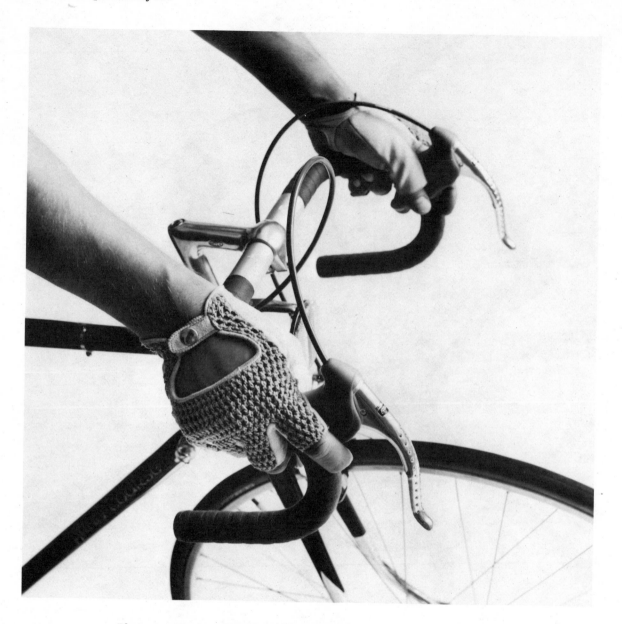

Photo 3–4B: **Handlebar Position 2.** The hands are resting on the gently sloping top part of the handlebars. This position provides a good balance between comfort and performance and easily allows the rider to actuate the brakes when necessary.

Photo 3–4C: **Handlebar Position 3.** The hands are located near the curves of the bars. This position causes maximum bend in the rider's back and is least comfortable for long periods of time. It is the most aerodynamic position and can be used effectively when facing a strong head wind.

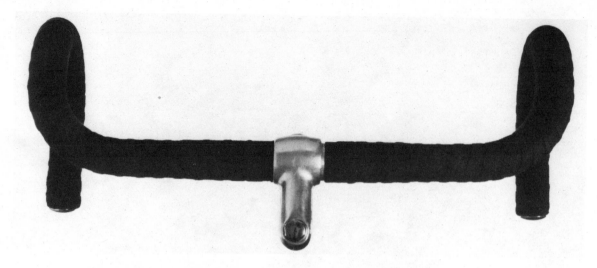

Photo 3–5: **Road Bars—Top View.** Road bars are designed to accommodate many comfortable hand positions. The bends are fairly square which permits a comfortable hand position behind the handlebar levers.

Photo 3–6: **Road Bars—Side View.** The top of an ideally shaped road bar slopes gently down to the handlebar levers, providing a comfortable hand and wrist position. The bottom of the bar forms a fairly tight curve since an extremely low handlebar is unnecessary and uncomfortable for road riding.

Touring Bar or **Randonneur**

The touring bar is designed to provide the leverage benefits of the *maes* bar with the comfort associated with flat 3-speed-type handlebars. The touring bar bends upward slightly when viewed from the front, providing several alternate positions for the rider's hands. The touring bar has an even smaller drop than the *maes* bar since low body position is less important to the tourist than the racer. The long reach of the touring bar provides a large flat surface for comfortable long-distance riding.

HANDLEBAR MEASUREMENTS

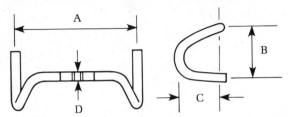

Figure 3–2: Handlebars have four important measurements:
- (A) Width—generally between 38 to 42 cm.
- (B) Drop—between 100 to 200 mm.
- (C) Reach—varies between 90 to 110 mm.
- (D) Mounting diameter—between 23.8 to 26.4 mm.

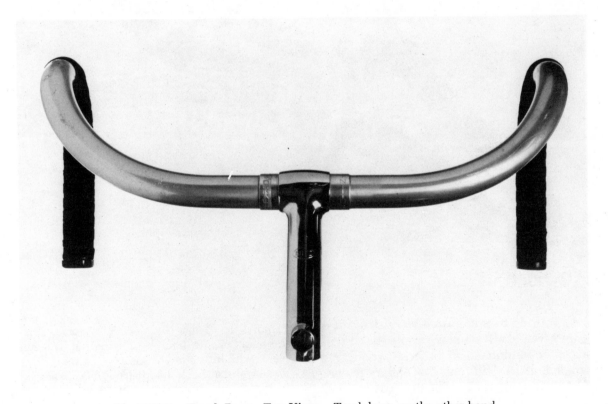

Photo 3–7: **Track Bars—Top View.** Track bars, on the other hand, have gradual curves. The handlebar is designed for racing and the position of the hands on the bottom of the bar is of primary importance.

Touring bars are usually constructed of a lightweight alloy and are rarely found with a center reinforcement because when touring, handlebar stiffness is secondary to comfort. When riding a bicycle that is laden with packs, handlebar stiffness is not a major problem since fast acceleration and quick, responsive handling are less important than overall stability.

Photo 3–8: **Track Bars—Side View.** Unlike the road bar, the track handlebar has sweeping bends with little straight areas. The drop is much greater on a track handlebar since increased leverage and aerodynamics are more important than comfort in sprint-type races.

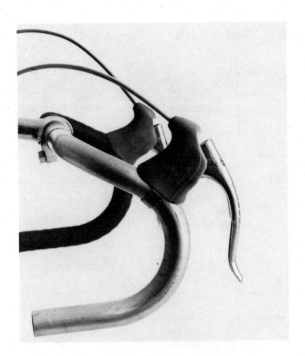

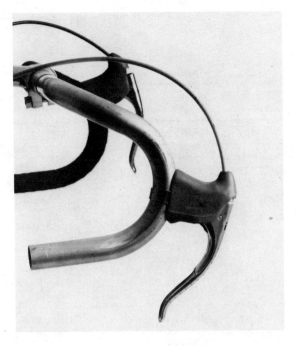

Photo 3—9: **Improper Position of Brake Lever.** If the brake lever is positioned too high on the handlebars, there will be insufficient room behind the levers for the hands. Moreover, it is difficult to reach the brake lever in either the top or bottom handlebar positions.

Photo 3—10: **Improper Position of Brake Lever.** If the brake lever is positioned too low, there is no comfortable position for the hands since the top of the bar curves too steeply. Also, it is very difficult to apply pressure to the brake lever in either the top or bottom handlebar positions.

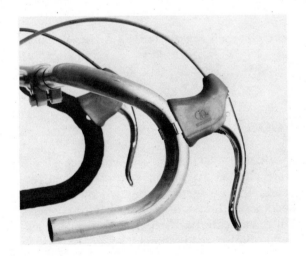

Photo 3—11: **Proper Position of Brake Lever.** A properly positioned brake lever permits a comfortable sloping surface for the hands, behind the brake lever. It also provides a satisfactory reach for the brake lever from the bottom as well as the top handlebar positions.

Handlebar Characteristics

	Touring *Randonneur*	Road *Maes*	Track *Pista*	Drop Bars*
Composition	Alloy	Alloy	Steel (chromed)	Steel (chromed)
Rigidity	Fairly stiff	Stiff	Very stiff	Very stiff
Weight	Light	Light [†]	Fairly light	Fairly heavy
Advantages	Several very comfortable riding positions	Several comfortable riding positions Good, stiff feel Many good-quality bars are very attractively finished and engraved	Strongest handlebar; designed for performance	Inexpensive
Disadvantages	Bottom handlebar position does not allow optimal aerodynamic efficiency. Bar not designed for sporting or high-speed use	Less choice of comfortable touring positions than touring bar	Few comfortable riding positions—performance considerations outweigh comfort	Poor design can reduce the number of comfortable riding positions Brake-lever position may be improper because of design limitations

*For comparison purposes, all handlebars found on inexpensive 10-speed bicycles are grouped under this category.

[†] Special lightweight bars are available. The decrease in weight is usually accompanied by a severe reduction in stiffness.

STEMS

To match the requirements of varying sizes of riders, handlebars are attached to the frame by a handlebar stem or extension which is available in a variety of styles and sizes. There are two basic styles: road and track.

Road Stems

In the past, both road and track stems were similar in design. Within the last ten years, the designs of the two stems have become distinct. Unlike the early road stems with an external expander bolt, recent good-quality road stems use an expander

BASIC HANDLEBAR STEM

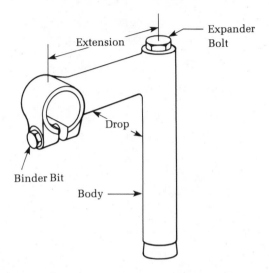

Figure 3–3: Handlebar stems are available in several extension lengths from 65 to 130 mm. The angle of drop is fairly consistent for road stems. However, some variation exists in track stems.

bolt that has a recessed hex head. Removal of the external bolt head reduces the incidence of rider injury; it is also more aesthetically pleasing. Similarly, the exposed binder bolt has been replaced by the recessed (allen key) binder bolt. Road stems are primarily manufactured with lightweight aluminum alloys. Top-quality manufacturers have developed lightweight alloy stems that are stiff and reliable.

Track Stems

Track stems have changed very little over the years. Most are still made of steel with a chrome finish. The majority of track sprinters prefer the extra stiffness and safety of the steel stem. Again, as a safety consid-

eration, an external expander bolt is utilized because the bolt can be tightened more securely when using an open-end wrench than by using an allen wrench (as on the road stem).

The Adjustable Stem

This stem is rarely used since it is heavy, expensive, and tends to slip under heavy stress. Nonetheless, it provides a handy way to determine a comfortable stem length as the length of the extension is completely adjustable without removing the handlebars. Once the proper stem length has been determined, there is no real advantage to the adjustable stem.

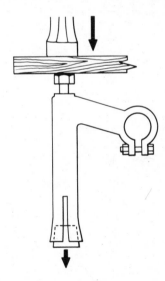

Figure 3–4: **To raise, lower or remove the bicycle stem, the following steps are required:**
1. Loosen the expander bolt 1½ to 2 turns (do not remove).
2. Using a brass hammer (or a piece of wood over the expander bolt), firmly tap the bolt once. The bolt should drop. If it does not, tap once again more firmly.

ROAD STEM

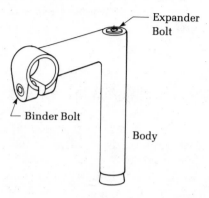

Figure 3–5: The road stem is usually made of lightweight alloy. Most road stems now include recessed (allen key) expander and binder bolts. This design results in superior aerodynamics and increased safety since the sharp bolt edges are eliminated.

TRACK STEM

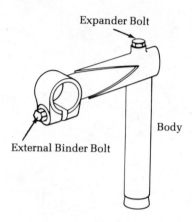

Figure 3–6: The typical track stem is made of chromed steel and has external nutted expander and binder bolts. This type of stem is preferred by track sprinters because of their need for extremely strong handlebars and stem.

3-SPEED-TYPE STEM

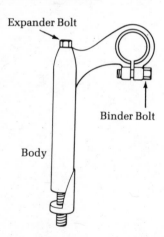

Figure 3–7: Three-speed-type handlebar stem. It is designed to provide an upright handlebar position at minimum cost.

ADJUSTABLE STEM

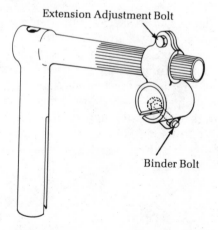

Figure 3–8: The adjustable stem offers varying extension lengths eliminating the need to remove the handlebars and replace the stem. To change the length of the extension, the extension adjustment bolt is loosened and the handlebars and holder slide back or forth to the desired position.

Handlebar Stem Characteristics

	3-Speed Type	Road	Track	Adjustable
Composition	Steel	Alloy	Steel	Steel or alloy
Weight	Very heavy	Light	Somewhat heavy	Very heavy
Advantages	Provides high, upright handlebar position Inexpensive	Allen-key binder and expander bolts provide good aerodynamics and safety Adequate strength for virtually all applications	Very strong—recommended for sprinters Nutted binder and expander bolts provide increased leverage to insure tightness	Permits varied extension adjustments without switching stems
Disadvantages	Improper design for normal performance riding Utilitarian finish	Requires special allen key to adjust binder and expander bolts	Very heavy Additional strength not normally required	Adjustable collar can slip under heavy use Weight penalty is not worthwhile since handlebar position is rarely changed after the optimal position has been realized

WORKING WITH THE HANDLEBAR STEM

The handlebar stem is a simple component that is easy to adjust once the rider understands the design of the expander bolt. Many frustrated cyclists have spent time removing the expander bolt without successfully loosening the handlebar stem.

The handlebar stem is held in the bicycle frame by the expander bolt and its internal wedge nut. To remove, raise, or lower the stem, first loosen the expander bolt approximately one-and-one-half to two turns. Tap the expander bolt with a brass hammer (or if using a steel hammer, place a piece of wood over the expander bolt to prevent scratches). The bolt should fall into its original (tight) position. If it does not, hit it again a little harder. The stem should be easy to remove once the bolt has dropped.

The design of the expander bolt becomes more obvious as the stem is completely removed from the bicycle. The wedge is forced up into the body of the stem as the expander bolt is tightened. As the wedge is pulled up, it expands the body of the stem

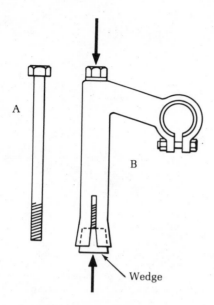

Figure 3–9: **Expander Bolt.** The expander bolt (A) is nothing more than a long, hardened bolt that attaches to a wedge-shaped nut.

As the expander bolt is tightened (B), the wedge is drawn into the body of the stem, expanding the stem against the steering tube of the fork.

against the head tube of the bicycle and firmly holds the handlebar in proper alignment. Once the expander bolt has been tightened, the wedge will be firmly "jammed" into place. *Complete removal of the expander bolt will not release the wedge;* a gentle tap with a hammer is required to dislodge the wedge and free the stem.

Warning: Do not adjust the handlebar stem in a position that is too high to insure safety. The expander wedge should be at least two inches inside the steering tube. If the wedge is forced against the threaded section of the steering tube, it can result in a fracture of the steering tube; a potential crash; and at the very least, a very expensive repair.

Handlebars and stems are available in widely varying styles and shapes. Unlike

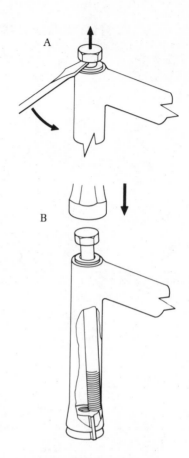

Figure 3–10: **Removing Expander Bolt.** If the expander bolt has stripped (turning the bolt does not loosen nor tighten the wedge), external force will be required to remove the bolt. (A) Place a screwdriver under the bolt head and force the head of the bolt up. Turn the bolt in a counterclockwise direction while applying upward pressure with the screwdriver. This will remove the bolt, but the wedge will still be firmly in place. (B) Take the bolt you have just removed and insert it back into the stem; but this time, insert it at an angle. Gently tap the wedge to lower one side. Continue to relocate the position of the bolt to permit the lowering of each position of the wedge until it falls free.

many components, it is more difficult to make a "bad" purchase (if the least expensive equipment is avoided) since the bars and stem are mechanically simple components.

HANDLEBARS AND STEM SPECIFICATIONS

Handlebar stems vary in diameter and should be matched to the size of the bicycle headset (which usually will match the country where the frame was built):

• French and Spanish bicycles use 21.9-mm. stems;
• Austrian, Danish, German, and Swiss bicycles use 22-mm. stems;
• Belgian, English, Italian, and Japanese bicycles use 22.2-mm. stems;
• Handlebar stems are usually available in 5-mm. increments with the extension varying between 65 mm. to 130 mm.

Better-quality stems are not usually available with extra-long bodies as the strength and stability would be adversely affected. If the body of the stem is too short to allow proper handlebar height, the frame is too small or the rider has set up the bicycle improperly.

The diameter of the handlebar stem (at the point where it attaches to the stem) varies by country of manufacturer. To insure proper fit, attempt to match the brand of stem with the brand of handlebars. The following measurements are intended as an interchangeability guide:

• The English use 23.8 and 25.4 mm.;
• The French use 23.8 and 25 mm.;
• The Italians use 23.8 and 25 mm.;
• The Japanese use 25.4 mm.

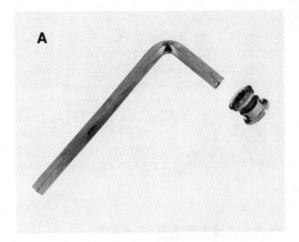

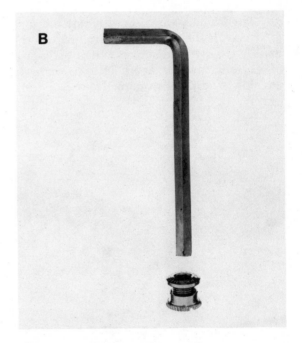

Photos 3–12A and 3–12B: In order to loosen or tighten recessed expander bolts, you will need the proper-size allen-key wrench. Where maximum leverage is required, insert the short end of the tool in the recessed bolt (A). In situations where speed is more important than leverage, insert the long end of the tool into the recessed bolt (B).

These specifications are not firm rules; they are intended only as a guide. Before purchasing handlebars and/or stem, the rider should measure each part to insure compatibility. For instance, although most Italian handlebars are 23.8 and 25 mm., the two top-quality bars (Cinelli and TTT) are not. Cinelli is 26.4 mm. and TTT is 26 mm. Even a slight size variation can result in unsightly scratches on the ornately engraved center support.

HANDLEBAR TAPE

The primary function of handlebar tape is to provide the rider with a firm grip on the handlebars. Long-distance riders soon discover that several layers of tape help to cushion their hands from road shock.

At one time, handlebar tape was produced in only two basic types: plastic and cloth. Because many recreational cyclists are incorrectly placing too much weight on the hands, several manufacturers have developed different materials designed to provide a nonslip surface to reduce road shock and enhance the appearance of the bicycle.

Plastic Tape

Plastic handlebar tape is usually the least expensive and most durable tape available. It is very easy to apply since it does not have adhesive backing, which also means it can be removed and reused if desired. Plastic tape is washable and retains a new look indefinitely. With all these positive points, why is the plastic tape found only on inexpensive 10-speed bicycles?

Photo 3–13: **Handlebar Wrapping.** Start wrapping the handlebar tape at the top and center of the handlebars to insure that it will not unwind. Apply the tape evenly with a carefully applied overlap each time you circle the handlebars. In addition to looking better, it will insure an even surface for your hands. Do not be concerned with the gap in the tape that occurs as you go from above the brake lever to below it; simply continue wrapping the bars until you reach the end. Cut off the tape with approximately one-inch excess, fold it over, and insert the end inside the handlebar. It will be held in place by the handlebar plug. To do a really first-class job, peel back the rubber brake hood and place a piece of tape (as shown) over the bare handlebar (sometimes two pieces will be required). Fold back the hood to its normal position. If you do this properly, the brake hood will hold the tape in place.

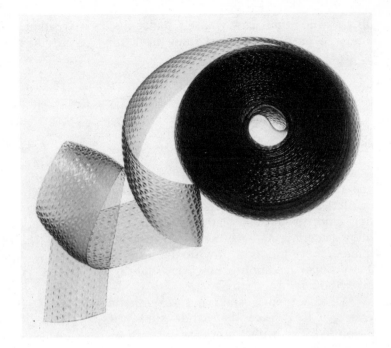

Photo 3–14: Plastic handlebar tape should have a textured surface to reduce slippage caused by sweaty hands.

Few serious riders use plastic tape; it cannot absorb the perspiration from the hands and therefore, tends to be slippery. Plastic tape (which is usually very thin and provides no shock-absorbing characteristics) is available in several different colors and in textured, transparent, or opaque styles.

Cloth Tape

Virtually all racing cyclists select cloth tape, because its textured surface provides a very good grip and absorbs perspiration. Some long-distance racers simply retape the handlebars as the tape gets dirty without removing the old tape. In this way they obtain some additional shock-absorbing effects. For added comfort some will place a rubber pad on the top surface of the handlebars and then wrap the bars. Small strips

of bicycle inner tube provide a comfortable surface, but the strips must be very carefully positioned and taped to insure stability. One advantage of adding a little padding on the top surface of the handlebar is that the overall grip of the bars is not significantly increased, as is sometimes the case with other handlebar grips.

Cloth handlebar tape is available from several different manufacturers in different colors and textures. We have found that the best cloth tape seems to be Tressostar. It is slightly more expensive than the average cloth tape, but Tressostar is comfortable and visually appealing.

But three notes of caution concerning cloth tape:

1. It takes two rolls of Tressostar to complete one set of handlebars.

2. Cloth tape gets dirty very quickly.

Unless you don't care what it looks like, choose a dark color. Black tape lasts the longest.

3. One side of the tape is sticky so you must be more careful in positioning it.

Specialty Tapes

Several American manufacturers have recently produced handlebar coverings that look like tape but are made of materials other than cloth or plastic. Many different synthetic materials and leathers are available. Some of these products provide the benefits of additional cushioning; however, some are not without faults.

We have seen several types of synthetic coverings that leave the hands sticky or discolored. The leather tapes are very attractive and comfortable but they have all of the disadvantages of leather in inclement weather. All in all, cloth handlebar tape provides optimum comfort and durability for the price.

If you tend to suffer from painful hands or numbed fingers when riding and if price is not a prime consideration, you should investigate the two popular alternatives:

1. Grab-On Products makes a handlebar padding that is made of a very dense foam that effectively reduces road shock and is unaffected by inclement weather or rider perspiration. Riders with very small hands should try the wrapping before purchasing it since the thicker padding greatly increases the circumference of the handlebar.

2. Dahltron Corporation manufactures a product they call No. 1 professional handlebar tape that is very popular. The tape provides a comfortable grip, is washable, and effectively reduces road shock. Although it feels like suede, the tape is weather resistant and long lasting.

Handlebar Tape Characteristics

	Cost	Durability	"Feel"	Shock Absorption	Ease of Application
Plastic	Very inexpensive	Excellent	Slippery when wet	Poor	Very easy
Cloth	Moderate	Fair	Retains feel wet or dry	Fair	Easy
"Special" Synthetic Tape	Moderate	Fair to good	Retains feel wet or dry	Good	Easy
Insulated Padding	Fairly expensive	Good	Retains feel wet or dry	Excellent	Somewhat involved
Leather	Moderate	Excellent	Absorbs moisture; however, takes a long time to dry out again	Good	Easy

HANDLEBAR PLUGS

Handlebar plugs are intended to prevent injury to the rider in the event of a crash. If the handlebars were left unplugged, a bar could impale the rider if he or she were unfortunate enough to fall on the end of the handlebars. Never ride without handlebar plugs; it isn't worth the risk! Handlebar plugs are available in two configurations—with or without tensioning bolts.

Standard Plug

The basic handlebar plug is plastic or steel. The most popular type is chrome since it is pleasing to the eye. The plug is held in place by the tension of its prongs against the inside of the handlebar. A distinct disadvantage is its tendency to fall out of the handlebars. This can be reduced, however, by proper tensioning (bending) of the prongs.

"Adjustable" Plug

Another popular handlebar plug is made of soft rubber and has a bolt running through its center. Like the expander bolt on the handlebar stem, tightening the bolt expands the handlebar plug and firmly holds it in position in the handlebar. If properly tightened, the handlebar plug will rarely fall out.

Troubleshooting Guide: Handlebars and Stems

Problem	Probable Cause	How to Repair
Handlebar wobbles under pressure	Improper match between handlebar to stem or stem to headset	Impossible to properly repair. Refer to handlebar and stem specification charts on pages 56 and 59. Temporary repairs can be made by using a shim between the improperly matched parts. (This shim can be made by cutting a small piece out of an ordinary tin can.)
	Loose, cracked, or broken binder bolt	Inspect binder bolt; replace if there is any evidence of stripped threads or fractures.
	Loose, cracked, or broken expander bolt	Inspect expander bolt; replace if there is any evidence of stripped threads or fractures.
Expander bolt turns without evidence of tightening or loosening the wedge	Expander bolt is stripped	Remove and replace expander bolt and wedge. Upward pressure will be required to remove expander bolt as illustrated in figure 3-10. The wedge is also removed.
Binder bolt turns without evidence of tightening or loosening the handlebars	Binder bolt is stripped	Remove binder bolt using external leverage.

Photo 3–15: Two types of handlebar plugs are available: on the right, the adjustable-tension plug, which is tightened with a screwdriver to fix the plug in position and, on the left, the standard plug, which is held in place by the force of the adjustable metal prongs. If the plug is too loose, the prongs can be bent slightly outward.

Rules of Thumb

- Never ride your bicycle without handlebar plugs; the risk of injury isn't worth it.

- Do not position your handlebar stem too far out of the frame. In addition to the increased chance of stem breakage, the top of the fork steering column can be damaged which is very expensive to repair.

CHAPTER FOUR

SADDLES
AND SEATPOSTS

Each component found on a modern 10-speed bicycle affects the operation and efficiency of this machine. Some of the parts are crucial to the smooth operation (such as the derailleurs or brakes) and others are largely unnoticed (cables, toe clips, and handlebar plugs). But the saddle is readily noticed and receives more negative comments from the novice than any other.

SADDLES

The importance of a good saddle is frequently overlooked because most riders presume that saddles must be uncomfortable because of their narrow shape. Dozens of different saddles are available, yet few are totally satisfactory. The selection process is made more difficult because rider discomfort may not be caused by the saddle itself. Rather, the position of the saddle, governed by the seatpost, may be part of the problem.

Sometimes the design of the seatpost will not allow proper saddle adjustment.

Before we review the characteristics of different saddles and seatposts, let's take a look at the relationship between the saddle and seatpost and proper cycling position.

Proper saddle adjustment is related to the following factors:

1. *Amount of extension of the rider's leg.* We have covered proper saddle height adjustment in chapter one. Improper saddle height causes a severe restriction on cycling efficiency and it can cause knee problems and saddle sores.

2. *The amount of weight concentrated on the rider's hands.* Too few riders realize that the tilt of the saddle will affect their overall weight distribution on the bicycle. As described in chapter fourteen, your weight should be distributed approximately 45 percent in the front and 55 percent in the rear of the bicycle. The height and tilt of the saddle will influence balance. If the nose of

SADDLE-FRAME WIDTHS

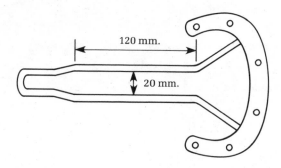

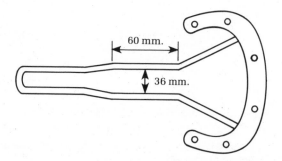

Figure 4–1: Most saddle frames and seatposts are designed to match the standard, 36-mm. saddle-frame rail width. Some saddles and seatposts are 20 mm. wide and are incompatible with the 36-mm. size. The 20-mm., saddle support-rail configuration is designed to allow greater fore–aft positioning of the saddle and is unnecessary in most applications.

the saddle is tilted down, the rider will have a tendency to slide forward. Although the cyclist may not be aware of the sliding effect, the rider's hands must resist this tendency. The inevitable result is sore or numb hands and tired arms and shoulders.

3. *The angle of force applied to the pedals.* The saddle is designed to be adjustable in fore–aft positioning to optimally conform to the variations in the individual rider's physique; specifically, the length of

the upper leg. Chapter one describes how to properly set the saddle to match your thigh length. Improper adjustment of the fore–aft saddle position results in reduced performance, since it tends to magnify the effect of improper gear selection.

4. *Saddle soreness.* No one who has ever ridden a 10-speed for the first time needs to have the term saddle soreness clarified. The pain is caused by the bruised skin which covers the area of the pelvic bone that supports your body by resting on the relatively hard saddle. Many riders ask if a wider saddle would be more comfortable. The answer is no. The saddle is designed to support the rider's weight on the two lower pelvic bones *not* the rider's buttocks. Widening the saddle will only result in a restricted pedaling motion and increased risk of chafing. Until recently, cycling had been a predominantly all-male sport. Accordingly, saddle manufacturers paid little attention to the particular requirements of the female rider who has a wider spread of up to one inch between the two supporting pelvic bones. Fortunately, several manufacturers have devoted their attention to this problem and saddles specially designed for women are now available.

Plastic Saddles

The least expensive and most popular saddle is made out of tough plastic. It has become standard equipment on less-expensive bicycles because of its durability and low cost. The chief advantage of the plastic saddle is its composition which makes it impervious to the weather. The plastic saddle has exactly the same "feel" in the cold winter as in the heat in summer. It is unaffected by rain, sleet, or snow and, in

Photo 4–1: The seat clamp is tightened by two nuts—one on each side of the seatpost. Loosen both nuts to adjust the angle of the saddle and/or fore–aft position.

addition, it is very light. In most cases, the saddle will remain completely unchanged through years of riding. If you don't like the way it feels when it is new, you won't like the way it feels a year from now, since it never "breaks in," softens, or changes. Although the plastic saddle sounds like a winner in theory, the cyclist is faced with a difficult selection process since all plastic saddles are not equal.

Usually, the plastic saddles that are included on inexpensive 10-speed bicycles are rock hard and of very poor design. At first glance, they appear to resemble the basic design of the good plastic saddles but close examination (and riding) demonstrates subtle differences. The shape of the top of the saddle is critical to insure reasonable comfort. Many of the inexpensive plastic saddles have tops that are curved far too much. This small design flaw causes the saddle to feel like it is a knife blade and it tends to position itself too high within the rider's extended pelvic bones. Since cost is a major considera-

tion, the saddle made of inexpensive plastic is thick and inflexible to insure minimum risk of cracking or breaking. Unfortunately, this design also provides a minimum amount of comfort.

Before you buy a plastic saddle, be aware of the enormous variations in comfort and cost. The most popular and probably the best plastic saddles in the world are made by Cinelli and branded UnicaNitor. They are virtually unbreakable, fairly comfortable, light weight—and recommended for racing. (Cinelli manufactures models that are more comfortable, although more expensive.) Compare any other plastic saddle to these saddles for overall softness and construction quality.

Since it requires no maintenance and is extremely durable, the plastic saddle has largely replaced the leather saddle on most bicycles. To increase comfort, a variety of coverings are used. Although Cinelli Unica-Nitor saddles are among the most expensive, we will use them as examples of each

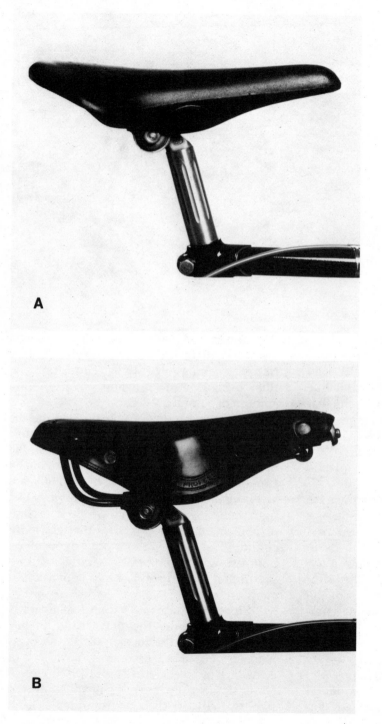

A

B

Photos 4–2A and 4–2B: Plastic saddles (A) are much shallower than leather saddles (B). This feature can be used to advantage when sizing very short riders. Assuming the smallest available frame size has been selected and the rider cannot lower the saddle far enough to properly adjust it, try replacing a leather saddle with a plastic saddle. This plastic saddle will lower the rider approximately one inch.

Saddle Characteristics

	Weight	Maintenance Required	Cost	Advantages	Disadvantages
Plastic	Very light	None	Inexpensive	Light weight Low cost Impervious to weather Long life Saddle comfort unchanged by use or weather	Uncomfortable for long-distance rides
Plastic with Leather Covering	Light	None	Expensive	Light weight Relatively unaffected by weather Shares part of comfort of leather saddle without maintenance requirements	Saddle shape designed to appeal to the racer or performance-oriented rider
Leather	Heavy	Regular application of saddle dressing to preserve and clean	Very expensive	Very comfortable after break-in period	Long break-in period Regular maintenance required Affected by water Improper maintenance reduces life of the saddle
Specialty*	Light	None	Expensive	Can be the answer to saddle soreness Light weight Unaffected by weather Several saddles are specifically designed for women	Inconsistent quality between manufacturers Harder to evaluate products since recent development does not provide a long history for evaluation

*Describes saddles that are specifically designed to include inserts for comfort, e.g., the Avocet saddles.

different type of design variation that is available. These saddles provide a good basis for comparison as the overall quality and comfort are unsurpassed.

Leather Top

Using the basic plastic saddle as the shell, a smooth leather covering is bonded to the top. This provides additional comfort, reduces heat transmission to the rider, and allows the rider's posterior to breathe. Because the leather is supported by the nylon shell, it is not harmed by adverse weather conditions. Another model is offered with an additional feature for the long-distance rider—a layer of dense foam padding is inserted between the nylon shell and the smooth leather covering.

You can compare the quality of other saddles by examining how the leather covering is attached to the shell. Some manufacturers use staples (that fall out) or poor-quality glue. Most riders agree that the smooth leather top is preferable to the rough-finished top which does not allow easy motion, thus denying a rider the opportunity to make essential adjustment in his or her riding position. The leather-top saddle, which requires no treatment to preserve it, will not stain your clothes to the same degree as the 100 percent leather saddle.

Buffalo Hide Top

This saddle is our personal favorite and frequently it is the top choice of serious cyclists. The buffalo hide is a premium-grade, extra-thick leather which becomes very smooth and shiny with use. Since the hide is thick and supple, it provides as much comfort as a foam-padded saddle. It is light weight, resistant to the weather, and does not stain clothing.

Leather Saddles

Until the arrival of leather-top plastic saddles on the market, the leather saddle was the only type available. After it is broken in, the leather saddle remains as the most comfortable saddle available. Unfortunately, there is only one way to properly break in a leather saddle—miles and more miles. Do *not* listen to the stories that tell of shortcuts for softening the saddles. For instance, some people believe that the best way to "prepare" the saddle is to drill out all the rivets that hold the leather top to the frame, remove the leather and soak in neat's-foot oil. While this does soften the saddle quickly, it also considerably reduces the life of the saddle. Although we are sure that some softening techniques like this one might work, we prefer to adhere to the advice of the manufacturers of the saddles. They do not recommend the soaking technique.

It is interesting to note that some professional riders had coaches who would prepare the saddles using this technique. Those saddles were identifiable by their new copper rivets which were larger than the original rivets (to cover the deformed leather where the original rivets were removed). To match the appearance of professionally "prepared" saddles, Brooks now produces its Professional saddle with large copper rivets, although this does not affect the characteristics of the saddle.

To care for your saddle you should apply saddle soap regularly. The saddle soap will help to preserve the leather as well as soften it. Cyclists who plan to do a lot of riding in the rain should apply liberal amounts of neat's-foot oil to the *underside* of the saddle. Remember water is the enemy of the leather saddle. Theoretically, you should saddle-soap the saddle each time it gets wet. Regular saddle-soaping also cleans the pores of the leather and helps to remove the salt that is deposited from your perspiration. Unfortunately, the regular use of saddle soap will cause stains on cycling shorts. For racers this is no problem since the shorts are black. However, the commuter or casual rider will develop embarrassing stains on the seat of his or her pants.

You'll have to ride up to 100 hours to break in a top-quality leather saddle, since one of the features of a top saddle is its thick leather. Generally, the thickness of the leather is a good indication of the quality of the saddle as leather is so expensive. With each hour of riding, the leather will soften and begin to shape itself. Eventually, it will become very soft and actual indentations will appear where your pelvic bones rest. The chief advantage of a leather saddle is its custom-fit surface to your individual physique. The importance of this is best demonstrated by a practice of professional racing cyclists; although they might get new bicycles on a regular basis, they always retain their broken-in saddle!

Leather breathes. It is very porous and helps to reduce the effects of chafing and irritation caused by perspiration. Unfortunately, this porosity can contribute to increased chances of infection. The plastic saddle is totally unporous. Some manufacturers drill ventilating holes in the saddle to reduce the problem associated with excess perspiration.

If you decide to select an all-leather saddle, compare the quality of the available saddles with the recognized quality leaders: Brooks and Ideale. It is hard to duplicate the quality designs of these two famous manufacturers.

With the increased number of recreational cyclists, manufacturers have been bombarded with complaints about uncomfortable saddles. These complaints were the result of marketing, not design problems. The manufacturers supply the basic 10-speed bicycles with a bicycle saddle that usually would retail for $6. All of the top-quality saddles that we have described cost at least four to five times that price. How can the manufacturer include a saddle that may cost one-fifth as much, by itself, as the whole bicycle? Accordingly, the cyclist should be aware that good, comfortable saddles do exist and they are easily changed.

You should also be aware that a saddle that is judged comfortable will never equal the comfort of sitting on your favorite couch at home. The term comfort is relative. Regular riding will toughen the tender flesh that surrounds the pubic bones. If the saddle is well designed and manufactured, the rider should not experience any appreciable saddle soreness. Even the experienced professionals encounter some tenderness when they first get on their bicycles after a winter break. If you continue to suffer from saddle soreness, several new saddles may be of interest.

Avocet, Inc., produces several well-thought-out and constructed bicycle saddles. Their leather-topped plastic saddles include special padding in the areas where your pelvic bones rest. The thickness and shape of the saddle vary with the type of use intended for the saddle, from racing to touring. This company has made significant progress in the design of saddles specifically for women.

Another saddle with similar features is the Celle Milano. You should be very careful in your selection of this type of saddle since some inferior designs exist. We have witnessed dozens of saddles that came apart with very little riding. Some riders even report that their unique shapes or design causes chafing.

The final selection of a saddle is primarily a subjective evaluation based on comfort. Think very carefully before you decide on a saddle other than the time-tested, and proven, famous brands. If you already own one of the top-quality saddles and you still have problems, double-check your overall bicycle setup; the instructions in chapter one serve as a good basic reference point. If you still have problems, review the recommendations concerning bicycle shorts in chapter ten. Proper bicycle setup, a good saddle, and proper clothing will eliminate problems for most riders.

SEATPOSTS

There are two basic types of seatposts: the plain pillar and the microadjusting seatpost. Since both reliably perform their intended function, let's review the purpose of the seatpost before we look at the features of each type.

The primary purpose of the seatpost is to provide a means of attaching the saddle to the bicycle frame. The outside diameter of the seat pillar should be matched with the inside diameter of the frame. Several sizes, which usually reflect the country where the bicycle was originally manufactured, are available. Once the saddle has been attached to the seatpost, it can be raised or lowered in the frame to provide the exact distance from saddle to the pedal as required by each cyclist's individual requirements. In addition, the clamp that holds the saddle to the seatpost allows adjustment of the fore–aft position of the saddle on the post and the angle of tilt for the saddle. Seat pillars are available in either chrome steel (chromed) or alloy. The difference between the two compositions is simple: steel is cheaper and

Photo 4–3: The microadjusting seatpost is the only way to insure precision adjustment of saddle tilt. To adjust the angle of the saddle, both bolts A and B should be tightened equally. Once the saddle has been attached firmly, the adjusting process can begin. To lower the *top* of the saddle, tighten bolt A (or loosen bolt B). To raise the *top* of the saddle, loosen bolt A (or tighten bolt B). Double-check the tightness of each bolt to insure proper tension before riding.

heavier than the more expensive lightweight alloy.

Standard Pillar with Clamp

Most inexpensive bicycles include a standard seat pillar which is little more than a steel or alloy tube with a separate saddle clamp that affixes the saddle to the seat pillar. Since it is reliable and inexpensive, this type of fastening system is popular. In fact, the standard pillar and clamp usually cost between one-fourth to one-fifth as much as the microadjusting seatpost described below.

Although the seat clamp allows an infi-nite number of adjustments in fore–aft saddle positions, it has a limited number of adjustments for its tilt angle. Disassembly of the clamp reveals a number of serrations in the circular part of the clamp that rotate to accommodate the desired saddle tilt. Since these serrations occur at fixed intervals, the saddle is not infinitely adjustable between those serrations. The saddle clamp will only hold if the serrations match. While there are several available positions for the angle of tilt, it seems that none are perfect. For the casual rider, exact positioning is fairly unimportant. For the serious cyclist who rides long distances, the adjustment is critical. For that reason, a seatpost with an infinitely adjustable tilt adjustment was developed.

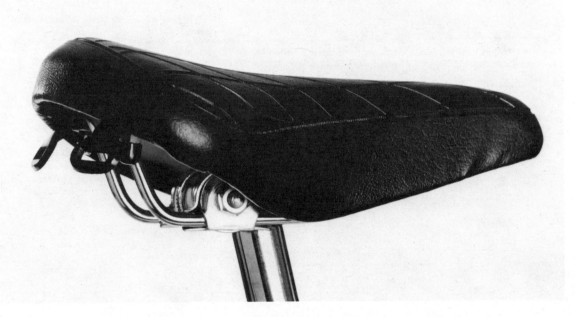

Photo 4–4: Some short cyclists experience difficulty in adjusting the saddle since it may not be low enough in its lowest position. Inverting the saddle clamp will result in a seat that is almost one inch lower without moving the seatpost.

Troubleshooting Guide:
Saddles and Seatposts

Problem	Probable Cause	How to Repair
Leather saddle drying out or cracking	Frequent use in rain or hot climates without treatment of the leather	Rub a generous quantity of saddle soap or Brooks Proofide into the leather until it becomes soft and supple. Apply regular treatments of saddle soap. Rub neat's-foot oil into the underside of the saddle until it is supple.
Leather saddle sags causing rider contact with seatpost	Saddle has been deformed from riding when wet or saddle has been oiled too frequently	Adjust the saddle tension by turning the adjusting nut clockwise at the front of the underside of the saddle frame. If the saddle is badly stretched and the tension nut cannot reduce the tendency of the saddle sides to spread under the rider's weight, the bottoms of the side flaps can be tied together with a piece of rawhide. *Caution:* Position the rawhide loop so it does not interfere with your cycling motion.
Saddle changes position while riding	Loose or damaged saddle clamp or loose seatpost	If the tilt of the saddle moves as you ride: 1. Check the tension on integral seatpost/saddle clamp pillars—it is probably loose. 2. On pillars using a separate seat clamp, tighten (clockwise) the saddle clamp nuts under the flaps of the saddle. If this does not eliminate the problem, check the condition of the serrated washers on the saddle clamp to see if they have been damaged. Replace as required. 3. If saddle is moving side to side, check tension of seat clamp. Also check tension of seatpost bolt (in frame).

Microadjusting Seatpost

As the name implies, fine adjustment is available with the microadjusting seatpost. It shares the feature of a standard clamp, which allows infinite adjustments for fore—aft saddle positions. In addition, the microadjusting post allows adjustment of saddle tilt to any desired position. Unlike the standard clamp that slips unless it is in a specific position, the microadjusting clamp will firmly hold the saddle in whatever position the cyclist desires. This is accomplished through a specially designed clamp that is an integral part of the seatpost. Most of these seat pillars have two bolts that are tightened to hold the saddle on to adjust it as pictured in photo 4-1. This seatpost design has several minor variations; however, they all utilize the same principle. All good-quality bicycles include a microadjusting seat pillar because of the critical importance of proper saddle adjustment, the only disadvantage is their cost.

Do not attempt to match a seatpost to your frame without careful measurement. There are many different sizes available. We have included the following chart as a rough guide to interchangeability.

Possible Sizing

Country of Manufacture	Sizes for Good Quality Tubing (in mm.)	Double-Butted Tubing
France	26.2	26.4
England	26.4, 26.6	27, 27.2
Italy	26, 26.2	26.8, 27, 27.2
Japan	26.2	26.4, 26.6, 26.8, 27

Rules of Thumb

- Always leave at least two inches of seat-post in the frame. If you must raise the saddle to a position where the post has less than two inches inside the seat lug, get a new, longer seatpost.

- Do not drill holes in your plastic saddle since it will weaken it and the rough edges will wear out your bicycle shorts prematurely.

- Do not dry out a wet leather saddle by leaving it in direct sunlight or by using an artificial heat source. Let the saddle dry naturally.

- Racing vs. touring saddles are easily identified. The touring saddle is wider to provide support for the rider who generally sits in a fairly upright position while the racing saddle is narrower since less support is required and freedom of unrestricted leg movement is important.

CHAPTER FIVE

THE DRIVE CHAIN: CRANKSET, CHAINWHEEL, AND FREEWHEEL

This chapter deals with the many components that comprise the drive chain. We decided to group these components together since each is an integral part of the transmission of power from the rider to the wheels and ultimately the road.

CRANKSETS

Since it must be strong enough to withstand years of use and is the primary device to transmit the power in a cyclist's leg to the rear wheel, the crankset is the most expensive single component on a bicycle. Furthermore, the drive chain must be precisely manufactured to reduce energy loss through friction.

Although the crankset is available in a large number of styles, relatively little controversy exists over design philosophies. Perhaps this is due to the fact that most cyclists know very little about the importance of proper pedaling and concern themselves primarily with the price vs. features of a crankset instead of which *type* of crankset they really need.

Basically, two major types exist: cottered crankset (crankarms attach to the bottom bracket axle hole with cotter pins) and cotterless crankset (it is bolted to the axle). Both of these styles are available in steel or in lightweight alloy materials.

A cottered crank is held on the bottom bracket axle by a cotter pin. This pin wedges the arm against the side of the axle and the position (and tightness) of the pin is maintained by a nut. Cotterless cranks, on the other hand, have no cotter pins. Instead, the cranks are attached to the end of the axle with a bolt that maintains their position. Cottered and cotterless cranks are not interchangeable. However, a bicycle that has been fitted originally with a cottered crankset generally can be fitted with a cotterless set. In this case, the whole system must be changed—axle, cups, bearings, and crankarms.

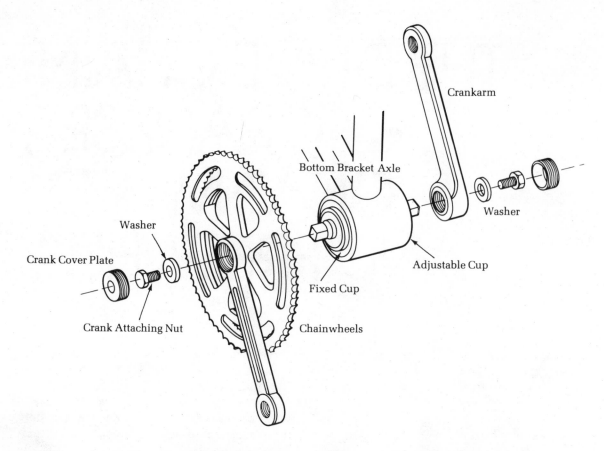

Figure 5–1: **Cotterless Crankset (Exploded View).** The cotterless crankset is standard equipment on top-quality bicycles. It has light-weight alloy cranks that are fixed to the bottom bracket axle by a nut on the end of the axle.

The cotterless fastening system is superior to the cottered method because it is easy to keep the cotterless crank tight on the axle. Under extremely heavy stress, the cottered crank can shift position as the crank works against the pin wedged between it and the axle. Because of the "working" action of the bottom bracket axle against the cotter pin and crankarm, cottered cranks are usually made of steel. Some manufacturers try to entice customers by offering cottered cranksets with alloy crankarms and steel chainwheels. We would advise staying away from these. An alloy cottered crank will very quickly develop an elongated cotter-pin hole since the aluminum alloys that are used on inexpensive cranks are much softer than steel.

Virtually every lightweight 10-speed bicycle now has an alloy cotterless crankset. As recently as 15 years ago, many racing bicycles had steel cottered cranks. Why the switch? As we have indicated, the racer is concerned with strength and weight; an

Photos 5–1A and 5–1B: Beware of cotterless crankset designs that can cause problems. (A) This crankset includes a two-piece, right crank-arm/spider combination. Heavy pedal pressure can cause the crank-arm to loosen from the spider. All good-quality cotterless cranks have a one-piece crankarm/spider.

We have also experienced difficulties with the bottom bracket axle on this type of crankset. Note the difference between this cotterless bottom bracket axle and the "normal" cotterless bottom bracket axle. (B) This axle has a threaded end and the crank is attached to the axle by a nut. The threads are easily damaged on this unit.

ultralightweight part is of no value to the racer if it breaks before the race is over. For that reason, until sufficiently strong alloy cranksets were developed, the racer used steel. Since every professional racing bicycle eventually became equipped with an alloy crankset, the general public believed that alloy cranksets were better as a group. This statement is not entirely true. Logically, a poorly manufactured alloy crankset is not necessarily better than a good-quality steel crankset. We will list the reasons why when we examine the advantages and disadvantages of each type.

CRANKS (OR CRANKARMS)

Every bicycle comes with two cranks. The right side (when seated on the bicycle) includes a means of attaching the front

sprockets or chainwheels. The left side merely serves as an arm that connects the pedal to the bottom bracket axle.

Cranks are manufactured with one of two basic materials—steel or aluminum alloy. Generally, the alloy cranks are more expensive because far more sophisticated manufacturing processes are required to achieve the strength and durability of steel. The primary advantage of aluminum alloys is their light weight. Unfortunately, they are more costly, more difficult to produce, and more prone to failure since steel is more malleable than aluminum alloys. The soft

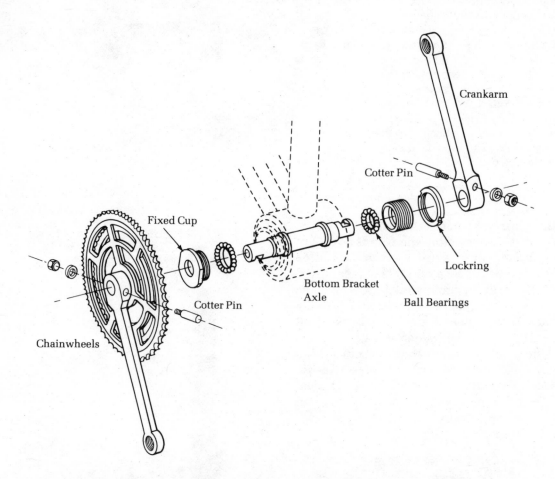

Figure 5–2: **Cottered Crankset (Exploded View).** Basic 10-speed, utility, and lower-priced sports bicycles usually have a cottered crankset that relies on a cotter pin to fix the crankarms to the bottom bracket axle. The all-steel construction results in a reasonable price without sacrificing strength. This crankset is adequate for most normal riding applications, although it does not have the close tolerances of the cotterless mounting system.

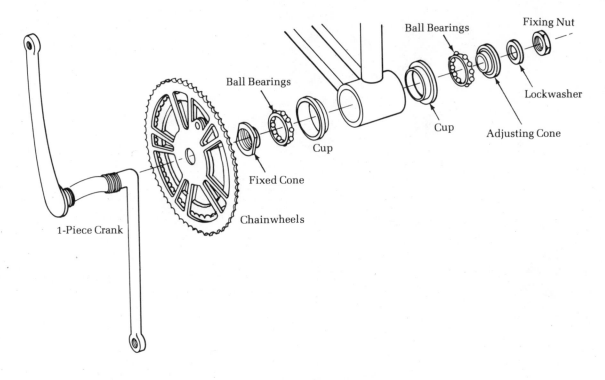

Ball Bearings

Fixing Nut

Ball Bearings

Cup

Lockwasher

Fixed Cone

Cup

Adjusting Cone

1-Piece Crank

Chainwheels

Figure 5–3: **One-Piece Crankset (Exploded View).** The one-piece crankset is found on inexpensive, utility, and children's bicycles. It is made of steel, is very sturdy and durable, but is very heavy and poorly finished. It is inexpensive to manufacture since the left crankarm, bottom bracket axle, and right crankarm are one piece. The crankarms are easily indentified by their round shape.

alloy surface scratches easier and it is more prone to damage from poor shop practices than a steel crank.

Although it is possible to purchase inexpensive alloy cranks that approximate the price of steel cranks, remember to consider the relative quality of each. To best understand the variations in cranksets, compare the difference between the price of the least expensive alloy crankset and the cost of the most expensive alloy crankset. Unlike steel cranksets, good alloy cranksets can be as much as three to four times more expensive as their inexpensive counterparts. If you are interested in buying an alloy crankset, take the time to examine all of the available brands. Line up, in order of price, each crankarm side by side and you will easily see the difference in attention to detail. Specifically, look at the right crankarms to get the true picture.

You should immediately notice that there are two major differences as the price

(continued on page 87)

Removing a Cotterless Crank and Cups.

Photos 5–2A and 5–2B: Use the recommended allen wrench (A) or screwdriver (B) to remove the crank cover plate (loosen in a counterclockwise direction).

Photo 5–3: Use recommended wrench to remove the crank attaching bolt (loosen counterclockwise).

Photo 5–4: Insert the recommended crank extractor until it stops turning (clockwise).

Photo 5—5: Using the appropriate wrench or tool, tighten the extractor slightly (clockwise).

Reposition wrench on the movable extractor bolt, turn clockwise until the crank is forced from the bottom bracket axle.

To Remove Cups:

Photo 5—6: Use the recommended tool to remove the outer lockring (counterclockwise). The bearing cup can usually be removed (counterclockwise) by hand.

Photo 5–7: **Cone Adjustment.** Use the bearing cup tool to turn the cup to the position where the bottom bracket axle turns freely without excess "play." Holding the cup in that position with the left hand, use the lockring tool to tighten (clockwise) the lockring which holds the cup in its proper position. Check the axle to see if it turns freely. If not, loosen the lockring and repeat the adjustment and locking procedures.

goes up. The quality of the finish and materials used improves noticeably. The best alloy cranks are cold forged, a process that provides the strongest, most durable product. As the price of the cranksets goes up, you will see the difference in carefully machined surfaces. Even more important is the *design* of the right crankarm. You will usually be able to correlate the design and the finish quality since certain basic rules hold true.

Generally, the number of arms on the crankarm (spider) increases as the cost and quality increase. All good-quality steel cranks (right side) have three arms; an arrangement that provides adequate strength for all applications because of the characteristics of steel. However, this is not true of alloy crankarms. In order to compete with the steel cranks in price, the alloy cranks represent many compromises, including the number of spiders in the crank. The impor-

tance of the strength of these arms should be immediately obvious. The normal pedaling forces generated by the cyclist will easily bend and distort all but the very best cranksets.

Three-pin alloy cranksets are commonly found on inexpensive 10-speeds. Not only does the three-pin design provide much less structural strength than the five-pin design, but the method of manufacturing the crank is completely different. All quality cranks are forged and the crankarms are an integral part of the crank. On some of the inexpensive, alloy three-pin cranks, they are two separate pieces that have been attached as a part of the manufacturing process. Look at the inside of the crank where it joins with the crankarms to determine if the unit is one or two piece.

Unfortunately, the three-pin, two-piece alloy right crank is satisfactory for only very

Photo 5–8: **Removal of Cottered Crank.** Remove the attaching nut on the cotter pin by rotating counterclockwise.

Photo 5–9: If you do not own a cotter-pin tool, use a hammer to tap the cotter pin from its position. To reduce the possibility of bending the bottom bracket axle, use a rubber mallet or heavy block of wood under the crankarm to absorb shock.

casual, recreational use. Hard pedaling results in severe chainwheel flexing since there just isn't enough strength in the assembly. Hard riding can result in a loosening in the joint where the crank and the arm connect. It is interesting to note that most experts agree that good steel cranks cost about the same as inexpensive alloy cranks yet they are far stronger and more reliable. Why then, in most cases, has the inexpensive alloy crankset replaced the steel crankset?

The answer is really quite simple. Since the generalization that cotterless cranks are better than cottered cranks is usually true, the generalization has been expanded to mean *all* cotterless cranks are better than all cottered cranks, which is not true. Correctly stated, the cotterless crank *design* is better than the cottered crank *design*. The evaluation of any product should include the manufacturer's effectiveness in matching the features of the design with appropriate manufacturing and assembly standards. As a result of the lack of good information, the consumer has been educated through advertising that cotterless cranks are "best." Consequently, many bicycles are offered with cotterless alloy cranks that are not as "good" as the steel cottered cranks that they have replaced as a result of marketing considerations.

We found a good example of this in our bicycle shop when we offered a $250 bicycle that had cotterless steel Campagnolo cranks (recently discontinued). Most cyclists were immediately "turned off" by the steel cranks even though the cranksets did include alloy chainwheels. Visually, we would show them the design and manufacturing difference between cranksets and after considerable sales pressure, would make the sale. Not one of those many customers ever regretted the purchase. Virtually every one of them returned to tell us how smoothly operating and

stiff their chainsets were compared to some chainsets owned by their friends. They were free of the fast wear, sloppy tolerances, susceptibility to scratches, and flexing associated with many alloy chainsets.

Why do we bring up the subject of steel cranks when they are rapidly becoming an anachronism? We feel that some of the popular trends are not based on real value or utility and, hopefully, this example will provide the reader with some insight into the need for looking carefully at every aspect of the bicycle before paying more for a "new feature" that may not provide any real benefit.

BOTTOM BRACKET AXLE

The bottom bracket axle is a carefully machined rod of steel that acts as the axis around which the cranks turn. To minimize energy losses through friction, the axle runs on two sets of ball bearings. Adjustments are made in the same manner as hub and headset bearings—with a set of bearing cones and locknuts.

Selecting a bottom bracket is easy for there are only two choices: (1) purchase the original equipment that is designed for specific cranks, or (2) purchase a "specialty" bottom bracket axle that is designed to fit specific cranksets. Under most conditions, you should replace any bottom bracket axle with original equipment. Specialty bottom bracket axles have been designed to provide (usually at a steep price) some additional technical advantages. Most popular is the conversion from plain ball bearings to sealed bearings. The sealed bearing units are usually maintenance free for life.

Since bicycles frequently encounter inclement weather, the bearing surfaces are subjected to abuse that greatly reduces the

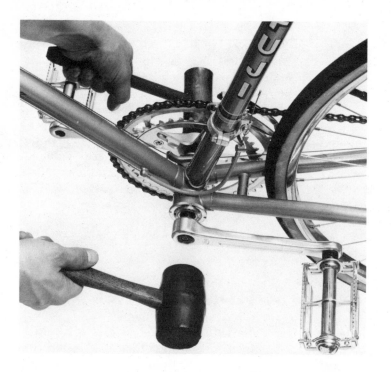

Photo 5-10: The crankarms should not be tightened into position with the bottom bracket axle bolt. Instead, tighten the bolt with your finger. Place a heavy object on one crank (at the axle) and hit the other crank (at the axle) with a rubber or wooden mallet. This will force the crank onto the tapered bottom bracket axle. After hitting the crankarm several times, tighten the nut with the crank wrench. Always use a heavy weight on the side opposite the hammer side to absorb the force of the shock. Without this shock absorption, the bottom bracket could be twisted out of alignment. Always retension the crankarm bolts regularly.

Photo 5-11: If you do not have bottom bracket axle tools, you can use a punch and hammer to remove the lockring. This should only be done when the proper tools are unavailable since it will cause some damage to the lockring. The lockring loosens in a counter-clockwise direction.

COTTER-PIN INSTALLATION

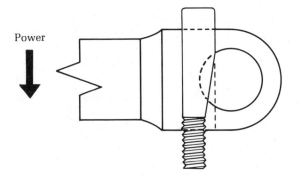

Power

Figure 5—4: The cotter pin should be installed with the direction of the cranks as the primary consideration. The threaded portion of the cotter pin should be at the bottom of the power stroke.

potential life of the components. The bottom bracket bearings in particular are subjected to considerable abuse because their position at the lower junction of the frame down tube, seat tube, and chainstays provides an excellent gathering place for water and dirt. Until sealed bearings were developed, the cyclist had no alternative except regular disassembly, cleaning, greasing, and reassembly.

The sealed bearing unit is a natural for the rider who cares about the condition of the bottom bracket, but doesn't have the time or the inclination to continually disassemble and clean it. Phil Wood makes an excellent sealed bearing unit that is reasonably priced; however, you should think twice before you decide to install one yourself. Unlike many repairs that can be economically performed at home, the Phil Wood bottom bracket assembly requires a specially designed wrench

at an approximate cost of $10 to properly install the unit. Those of you with British threads in the bottom bracket will require two wrenches because of the unique English thread pattern. Since the unit requires no maintenance or adjusting, purchase of the tools is really unnecessary. Let your bicycle shop handle the installation with *their* tools. It will be cheaper in the long run.

One other popular specialty bottom bracket exists—the lightweight titanium axle. The weight savings of the titanium vs. a standard all-steel axle can be up to 100 grams. But the savings is not cost efficient. The standard Campagnolo axle is $20, the titanium is $100.

As we have stated before, weight savings should never be considered without analyzing if any loss of strength results. Presuming the strength of the lightweight component is satisfactory, is it worth it to spend the greatly increased costs of titanium or other exotic alloys? Of the many expert coaches, trainers, and equipment manufacturers we have spoken to, none thought the marginal weight savings and minimal performance improvement could outweigh the cost of the item or the potential problem of reduced reliability. Unless you are a racer whose winnings will be substantially affected by gaining a few inches at the finish line, save yourself the money. Buy the best lightweight components, not the ultralightweight. The weight difference between the lightweight and ultralightweight components isn't enough to spell success or failure—your cycling technique, tactics, and conditioning are, however.

In short, unless the idea of the nomaintenance sealed bearing units appeals to you, stay with the manufacturer's recommendations for original equipment on your specific crankset.

CHAINWHEELS

Like bottom bracket axles and cups, chainwheels are provided by manufacturers to fit their own particular designs. There is much more to consider than the number of teeth on the sprockets. The choice between aluminum or steel chainwheels isn't offered. Usually, steel cranksets have steel chainwheels and alloy cranksets have alloy chainwheels. Steel chainwheels are best for the casual rider or commuter because they last far longer than even the best alloy chainwheels. This is particularly important for the commuter who generally rides in all types of weather. Chains accumulate salt,

dirt, and dust which are abrasive and quickly wear the chainwheel teeth—another reason why some riders might elect not to purchase alloy cotterless chainwheels.

Generally, the better alloy cranksets will outlast the inexpensive ones. Fortunately, you can determine which ones will last longest by physical inspection. The longest wearing chainwheel is the Campagnolo. Like other good-quality cranksets, it is cold forged and the alloy is very hard. The inexpensive chainwheels are usually very soft. Cheap alloy chainwheels are stamped; the good ones (like Campagnolo) have gear-cut

Photos 5–12A and 5–12B: **Chainwheel Tooth Patterns.** Different manufacturers use different designs for the teeth on their chainwheels. The industry standard, Campagnolo (A), has a semicircular cut between each gear tooth that is exactly the same size as the chain roller. Other designs (B) contribute to quick wear since the shape of the area between the teeth is greater than the size of the roller in the chain and some slippage occurs.

teeth. Not only does the accuracy of the manufacturing process help smooth shifting due to the consistency of the teeth, but it also increases the chainwheel life.

The shape of the teeth on the chainwheel is one of the most important factors that govern both shifting performance and wear. Campagnolo chainwheels have perfectly cut semicircles between each tooth which are exactly the size of the rollers on the chain links. Since the chain fits each slot perfectly, little abrasion results. Some Japanese chainwheels have a square cut area between the teeth. We have found that this area provides a small degree of movement that can lead to premature chainwheel wear.

Most cyclists raise an eyebrow when this point is discussed since really fast wear seems so improbable. We have spoken to more than one bicycle shop owner who has confirmed that some customers have complained of severe chainwheel wear with as little as 1,000 miles on the bicycle. Compare that to most riders who claim to exceed 10,000 miles with a Campagnolo chainwheel with no wear problems.

As we wrote this we came across an ad in a popular cycling parts catalog that listed a closeout price on one of the chainwheels with which we had encountered many problems. They were offering the chainwheel for $1.98. Perhaps our criticism of these parts is not justified when the actual price of the part is so cheap (most chainwheel sets are between $8 to $30). We believe that some of the least expensive chainwheels are little more than cutout pie pans and maybe no one should expect over 1,000 to 2,000 miles of use.

The strength of a chainwheel is an important advantage. We explained how the number of support arms on the crank spider contributes to the strength, but there are other factors. Figure 5-2 illustrates how the better chainwheels offer an additional strengthening ring. The only reason to eliminate this ring is for the benefit of reduced weight since it contributes greatly to the stiffness of the crankset. Some of the lightest cranksets include drilled-out holes to further reduce weight. Remember the lack of stiffness of a chainwheel may result in less benefit to the rider than the benefit of the reduced weight.

Another advantage that is found with the better chainwheels is their overall accuracy of manufacture. They tend to wobble less from side to side and they are round. Although it sounds hard to believe, not all chainwheels are accurately cut and some shifting problems can occur. This problem is particularly obvious on direct-drive (fixed gear) track bicycles; the chain tension may vary considerably as the cranks are rotated.

Elliptical Chainwheels

Just a few quick words: *don't buy one.* Many articles and magazine ads have extoled the virtues of the elliptical chainwheel but why doesn't the serious cyclist use one if they are so great? Not one professional racer uses one. The elliptical chainwheel was designed by a cycling novice who did not properly understand how to pedal (see chapter fourteen).

CHAINS

Everyone knows where the bicycle chain is located. . . . It's adjacent to the black grimy stains on your right calf or pants leg. Chains are dirty because they require constant lubrication to prevent losses through friction resulting in premature wear of those

Crankset Characteristics

	Advantages	Disadvantages	Recommended Use
Steel One-Piece Crank	Inexpensive Little maintenance Reliable Durable Strong	Very heavy Poor finish Poor fits Selection among chainwheels is limited	Utility and commuter bicycles where cost outweighs performance
Steel Cottered Crank	Relatively inexpensive Reliable Improved finish over one-piece cranks	Heavy Cotter pins can loosen under heavy stress May be difficult to obtain chainwheels	Commuter, recreational, and sports bicycles where cost is a factor
Alloy Cottered Crank	Relatively inexpensive Lighter than steel cottered crank Improved finish over one-piece cranks	Cotter pins can loosen under heavy stress May be difficult to obtain chainwheels Inordinate wear on alloy crankarms where cotter pins are inserted Alloy arms bend more easily under heavy stress	Commuter, recreational, and sports bicycles where cost is a factor
Steel Cotterless Crank	Reliable Strong Good finish Superior cotterless fastening system	Heavy Few manufacturers distribute or include on bicycles in United States	Commuter, recreational, and sports bicycles where cost is a factor and increased reliability is important

	Advantages	Disadvantages	Recommended Use
Alloy Cotterless Three-Pin Spider	Inexpensive Very light weight Superior cotterless fastening system	Crankset may be weak Insufficiently stiff chainwheels may wear rapidly Replacement parts may be hard to find	Sports and recreational bicycles
Alloy Cotterless Five-Pin Spider	Light weight Reliable Strong Good finish Superior cotterless fastening system	Expensive Wide variation from fair to superb cranksets are available Some cranksets may not have wide distribution of replacement parts	Recreational, sports, and performance bicycles where superior finish, strength, reliability, and light weight are important

expensive chainwheels and freewheel cogs on the bicycle.

The function of all bicycle chains is the same: transfer of the cyclist's power from the crankset to the rear wheel. All bicycle chains are not the same, however; different requirements have resulted in some variation in chains. Basically, there are two different sizes: $1/2'' \times 1/8''$ for nonderailleur bicycles and $1/2'' \times 3/32''$ for derailleur-equipped bicycles.

The narrower $3/32''$ wide chain is designed for derailleur-equipped bicycles, since the 5- and 6-speed freewheels have cogs that are close together which require a narrow chain. Utility bicycles, 3-speeds, and track bicycles use the heavier $1/2'' \times 1/8''$ chain. Another difference between the two chains is their method of fastening. The $1/2'' \times 1/8''$ chains use master links. Every link in the chain is identical except for one, the master link, which is designed to be disassembled without any special tools. The master link is slightly wider than any of the other links in the chain. Consequently, it is not used for derailleur-equipped bicycles since the chain would hang up on the rear derailleur. The derailleur chain ($1/2'' \times 3/32''$) has no master link and removing the chain requires a special tool to force one of the rivets out of the chain (photo 5-14A). Several such tools are available for a reasonable price.

Many cyclists are overly concerned with the selection of chains. Frequently, shifting problems are attributed to the chain which has very little to do with the problem unless it is dirty. Chains are available in many different colors and styles—including gold and silver—with holes drilled in the plates for lightness and titanium chains to reduce weight (which some manufacturers are offer-

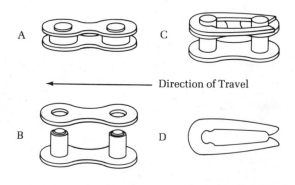

Figure 5–5: **Chain Parts.** A chain consists of many inner links (A) and outer links (B) that are alternated. Derailleur chains require a special tool to remove one of the pins (or rivets) from an outer link. Utility and track bicycle chains (½″ × ⅛″) both use a master link (C). The master link is removed by prying the ends of the spring clip (D) off the special outer link (C). Always install the spring clip with the closed end facing the direction of travel.

ing at a staggering price). Most cyclists would do better to carefully match his or her choice of drive-chain components rather than selecting any specific chain because of the manufacturer's claims.

Regina chains, for instance, are superb chains that are manufactured in a width slightly narrower than ³/₃₂″. They work best on Regina freewheels and Campagnolo chainwheels. Typical of many Italian products, the chains were designed and tested in collaboration with Campagnolo. Most racers use Regina Oro chains since Regina makes one of the best freewheels with specially prepared bearings to insure minimum friction.

On the other hand, the Japanese freewheels have different tooth patterns than the European cogs and they offer chains to match. Recently, the Japanese have been offering many new chains with specially designed links to ease shifting. We have

Photo 5–13: To correct a stiff chain link, first isolate the problem link. Place your thumbs on the adjacent links and, with your hands wrapped around the chain, work the link back and forth a few times.

Photos 5–14A and 5–14B: **Using a Chain Tool.** Insert the chain into the tool (A) and rotate the extractor pin until the rivet loosens (B). *Do not remove* the rivet completely since it is very difficult to reinstall.

always felt that most shifting problems are from (1) the rider who never learned how to shift a derailleur-equipped bicycle or (2) the equipment or the bicycle which had been changed or damaged so that alignment problems occurred.

Most chain problems originate from lack of proper maintenance. The chain becomes covered with grit which results in two problems: poor shifting and premature wear. The chain should be oiled and cleaned regularly depending on the riding conditions. When the dirt begins to accumulate, it's time to remove the chain and clean it as follows:

1. Immerse the chain in mineral spirits or kerosene. A canning jar filled three-quarters full with the solvent will usually hold the chain. Do not use gasoline to clean chains; many chains have a semipermanent lubricant inside the links that is destroyed by gasoline. Gasoline is also highly flammable

and too dangerous to use in any type of cleaning procedure. A chain cleaned in gasoline will sound like it's 100 years old even though it may be brand new.

2. After all grit has been removed, hang the chain up to dry (away from any open flames). Wipe the chain with a clean rag. Look over the chain to determine if there is any remaining grit. If dirt is evident, clean the chain again.

3. Using another canning jar, this time filled with light machine oil, submerge the chain and let it soak. After the chain is thoroughly saturated, hang it up to "drip dry." Place the open canning jar under the chain so the excess oil will drip back into the container.

4. After the dripping process has ended, take another clean rag and thoroughly wipe off the outside links of the chain. Any oil on the outside of the chain will attract dirt and necessitate prematurely recleaning the chain.

Chains cleaned using this system will last substantially longer than those cleaned with gasoline or those merely receiving an external oiling.

FREEWHEELS

The explanation of what a freewheel does is simple. However, repair procedures are complex and time consuming. Generally, you would be further ahead to buy a new freewheel if any bearing problems occur. With some brands of freewheels (i.e., Regina and Sun Tour), it is possible to purchase the freewheel body without the sprockets.

The two major components of the freewheel body are the ratcheting mechanism bearings and their casing. The outside of the body is either splined or threaded (or a combination of both) to accept various-size cogs which will in turn provide 10 different gear ratios, when 2 front chainwheels are

Freewheel Threads

Thread Type	Thread Pitch (in mm.)	Threads per Inch
Italian	1.058	24
British	1.058	24
French	1	25.4
Proposed Standard	1.058	24

This chart illustrates why some freewheels and hubs are not interchangeable and why the industry proposed standards to be used by all manufacturers.

Although they are not identical, British and Italian hubs and freewheels can interchange, but the French components are unique and are not interchangeable with any others.

used, or 15 different speeds if 3 front chain-wheels are used.

The freewheel body is engaged when the cyclist pedals forward (in a clockwise direction). The wheel turns, moving the bicycle ahead. The freewheel ratchets when the cyclist's feet are held motionless while the bicycle is moving. This coasting results in a tic-tic-tic sound, just like a 3-speed bicycle. The freewheel also ratchets (or "freewheels") when the pedals are moved counterclockwise. This clicking sound is caused by tiny pawls that are tensioned by minute springs. These pawl springs are the reason why you don't normally want to take your freewheel apart. The inside of the freewheel is a little like the inside of a watch.

The freewheel is probably the least reliable component on a bicycle. Usually little warning is given before a pawl spring breaks or one of the tiny ball bearings crumble. Many times this will result in a freewheel that is still ridable but the freewheeling or coasting will be very noisy and jerky. Replace or repair the unit as soon as possible.

Sometimes this noisy condition can be caused by dirt that has entered the freewheel body. Before you replace the freewheel, flush it out with WD40 or lightweight oil. Pouring oil through the body will sometimes flush out the offending particles of dirt (photo 5-15). Always wipe off all oil on the outside of the freewheel because as on a chain, this oil attracts and holds dirt.

The Regina Oro is probably the number-one freewheel choice of the racer since the bearings are carefully lapped to insure smooth, quiet operation. Another very important feature to the racer is the wide-spread availability of different cogs for the Regina freewheel body. With proper selection of cogs, the rider can select whatever gear ratios are best for his or her style and individual needs.

Photo 5–15: **Oiling the Freewheel.** Lay your wheel on its side with the freewheel at the top. Spread oil along the seam that separates the fixed part of the freewheel body and the portion that rotates. Spin the freewheel several times to work the oil into the bearings and remove excess oil with a cloth.

Recently, the Japanese introduced a number of fine inexpensive freewheels, some of which offer a selection of alternative cogs. Because of the overall minimal reliability level of freewheels, most riders would be better off using the basic Japanese freewheels. They are no less reliable, yet they are usually less expensive. The Sun Tour freewheels seem to offer the best combination of reliability, quality, economy, and they are universally available.

Whatever freewheel is selected, you should try to purchase the same freewheel brand as a replacement, since freewheel widths vary and shifting problems will require readjustment of the rear derailleur. Worse yet, some freewheel designs are different enough to cause the chain to rub on the chainstay when the chain is in the high-gear (smallest cog) position. This problem is common on bicycles with short chainstays. Racers must be particularly conscious of freewheel selection because they usually have a set of racing wheels for competition and a different set of wheels for training or everyday riding. Unless the freewheels are the same, the derailleur may have to be adjusted with each wheel change.

Inexpensive freewheel spacers are available to correct this problem. The spacer is installed on the threaded side of the rear hub before the freewheel is mounted. Varying thicknesses of these spacers can insure that all the cogs, from one wheel to another, are in the same position when mounted in the frame.

The latest fad in cycling seems to be the freewheel-and-chain combination. Although the 5-speed freewheel provides virtually every gear choice a rider normally needs, 6- and 7-speed freewheels are being advertised. If you decide to get a special 6- or 7-speed freewheel, be aware that several modifications will be required.

A 6- or 7-speed freewheel usually requires a different rear hub than the standard 5-speed. The ordinary 6-speed hub is 125 mm. wide while the 5-speed hub is 120 mm. wide. This means that the bicycle chainstays will have to be spread and realigned for the larger hub. Also, some freewheels *require* matching chains. Specialization of this type can be a problem, especially on a long tour.

If trouble strikes, you may be required to make several modifications to get yourself back on the road.

One word of advice: Before you select special 6- or 7-speed cog freewheels or special titanium chains or cogs, ask yourself if you really need the small benefits that will result.

Rules of Thumb

- Always check the tightness of the crank attachment bolts (for cotterless cranksets) on a weekly basis. These bolts tend to loosen, and damage to the crankarm is likely if the rider isn't careful.

- Carefully match pedal axle threads with the crank threads. A small quantity of light grease should be smeared on the pedal axle threads to reduce the chance of thread damage. This is particularly important when fitting steel pedal axles into alloy cranks—the soft threads on the alloy cranks are easily damaged.

- If your chainwheel rubs against the rearstay, first check to insure that the chainwheel is not warped. If it is OK, you must bend in a section of the rearstay to provide adequate clearance. Although this is best accomplished by a competent bicycle shop, you can do it by laying the oval wooden handle of a hammer on the place where an indentation is required. Using another hammer, hit the wooden handle sharply to create the dent. Do not hit the steel tube directly. Also, do not file the tube to obtain the necessary clearance. The tube wall is too thin to file without causing a weakening.

CHAPTER SIX

PEDALS AND TOE CLIPS

All of the rider's pedaling power is transmitted to the pedals which are attached, at right angles, to the ends of the cranks. Two basic types of pedals are made: rubber and rattrap. The rubber pedal is designed for the recreational cyclist. It can be used barefoot (not a safe practice) or with tennis shoes, loafers, and sandals; the large soft, flat surface will not bite into the rider's shoes. These are the least expensive pedals manufactured and they are usually seen only on children's bicycles or 3-speed commuting-type bicy-

Photo 6–1: The basic utility pedal is designed for use with any type of shoe. Instead of a pedal cage, it has a solid platform of rubber to evenly distribute the pressure of the foot on the pedal. Generally, these pedals are inexpensive, do not permit bearing adjustment, and are found on utility bicycles.

Photo 6–2: The basic rattrap pedal is an inexpensive imitation of the better alloy-cage pedals. It is made of steel, and like the rubber pedal, it does not have adjustable bearings. Frequently, the design precludes the use of toe clips and straps since there are no mounting holes.

cles. Toe clips and straps cannot be attached. Rattrap pedals have steel or alloy cages that are designed to be used with cycling shoes, toe clips and straps, and shoe cleats (see chapter ten).

When combined with shoe cleats, the rattrap pedal holds the foot in the optimal position for efficient pedaling. Its design makes cycling in soft-sole shoes, such as tennis shoes, uncomfortable. The rattrap is intended for hard-sole shoes that will distribute the pressure from the contact points throughout the sole of the foot.

PEDALS

Inexpensive rattrap pedals do not have adjustable bearings and consequently, they can wear quickly. The bearings can easily become too tight or too loose. Most inexpensive 10-speeds are equipped with this type of pedal as standard equipment. The serious

rider who intends to ride in all conditions and likes to maintain a bicycle, will probably want to change to a set of pedals that allows bearing adjustment. Pedals with adjustable bearings are usually of sufficient quality to provide an additional benefit—more accurate tolerances. Although the tolerances don't seem too important for pedals since only the axle moves, an equally important tolerance exists: the perfect 90-degree installation into the crankarm. If the axle is bent, the pedal will wobble with each pedal stroke. This is not overly important for the casual rider, but can become a real aggravation to the long-distance rider as the wobbling motion can adversely affect ankle and knee joints.

Before you attempt to switch pedals, make sure you select pedals that have the appropriate threads. Installing or removing pedals is made somewhat complicated because the right pedal has a righthand thread and the left pedal has a lefthand thread. The easiest way to remember the thread direction

(continued on page 107)

Pedal Characteristics

	Advantages	Disadvantages	Recommended Use
Rubber Utility	Inexpensive Durable Does not require special cycling shoes No maintenance (except occasional oiling) required	Heavy Nonadjustable bearings	Utility or commuting bicycles
Steel Rattrap	Fairly inexpensive Durable May accommodate toe clips	Fairly heavy Cannot be used with bare feet or sandals Poor overall finish and fits	Commuting bicycle or basic recreational 10-speeds
Alloy Sports Pedal	Moderately expensive Adjustable bearings Will accommodate toe clips and straps Improved precision and finish Width will accommodate sports and "street" shoes Fairly light weight	Excessive width may hinder high-speed cornering	Recreational and sports 10-speeds where owner desires precise, adjustable bearings—reasonable compromise between features and price
Alloy Racing Pedal (steel axle)	Designed for toe clips, straps, and cycling shoes with cleats Adjustable bearings Very precise fits and finish Light weight Reliable	Expensive Designed to be used with cycling shoes—may be too narrow for "street" shoes	Sports and performance riding where reliability, performance, and appearance are more important than price

	Advantages	Disadvantages	Recommended Use
Racing Pedals Extra-Lightweight Black Alloy Cages (steel axle)	Marginally lighter than regular alloy racing pedal (same features)	Very expensive Black lightweight pedal cages require plastic shoe cleats Cage breakage can occur from a crash	Racing
Racing Pedals Extra-Lightweight Black Alloy Cages (titaium axle)	Lightest pedal available Other features same as racing pedal	Incredibly expensive Weight reduction is hard to justify when comparing increased cost vs. performance improvement	Racing uses where budget is unlimited

Photo 6–3: The basic sports pedal includes mounting holes for toe clips and reflectors. Like the top-quality pedals, it has a quill that extends outside the pedal axle. This assists in positioning the foot and provides comfortable routing of the toe strap. This pedal has adjustable bearings which can usually be identified by the flats on the bearing cap which are built to facilitate a wrench for removal.

Photo 6–4: The standard, top-quality road pedals look like this one by Campagnolo. Many manufacturers produce a pedal that looks exactly like the Campagnolo pedal. In addition to the features found on a basic sports pedal (photo 6–3), it includes a better finish, high-quality alloys, and two small tangs. The rear tang is designed to tip the pedal into position for easy entry of the foot into the toe clip. On the inside of the pedal, another tang is provided to keep the toe strap close to the pedal cage so it does not rub against the crank while pedaling.

Photo 6–5: The top track pedals are similar in quality to the top road pedals (photo 6–4). Again, many manufacturers produce copies of this accepted Campagnolo design. The track pedal does not include the wraparound quill since it could contact the track banking on steeply banked tracks.

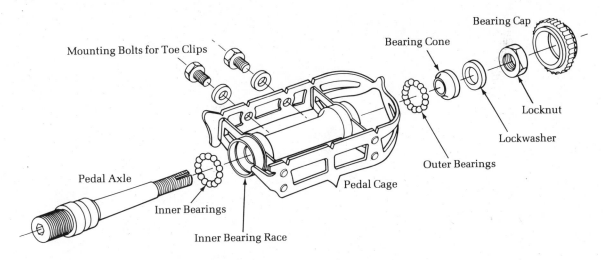

Figure 6—1: **Exploded View of Pedal.**

is to remember this: To loosen the pedal always turn the wrench toward the rear of the bicycle. To tighten, always turn the wrench toward the front of the bicycle. Assuming that you can get the pedals on and off properly, all you have to do is identify the proper thread size. This is extremely critical with alloy cranks, since any error will result in damage to the soft threads in the cranks. English, Italian, and Japanese pedal axles are 9/16″ × 20 tpi, but the French pedal axles are 14 mm. × 1.25 mm. Most manufacturers stamp the end of the axle with a letter which indicates which side of the bicycle the pedal belongs on.

The Japanese make the best pedals for the price. While Campagnolo still makes what is probably the best pedal, several Japanese companies offer pedals that look the same and feel almost as good. This is one item where the best isn't necessary for the average rider.

The Cinelli pedal, designed to hold the foot tightly on the pedal without toe clips or straps, is unique. The pedal is light weight, since it has no cage. Rather, it has an over-size shoe cleat which locks onto the pedal. As with all Cinelli products, the quality is first class and the price is staggering. Unlike most Cinelli products, the pedal hasn't met with

Country of Manufacture	Marking on Right Pedal Axle	Marking on Left Pedal Axle
France	D	G
England	R	L
Italy	D	S
Japan	R	L

Troubleshooting Guide: Pedals

Problem	Probable Cause	How to Repair
Clicking or scraping noise while pedaling (pedal binding)	Bottom bracket axle bearings (see Troubleshooting Guide: Derailleurs in chapter seven or Cranks in chapter five)	Disassemble, inspect, regrease, and reassemble pedal bearings
	Pedal bearings dirty or damaged	Inexpensive, nonadjusting pedals must be replaced
		Adjust pedal bearing cones
Pedal does not rotate at constant position to crankarm (wobbles)	Bent pedal axle	Disassemble pedals and replace axle (if replacement parts are available) or replace pedal
Pedal cage wobbles on pedal axle	Loose pedal bearing cones	Adjust as appropriate
Pedal rotates smoothly but "grabs" occasionally	Broken or damaged ball bearing	Disassemble pedal, inspect bearings, and replace as appropriate. Regrease and reassemble.
		Replace nonadjusting pedals

any popularity because the foot *cannot* be removed without reaching down and releasing a lever by hand. The shoe cleat is also hard to latch into the pedal without someone holding the bicycle upright. For these reasons, the Cinelli pedal is rarely seen except at track racing events, and even there, is not particularly popular.

TOE CLIPS

Toe clips are very simple, inexpensive spring steel attachments that fit on the front of rattrap pedals. Used in conjunction with a toe strap, they keep the foot in its optimal position on the pedal. While all toe clips look pretty much alike, most cyclists prefer

Men's Shoe Size	Recommended Toe-Clip Size	Christophe Identification
5–7	Small	Stamped: Christophe D
8–10	Medium	Stamped: Christophe
11–13	Large	Stamped: Christophe Special

the Christophe, named for the famous bicycle racer Eugene Christophe, winner of the important Milan–San Remo in 1910, Paris–Tours in 1920, and the Bordeaux–Paris in 1920 and 1924. The Christophe toe clip is good looking, virtually unbreakable, and it comes in three sizes to accommodate most feet.

TOE STRAPS

The toe strap is little more than a thin strip of leather with alloy buckles. Used with the toe clip, it anchors the cyclist's foot to the pedal and permits the rider to pedal in a circular motion rather than simply pushing at the pedal. There are many different brands of toe straps; however, only two are really satisfactory for the serious cyclist. Most non-racers use Lapize toe straps, named after the famous three-time winner of the grueling 165-mile Paris–Roubaix and three-time winner of the 180-mile Paris–Brussels race (1911, 1912, 1913). This strap is satisfactory for virtually all riding. The high stress requirements of the racers call for a stronger buckle and a thicker toe strap which stretches less under pressure. Almost universally, racers use the Alfredo Binda toe strap. It was named for the famous Italian cyclist that virtually dominated Italian racing from 1925 to 1933.

Photo 6–6: **Correct Position of Toe Strap.** The toe strap must be properly inserted into the pedal or it will not work as designed. In this position, the buckle end of the strap is on the bottom and the plain end of the strap goes through the buckle from the top. This permits the strap to tighten by pulling the strap up and to loosen by pushing the buckle down.

Photo 6–7: **Proper Toe Strap Installation.** The toe strap should be twisted as it is placed into the pedal. This twisting will keep the strap in its proper position when it is tightened since the twist will prevent the strap from slipping through the pedal.

CHAPTER SEVEN

DERAILLEURS

Derailleurs rival brakes in terms of complexity and the number of types available. However, if you know how each design is related to its intended function, derailleurs are really not too difficult to understand. Most problems with derailleurs occur as a result of abuse or improper handling rather than poor adjustment or faulty workmanship.

PRINCIPLES OF GEARING

The principle of gearing is simple if you understand the relationship between the human body and the bicycle. Even a child's bicycle uses the benefits of gearing for mechanical advantage. For instance, a tot's tricycle employs pedals that are attached to a large front wheel. One revolution of the pedals will rotate the wheel once and the bicycle will go forward (or backward) a distance equal to the circumference of the wheel.

Since a child is relatively weak (and a high speed is undesirable), the diameter of the wheel is kept small. One revolution of the pedals will move the tricycle ahead a comparatively small distance. As the size of the wheel increases, the distance traveled with each revolution will also increase. Very early penny-farthing, or high-wheeler bicycles used this principle. These bikes had a very large front wheel which propelled the machine a considerable distance with each revolution of the pedals. Although the high-wheeler could cover distances in far less time than a person walking, its top speed was limited to the speed that the riders could pedal (the size of the wheel couldn't get any larger without severe handling, mounting, and dismounting problems). Therefore, the next logical step was to develop gears to multiply the distance traveled with each revolution of the pedals.

To illustrate the principle of bicycle gearing, let's use a hypothetical example of a bicycle that has 50 teeth on the front sprocket where the pedals are attached. Another

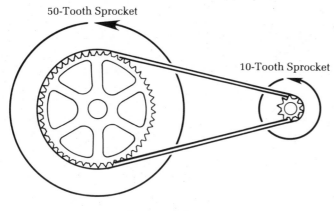

50-Tooth Sprocket

10-Tooth Sprocket

Figure 7–1: **Sprocket Revolutions.**

1 Revolution = 5 Revolutions

sprocket is attached to the back wheel and the two sprockets are linked by a chain. With each revolution of the pedals, the front sprocket rotates once. Assuming that there are 50 teeth on the front sprocket and 10 teeth on the rear sprocket, the back sprocket will rotate 5 times for every revolution of the front sprocket (figure 7-1).

As soon as designers equipped the bicycle with front and rear sprockets, new speeds were possible. The only limitation on the relationship between the front sprocket and the rear sprocket is the strength of the rider. As the difference between the front sprocket increases, so does the amount of power required to propel the bicycle. Eventually, optimum proportions between the two sprockets were reached. This subject is covered in more detail in chapter five, under chainwheels and freewheels. For the purposes of this chapter, we do not need to concern ourselves with how to calculate gear ratios; we only intend to show the benefits, use, and maintenance of derailleurs. Before we describe what a derailleur does, let's look at

why its development and evolution was necessary and inevitable.

On the early bicycles, the front and rear sprockets were chosen to satisfy the needs of the average cyclist under average conditions. The obvious problem is the lack of "average" people or riding conditions. Although the optimum pedaling speed might be 80 rpm's (revolutions per minute) for a cyclist, this speed is impossible to maintain while going up a steep hill (the rider might not be strong enough) or down the other side of the hill (the rider can't pedal as fast as the bicycle wants to go).

Remember, the early bicycles had fixed gears; that is, the chain was a direct drive between the front gear and the back gear. The rider could not coast. To solve the problem of going downhill faster than the cyclist could pedal, a freewheel was designed. Using the principle of a ratchet, the rider could pedal when desired or coast when appropriate. Still, the problem of going uphill was not solved.

Recall that the child's tricycle is easy to

pedal as the distance traveled is relatively small with each revolution of the pedals. Someone figured out a method of calculating gear ratios as the need for more than one available gear ratio became obvious.

The immediate solution which involved two sprockets, one on each side of the hub, was not very convenient. The rider was required to reverse the position of the rear wheel to select a different ratio. Generally, riders would select one gear ratio for riding on flat ground, and another for ascending steep hills. Imagine a race during which everyone stopped at the foot of a hill, removed the chain from the rear sprocket, removed the wheel, turned the wheel around, reinserted the wheel, reinstalled and adjusted the chain, tightened the wheel, and hopped back on the bicycle to ascend the hill! At the top, the riders would repeat the drill prior to their descent! Although this system of two sprockets was an advantage over one, the inconvenience led to two inventions: the quick-release wheel and a gear-changing system that didn't require the rider to dismount.

MODERN-DAY DERAILLEURS

Although many different forms of shifting mechanisms were developed, the modern-day derailleur system has proven to be the most efficient. Even though the internal-hub 3-speed is simple, it is heavy and mechanically inefficient. Its design also limits the possible number of different gear selections. The basic derailleur system uses a combination of two sprockets (called chainwheels) on the front where the pedals are joined, and five sprockets (called the freewheel) at the rear attached to the wheel. To utilize all of the potential gear variations, a method to move the chain from sprocket to sprocket was developed. Using a control lever, the rider can move the derailleur which in turn forces (derails) the chain to adjacent sprockets. While refinements changed specific characteristics, essentially all derailleurs do the same thing—they derail the chain from sprocket to sprocket.

The front and rear derailleurs are completely different in design and appearance, although they both rely on centrifugal force to help them move the chain. As the sprockets are spinning during the normal pedaling motion, the laws of physics dictate that the chain will tend to fly off the sprockets because of centrifugal force. To keep the chain in place, the rear derailleur includes a spring-tensioned roller that counteracts the centrifugal force of the spinning sprockets. Movement of the derailleurs is controlled by a lever that is located within easy reach of the rider. Shifting the control lever moves the derailleur which, in turn, forces the chain from one sprocket to the other. This movement occurs only when the rider is pedaling. It is impossible to shift gears without pedaling.

All 10-speed bicycles have two derailleurs, one for the front chainwheels and one for the rear freewheel. A 5-speed bicycle has only one derailleur (rear) since all 5 speeds have only a five-cog freewheel and one chainwheel. Although several gear variations occur (two or three chainwheels and four, five, and six freewheel cogs) only two derailleurs are required. Each derailleur is activated by a separate control lever. These levers are located in one of the following three positions:

1. *On the frame down tube near the head tube.* This position is preferred by the

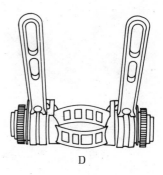

A   B   C   D

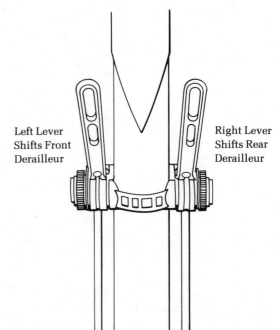

Left Lever
Shifts Front
Derailleur

Right Lever
Shifts Rear
Derailleur

Figure 7–2: **Derailleur Shift (or Control) Levers.** All of these shift levers are designed to be mounted on the down tube of the frame. Although they all perform the same function, each has slightly different features.

(A) This style requires a screwdriver or a thin coin to tighten the tension screw.

(B) This type has a knurled nut that provides easy adjustment of the tension screw using only the rider's fingers.

(C) This model includes a wing nut that performs the adjustment function without tools.

(D) Some models are available with cutouts to reduce weight.

vast majority of serious cyclists and racers. Shifting gears with levers in this position is smooth and positive because the control cable has relatively few bends between the lever and the derailleurs. Since this position is efficient, cable breakage is held to a minimum.

2. *Handlebar end shifters.* These are located at the ends of the handlebars. They take the place of handlebar plugs. Some cyclists prefer this control-lever position. A

major disadvantage is the extra-long cables that are required to reach from the ends of the handlebars. Two problems result from this extra length. First, the cable tends to stretch more during the shift. Second, the cable must be covered by a cable housing since it runs against the side of the handlebars and will therefore be subject to pressure from the rider's hands. This outer cable housing causes increased friction and less precise shifting. The down-tube shift lever

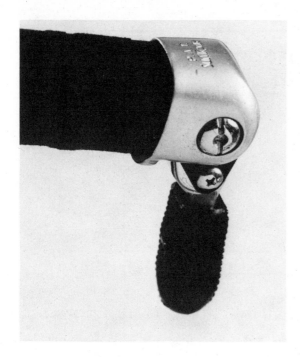

HANDLEBAR END SHIFTER

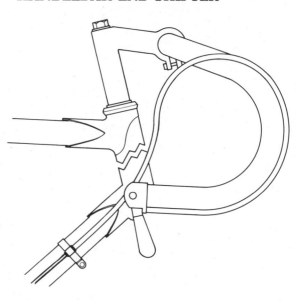

Photo 7–1 and Figure 7–3: The handlebar end shifter is mounted in the open end of the handlebars, replacing the handlebar plugs. The control cable must be routed through a cable housing (which is under the handlebar tape) before it runs without housing at the point where down-tube levers are normally mounted.

does not require an outer cable housing in most designs. Some riders also complain that a cable housing that is taped to the handlebars is uncomfortable.

3. *Stem shifters.* Unfortunately, a very high percentage of the middle-range 10-speeds include derailleur control levers that are attached to the handlebar stem. We say this is unfortunate because it is much harder to get a good, precise shift with these levers because of the extra cable length. This inefficiency is made obvious by the difference in size between shift levers that are mounted on the down tube (short) vs. stem shifters (very long). The extra length on the control lever is intended to provide more shifting leverage.

Cable breakage with the stem shifters is disproportionately higher than with down-tube shifters. Improperly mounted stem shifters also present a potential safety problem in a crash. Due to their positioning, they often protrude above the handlebars and stem. The fact that stem shifters are never found on high-quality sports bicycles (in this case, the definition includes bicycles with a lightweight, double-butted tubing frame and alloy components) says a lot about stem shifters. They offer no real advantage and are primarily a marketing tool.

Although there are three different positions for the control levers, certain general

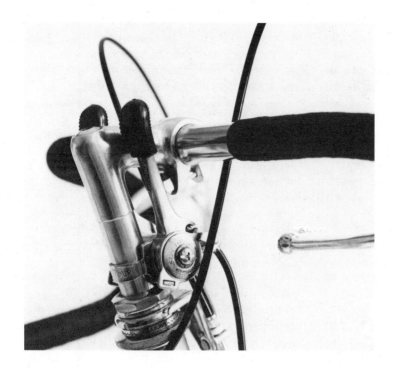

Photo 7–2: The stem shifter is attached to the handlebar stem. Its long levers and great cable length result in a slow, unresponsive shift.

design rules of thumb are consistent. All right-side derailleur levers control the operation of the rear derailleur. It's easy to remember: right-side lever—rear derailleur (right—rear). The left lever controls the front derailleur. All right-side derailleur controls (with the exception of the Japanese) work the same: moving the levers back (toward the back of the bicycle) results in a lower gear. The opposite is true with the left-side control lever. Moving the lever forward results in a higher gear. For some reason, the Japanese decided to use the opposite for the left-side lever on some derailleurs. Moving the left lever back results in a lower gear; moving it forward results in a higher gear.

Proper gear shifting requires an understanding of multiple gears and of the easiest way to actuate the derailleurs. Let's take a look at when you need to shift before we review how to shift.

SHIFTING GEARS

For the novice, proper use of the available gears on the 10-speed is probably the least understood part of cycling. To explain when to shift we must explain how the gears can benefit the rider. Although the human body is very versatile (it can pedal high gears slowly or it can pedal low gears fast), each person has an optimum pedaling speed. This optimum speed is usually developed after years of cycling experience. However, near-optimum pedaling speed is easy to attain if you know where to start. Let's begin with simple physiological characteristics of the human body.

Over a long distance it is easier to pedal with quick, light pedal strokes rather than by pushing high gears at a slow rate. The effects on your muscles can be easily demonstrated off the bicycle. To prove it yourself, try lifting a 2-pound weight over your head 50 times. Now compare the effect on your arm muscles as you try to lift a 50-pound weight over your head twice. This example is an exaggeration but proves a point. In the final analysis, how fast, and how hard, you pedal will depend on two factors:

1. *Your individual physique.* Generally, heavily muscled individuals can push harder but are less agile; lightly muscled individuals can't push as hard but they can pedal faster since they are more agile.

2. *The type of equipment you are riding.* It is more difficult to pedal a bicycle with heavy wheels and balloon tires than to pedal a bicycle with alloy rims and lightweight high-pressure tires. As a rule, you should attempt to pedal between 80 to 100 rpm's on a lightweight bicycle with tubular tires and 60 to 80 rpm's on a bicycle with heavier wired-on tires. Variations within that range reflect individual anatomy, age, physical conditioning, and cycling experience.

The beginner should ignore any reference to gear nomenclature and, instead, concentrate on understanding the differences between a high gear and a low gear. At this point, don't worry about how to locate first gear or seventh gear or tenth gear. Forget it. You should direct your attention to understanding how to use the gears efficiently. Let's assume that you have analyzed your age, conditioning, and type of bicycle and determined that you should pedal at 80 rpm's. Find a level road, select a gear that is fairly easy to pedal, and count the number of times your right leg rotates in a minute. Ride along for a while concentrating on maintaining your selected pedal speed. Again, time your pedal strokes to check the actual rpm's. With very little concentration, you should be able to tell if your pedal stroke varies significantly from your selected pace. Now that you are able to "feel" the proper pedaling speed, take your bicycle on a normal ride.

You will undoubtedly experience road conditions that make maintaining your selected pedal speed difficult. For instance, as you climb a hill, a great deal of effort is required to maintain pedal speed. On the other hand, going downhill causes you to pedal much faster than your selected speed. Although the effects of wind are usually less drastic, you will find that it is difficult to pedal at the same speed when riding with the wind or against the wind.

To better understand when to shift, let's define two basic terms that describe gear ratios: high and low. A high gear is one that requires large amounts of pressure on the pedals. A low gear is one that requires a relatively small amount of pressure on the pedals. The terms high and low are relative to the conditions.

Consider the following example: as the rider approaches a hill, he or she pedals easily at 80 rpm's. The hill is very steep and in order to maintain 80 rpm's, the rider must push very hard on the pedals. If the hill is extremely steep, the rider may be required to stand up on the bicycle to provide enough force on the pedals. Although the gear ratio had not been changed, the steep hill effectively made the gear ratio too high for comfort. As the rider reaches the top of the hill and then starts the descent, less pressure is required on the pedals. If the hill is very steep, the rider may not be able to spin his or her legs fast enough. In this situation, the gear is too low to allow the rider to maintain 80 rpm's. Proper gear shifting does not require you to memorize complicated gear charts. You only have to shift gears to match the gear ratio with your desired rpm's.

If you are having trouble keeping the

80-rpm pace because you are going uphill, shift to a lower gear. With very little practice, you will learn how to judge which gear to shift into if you always concentrate on pedaling at your preselected rate. The actual shifting procedure to obtain a lower gear is done in one of two ways:

1. *Rear derailleur.* Bring the right control lever back toward you. This will move the derailleur to one of the larger sprockets on the freewheel.

2. *Front derailleur.* Push the left control lever forward to select the lowest gear ratio on the chainwheel (the inside sprocket). If you have a Japanese derailleur the opposite may be true—pull to obtain a lower gear.

Remember that you *must* keep pedaling as you shift. After practicing the use of the rear and the front derailleurs, you will discover that the *amount* the gear is lowered is not the same with each derailleur. The jump (difference between the small chainwheel and the large chainwheel) is much larger when shifting the front derailleur than the back derailleur. In other words, if the gear you are riding is much too high you should change to a lower gear using the front derailleur. That change will result in a gear that is much easier to pedal. If, on the other hand, you would like a gear ratio that is slightly lower than the gear you are riding, you should shift one sprocket lower on the rear derailleur. Let's demonstrate how this could work in actual use.

The rider is pedaling at 80 rpm's with the chain on the large (outside) chainwheel in the front and middle gear on the freewheel in back. The rider approaches a very steep short hill. To maintain 80 rpm's, a lower gear is required. How much lower? The rider has a feel for the amount of gear reduction with the use of each derailleur and determines that since the hill is very steep, a much lower

gear is required to maintain pedal speed. As the rise in the hill is approached, the rider reaches down with the left hand and pushes the control lever forward to move the chain to the small (inside) chainwheel. The rider's guess was correct and pedal speed remains at 80 rpm's until the top of the hill is reached. As the hill slopes downward, the rider's legs begin spinning without any real force applied on the pedals. Once again the left control lever is actuated and the chain is moved to the large front sprocket. The rider once again reaches the comfortable 80-rpm pedal rate.

A slight head wind starts, requiring more pedal pressure to maintain 80 rpm's. The rider's legs tire in an effort to maintain rpm's and a lower gear is selected. This time the rider decides to shift the rear derailleur since the necessary reduction is not as drastic as that required by the steep hill. The rider grasps the right control lever in his or her right hand and pulls back just enough to move the chain over one sprocket, closer to the inside. Once again the rider is able to pedal comfortably at 80 rpm's. While this is an oversimplified situation, it demonstrates that no calculations or "mental" gymnastics are required. The rider only needs to know whether a lower or higher gear is required and how to shift each derailleur to find the proper gear ratio.

Most riders have little trouble understanding how to shift once the use of the derailleur has been explained. Many riders, however, are unaware of how proper or optimum pedaling speed is determined. There is no textbook formula for determining proper pedaling speed because of the individual differences among riders, but there is a general rule that always works.

If the gear you have selected is too high, your legs will fatigue before your lungs. If the selected gear you are using is too low, your lungs will fatigue first.

Sounds too easy, doesn't it? It is easy and it always works! To prove it to yourself, try the following tests. First, select the lowest gear on your bicycle (the inside chainwheel on the front and the inside sprocket on the freewheel). Pedal as fast as you can, and maintain that pace for 15 seconds. You will notice that your legs will not be tired; however, your lungs will be "burning." After resting, perform the second test. Select the highest gear on your bicycle (the outside chainwheel and the outside sprocket on the freewheel). Pedal as fast as you can for 15

seconds. Your lungs will not be "burning" this time; instead, your legs will feel "tight."

Practice this rule to maximize your performance whenever you ride. If you experience abnormal fatigue in your legs, *reduce* the gear you are riding. If you find yourself breathing too hard, *increase* the gear. Proper attention to the gear ratio you are using will result in the optimum relationship between energy expended and the speed maintained.

By now you should understand how and when to shift. Let's take a look at the technical part of shifting—how the derailleurs work and the characteristics of each design.

POSITIONING AND ADJUSTING FRONT DERAILLEUR

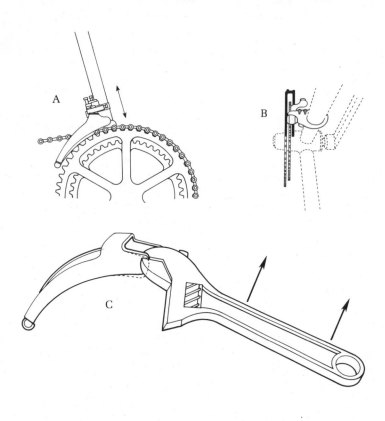

Figure 7–4: The front derailleur must be properly positioned on the seat tube of the frame so that the derailleur cage does not touch the outside (large) sprocket (A). Check manufacturer's specifications for the proper distance.

Before you tighten the bolt(s) that hold the derailleur to the seat tube, make sure the derailleur cage is parallel to the chainwheel as illustrated in B. Sometimes the chain will continue to shoot off the big chainwheel in spite of perfect cage alignment and setting of the limiting screw (occurs more frequently under hard pedaling). Remove the chain and sight down the chainwheel as you rotate the cranks—chainwheel wobble of more than 5 mm. should be corrected (see chapter five). If a bent chainwheel is not the problem, try bending the outside front section of the derailleur cage in slightly (C).

FRONT DERAILLEURS

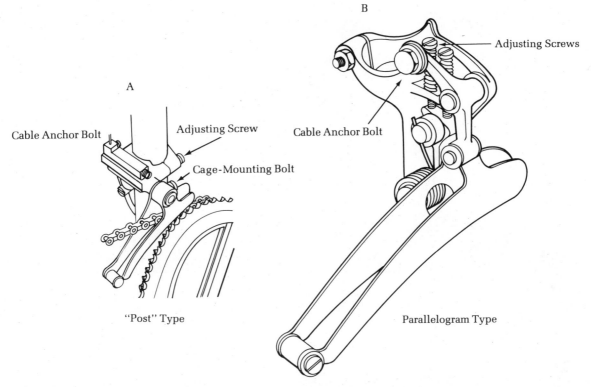

A

Cable Anchor Bolt

Adjusting Screw

Cage-Mounting Bolt

"Post" Type

B

Adjusting Screws

Cable Anchor Bolt

Parallelogram Type

Figure 7—5: Basically, there are just two types of front derailleurs:
The post type (A) merely pushes the chain from one chainwheel to the other. It does not rise as it shifts to the larger chainwheel. This derailleur is somewhat difficult to adjust since it has only one limiting screw. The other adjustments are handled by loosening the cage-mounting bolt.

The more sophisticated, parallelogram front-shifting derailleur (B) rises as it pushes the chain onto the larger chainwheel. This design is more costly, and is used on all quality bicycles.

FRONT DERAILLEURS

The front derailleur is always attached to the seat tube of the bicycle near the chainwheels. When properly adjusted, the front derailleur rides about 1/16 inch higher than the largest sprocket. The chain goes through the derailleur cage which is moved by the control lever. All good-quality front derailleurs use a parallelogram action or movement. This design keeps the derailleur cage vertical as it is moved. In addition, the derailleur cage rises as it moves the chain out to the larger chainwheel sprocket. This

119

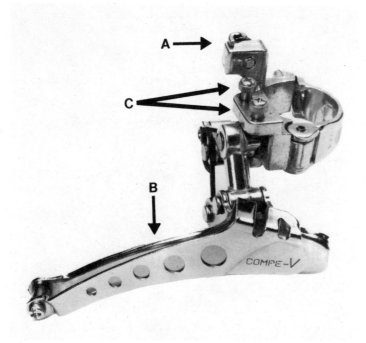

Photo 7–3: The typical front derailleur includes a cable anchor bolt (A). The cable is controlled by shift levers which move the derailleur cage (B). The derailleur is fixed to the top tube by a bolt or bolts. Two screws (C) provide the necessary adjustment to limit the travel of the derailleur cage.

action results in a smooth, positive shift.

Years ago, the front derailleur did not have this dual action. Instead, the cage was merely moved from side to side by a bar that was activated by the control lever. This type of derailleur (push-rod action) is still manufactured today; however, it is not very popular since it does not shift as smoothly as the parallelogram derailleur. Most parallelogram front derailleurs shift very well.

Little differences in performance exist between the good and the best front derailleurs. Extra-lightweight alloys and careful machining and polishing are the primary reasons for higher prices. If you are price conscious, you should be aware that the lightweight-alloy front derailleur performs similarly to its heavier steel counterparts but, the alloy derailleur costs substantially more.

Before you purchase a front derailleur, check the manufacturer's specifications to make sure that its capacity is compatible with your specific chainwheel sprockets. All derailleurs have a recommended capacity, which is the difference between the number of teeth on the large chainwheel less the number of teeth on the small chainwheel. For instance, if the front derailleur has a 14-tooth capacity, you cannot use it on a bicycle that has a 38-tooth and 54-tooth chainwheel set ($54^T - 38^T = 16^T$).

REAR DERAILLEURS

Unlike the front derailleur, rear derailleurs come in a bewildering array of shapes and sizes. All rear derailleurs are mounted on the right rear dropout by means of an attaching plate or they are bolted to a fitting that is brazed on the fork tip. Although rear derailleurs are available in many configurations, they all perform the same functions in very much the same way.

There are two basic types of rear derailleurs: the standard European-style parallelogram and the Japanese slant "pantograph." Both types of derailleurs work well, though each design type works best when matched to specific riding requirements.

The European parallelogram (like the parallelogram front derailleurs) keeps the derailleur pulleys in a vertical plane in every gear position. Although the relationship between the jockey wheel and the tension wheel will vary with each gear, the relative position of the jockey wheel remains the same in every gear position. The European

Photo 7–5: The body of the derailleur must be parallel to the chainstay with this type of derailleur.

Photo 7–4: This Schwinn rear derailleur is an extremely rugged design that is primarily designed for the abuse of children. Its slow, unresponsive shifting is compensated for by its ability to withstand rough treatment.

parallelogram, a very fast-acting and responsive derailleur, works best when matched with relatively close gear ratios. Less control-lever movement is required to complete a shift. The control-lever barrel is much smaller on the European derailleur systems. For this reason, we recommend you do not use European control levers with a Japanese derailleur. People frequently complain about shifting problems with European derailleurs. In most cases, the derailleur is not at fault. Because the European-style derailleur is so much more responsive than the Japanese style, it requires a more careful shift.

Although our opinion is not in keeping with recent derailleur trends, we found that the inexpensive Simplex plastic-bodied de-

(continued on page 125)

Derailleur Characteristics

	Price	Responsiveness	Gear Range	Weight
Front: Post-Type	Very inexpensive	Not smooth; fussy	Narrow	Light
Parallelogram (steel)	Inexpensive	Responsive	Wide	Light
Parallelogram (alloy)	Fairly expensive (much less than rear)	Responsive	Wide	Very light
Rear: Parallelogram (alloy)	Expensive to very expensive	Most responsive	Fairly wide	Very light
Parallelogram (plastic)	Very inexpensive	Responsive	Quite narrow	Light
Parallelogram (short body)	Very expensive	Responsive	Fairly wide	Very light
Parallelogram (long body)	Very expensive	Not quite as responsive	Wide	Light
Pantograph (alloy)	Inexpensive to moderately expensive	Fairly responsive	Wide	Fairly light
Pantograph (steel)	Inexpensive	Fairly responsive	Wide	Heaviest
Pantograph (short body)	Inexpensive	Fairly responsive to responsive, depending on design	Wide	Light
Pantograph (long body)	Inexpensive	Not very responsive	Very wide	Fairly light

Use	Advantages	Disadvantages
General transportation	Inexpensive	Difficult to adjust
		Requires frequent readjustment
Recreational riding with cost emphasis	Inexpensive	Quality control and tolerance not as good as alloy model
	Reliable	
	Will handle wide gear ranges	
Any use (touring or racing)	Fairly inexpensive	Cost rises quickly as exotic alloys are used.
	Will handle wide gear ranges	
	Light weight	
Racing or performance riding	Quick, responsive shifts under all conditions	Top models are very expensive.
	Light weight	Since riders frequently do not develop their skills, the derailleur is "too good" for their needs.
	Reliable	
	Parts are available from Campagnolo down to the smallest nut or bolt.	
Performance riding with cost emphasis	Inexpensive	Fairly fussy shift
	Light weight	Not as durable as top-quality alloy
Racing or performance riding	Quick and responsive	Cannot handle wide gear ratios smoothly
Serious touring	Will handle wide gear ratios	Not as responsive as short body
		Does not usually work as well as the pantograph
All-around use (racing and touring)	Good value for cost	Parts are not always available.
	Shifts well under most conditions	Some models wear out quickly.
General recreational riding	Indestructible	Fairly heavy
	Low price	Tolerances are not as accurate as on better models.
Sports riding	Relatively responsive shift	Parts are not always available.
Serious touring	Will handle very wide gear ratios	Not very responsive

Photo 7–6: Both derailleurs include a strong spring that will automatically shift gears if the control-lever tension screw is not tight. Adjust each control lever to a compromise tension that allows fairly easy shifting without the danger of the derailleur shifting itself. The rear derailleur will always shift to a higher gear if the tension screw is too loose.

Photo 7–7: Derailleur A is designed for fairly close gear ratios. The short distance between pulleys will result in responsive shifting.

Although the body of derailleur B is the same as A, the latter is easily recognizable as a touring derailleur by the distance between pulleys. The spring-loaded long cage allows wide-ratio gears since it can handle a larger amount of chain slack. Shifting with a long-cage derailleur is less responsive than the short-cage derailleur.

railleur shifts very well on a bicycle with a fairly close gear ratio. It is inexpensive, light weight, and surprisingly durable. Most novices have more trouble with the Simplex unless shifting instructions are provided.

The Campagnolo Nuovo Record derailleur, which is light weight, strong, responsive, and expensive, is a perfect example of the potential of the parallelogram derailleur. It handles fairly wide ratios; it will handle a 7-speed freewheel. No other derailleur can shift while the rider is going uphill as well as the Campagnolo.

As we have indicated, the basic parallelogram rear derailleur works best with fairly narrow gear ratios and, accordingly, it is the first choice of racers and riders interested in performance. (Very close ratio freewheels are popular with racers who are riding on flat terrain—13–14–15–16–17 and 14–15–16–17–18-tooth freewheels are quite common.)

With the exception of a few specific European models, slant pantograph rear derailleurs are always of Japanese manufacture. They are distinctive in the alignment of the derailleur body which runs parallel to the chainstay of the bicycle. This design allows the jockey wheel of the derailleur to maintain the same relationship with each individual rear cog (figure 7-6). In other words, the jockey wheel does not stay on the same horizontal plane (like the basic parallelogram). Instead, the pantograph maintains the same distance from each cog. This feature results in a more consistent feel when shifting between gears that "jump" several teeth. For this reason, this type of derailleur is very popular with wide-ratio freewheels like 14–16–21–23–28. With this freewheel, the unequal jump from cog to cog (14 to 16 is a two-tooth jump; 16 to 21 is a five-tooth jump; 21 to 23 is a two-tooth jump; 23 to 28 is a five-tooth jump) creates an inconsistent

PANTOGRAPH DERAILLEUR JOCKEY WHEEL

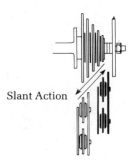

Slant Action

Figure 7–6: The unique pantograph design of the better Japanese derailleurs guarantees a constant distance from the jockey wheel to each freewheel cog. This feature permits consistent shifting even when unequal "jumps" occur between cogs (for instance 14–17–21–23–28 has changes of three, four, two, five teeth vs. 14–16–18–20–22 with changes of two teeth between each jump.

The standard parallelogram derailleur does not move with the slant action as illustrated here.

feel with a basic parallelogram derailleur. The pantograph handles those unequal jumps easily. This ability to make the shifting feel more consistent results in a less-responsive derailleur overall. For the tourist or the novice, this unresponsive shifting is actually welcomed because the derailleur is less fussy. Minute control lever adjustments are not as critical.

The pantograph design requires more derailleur movement than the parallelogram; therefore, the control lever barrel on the former is larger to move more cable. Consequently, the lever must also be moved a greater distance to complete each shift. The vast majority of the Japanese pantograph

PARALLELOGRAM DERAILLEUR VERTICAL PLANE

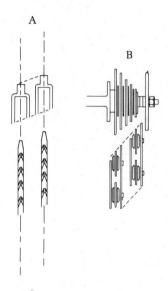

Figure 7–7: The parallelogram derailleur mechanically maintains the same vertical plane as it is shifted.

On the front (A), the derailleur cage is always in the same plane as the chainwheel in either the inside or outside chainwheel position.

At the rear (B), the chainwheel pulleys are always in the same plane as the rear cogs. If you experience shifting problems, always check to see that the derailleur is not bent. If it is bent, the pulleys will not run parallel to the freewheel cogs. This misalignment will result in noisy, slow shifts, energy loss, and premature wear.

derailleurs are rugged and easy to shift. One positive feature about the popular Sun Tour derailleurs is the number of models to choose from.

You can get the same basic shift and gear-handling capacity with a steel or alloy derailleur. For the price-conscious cyclist, the steel-bodied derailleur is a good place to save money because the overall weight dif-

DERAILLEUR ATTACHMENT METHODS

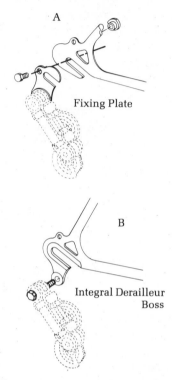

Figure 7–8: Although these derailleurs are the same, they are attached to the bicycle frame by two different methods:

A fixing plate (A) secures the derailleur to frames that do not include a mounting bracket.

Most good-quality frames include fork tips with integral derailleur fittings (B).

ference is relatively small (and the weight savings is not as critical as it is on the wheels) but the shifting qualities are still good.

You should now have a good idea of how to recognize the different designs and should know the characteristics of each type. If you have selected a good-quality derailleur which is properly mounted, it will require very few adjustments to keep it in shape. Cleaning and lubrication are the only real needs.

Caution: If you own more than one set of wheels, be very careful when changing the wheels to insure that the derailleur is properly adjusted. Many riders forget that all freewheels are not exactly the same size; this means you may shift the derailleur into the spokes, which can damage the wheel and the frame in severe cases. Always check to insure that the rear derailleur will not touch the spokes when shifted into the inside position.

Do not drop your bicycle on the right side or the derailleurs can be bent. Similarly, be careful when putting your bicycle in a car to keep any weight off of the derailleurs. Unless the derailleur gets bent, you will not need to do anything except keep it clean for many, many miles.

(continued on page 133)

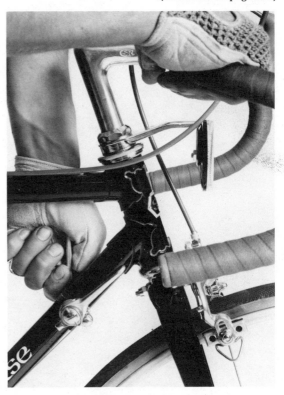

A

B

Photos 7–8A and 7–8B: **Proper Use of Shift Levers.** Many riders experience trouble when shifting gears because they do not have a "feel" for when the derailleur is correctly aligned with the desired gear. This difficulty can be the result of shifting with the fingertips (A). Use the palm of your hand (B) to shift gears and you will have increased leverage and better "touch."

Troubleshooting Guide:
Derailleurs

Problem	Probable Cause	How to Repair
Derailleur shifts by itself (front or rear)	Loose control-lever tension screw	Tighten as required. Many derailleurs have a tension screw that can be adjusted by hand. These are best since the rider can perform adjustments as he or she is riding.
Chain falls off of inside chainwheel and chain falls off outside chainwheel (front derailleur)	Improper adjustment of limiting screw	Check adjustment-limiting screw to determine that the derailleur body is not moving the chain too far.
	Improper chain tension	Check to see that chain is not too long.
	Bent or misaligned front derailleur	Check to see if the gear ratios are within specifications required by derailleur manufacturer.
	Bent chainwheels	Check to see that a fall has not bent or twisted the front derailleur. The derailleur cage should be parallel to the chainwheels.
	Loose chainwheel, crank-arm, or bottom bracket	Check to see that the chainwheel is not bent (see chapter five, Cranksets).
		Check to determine that all components are tightened securely.
Difficult to shift from small chainwheel to large chainwheel (front derailleur)	Loose or stretched control cable	Tighten control cable.
	Dirty or sticking derailleur	Remove derailleur and clean in solvent. Oil all pivot points. Make sure that all pivot points move freely.
	Improper adjustment of limiting screw	Check adjustment of limiting screw to insure that derailleur body is moving far enough to allow the chain to reach the large chainwheel.

Problem	Probable Cause	How to Repair
Slow, sticky shift	Dirty derailleur body	Remove derailleur and clean with solvent. Lubricate all pivot points and check to determine if all parts move freely.
	Kinked or frayed cables	Remove derailleur cable from housing. Inspect for kinks or fraying. Replace cable if required. Lubricate outer housing with Dri-Slide and reinstall cable.
	Control-lever tension screw is too tight	Check to determine if tension screw is too tight.
	Dirty chain and/or free-wheel or chainwheels	Remove chain from bicycle and clean with solvent.
		Remove rear wheel from bicycle. Use solvent to clean rear cogs or chainwheels. Reassemble.
Chain slips	Improper tension	Check to determine that chain length is correct.
		Check to see that the derailleur is clean and the tensioned position moves freely. Increase tension of derailleur in accordance with manufacturer's recommendations.
	Worn-out chain, freewheel, or chainwheels	Check chain for wear.
		Inspect freewheels and chainwheels for uneven wear or too much wear. Chain and freewheel should be replaced as a unit if possible.
	Cog is moving on a new freewheel body	Tighten all cogs prior to riding the bicycle.
	Stripped freewheel	Check to determine if the freewheel body is stripped and is slipping on the hub.

Troubleshooting Guide: Derailleurs

(continued)

Problem	Probable Cause	How to Repair
Chain falls off inside cog of freewheel (rear derailleur) and chain falls off outer cog	Bent or misaligned front derailleur	Check to see that a fall has not bent or twisted the front derailleur. The derailleur cage should be parallel to the chainwheels.
	Improper adjustment of limiting screw	Check adjustment of limiting screw to insure that derailleur body is not moving too far.
	Improper chain line	Check to insure that rearstays are not bent or that improper rear hub or bottom bracket is installed. Correction should be done by a qualified bicycle shop.
	Bent or twisted derailleur	Check to determine that the derailleur pulleys are in the same vertical plane as the freewheel (photo 7-7). Unless you consider yourself an excellent mechanic, you should not attempt to bend the fork end or derailleur back to position. Leave it to a qualified bicycle shop.
	Bent freewheel cog	Remove chain from freewheel. Spin the freewheel and look to see if the inside cog has been bent.
Scraping noise while pedaling	Chain is rubbing on front derailleur	Readjust position of front derailleur using control levers. If noise persists, readjust limiting screws or check alignment of derailleur cage body.
	Rear derailleur is improperly positioned	Adjust control lever to move derailleur pulleys in line with desired cog.
Clunking noise (or click) while pedaling	Front derailleur is misaligned and is connecting with crankarm with each pedal stroke	Reposition front derailleur (figure 7-4).
	Stiff link in chain	Examine chain to determine if a link is stiff (see chapter five, Chains).

Step 1.

Removing the Rear Wheel on a Derailleur-Equipped Bicycle.

Shift the rear derailleur to the high gear (outside sprocket).

Step 1.
Photos 7–9A and 7–9B: Release the quick-release hub.

Step 2.
Photo 7–9C: Pull the derailleur body back—which will permit the rear wheel to drop out of the frame without becoming tangled with the derailleur pulleys.

Step 2.

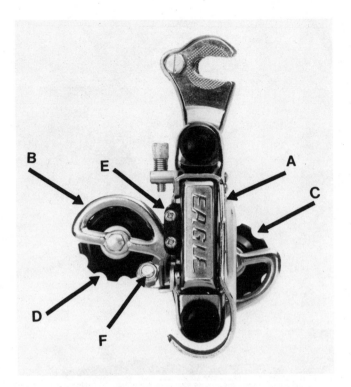

Photo 7–10: The typical rear derailleur consists of the derailleur body (A) and the cage (B), which holds the small guide wheels. The top wheel is called the jockey wheel (C); the bottom is called the tension wheel (D). Two screws limit the travel of the derailleur (E). Differently designed derailleurs have the screws in varying positions. The cable-fixing bolt is also located in different positions (F). As the shift lever is moved, the cable pulls the body of the derailleur and the chain is "derailed" from cog to cog.

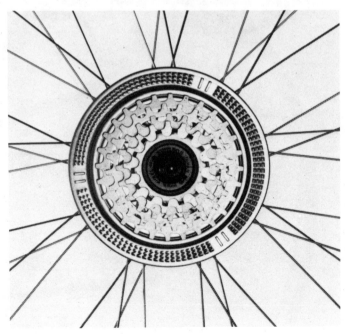

Photo 7–11: Most recreational 10-speeds use a spoke protector to eliminate the risk of the derailleur getting caught in the spokes. The spoke protector is inexpensive, light weight, and it is an excellent safeguard for the rider who isn't careful about the adjustment of the rear derailleur.

Rules of Thumb

- If you are riding uphill and you need to shift to a lower gear, reduce the amount of force on the pedals as you shift. Few derailleurs shift smoothly under heavy loads.

- Remember to shift the front and the rear derailleurs with different techniques—the control lever for the rear derailleur should be moved in small increments. The control lever for the front derailleur should be moved *all the way* in one complete, smooth motion.

- If the rear derailleur cable breaks on a trip and you don't have a spare but you must still ride home, adjust the high-gear limiting screw to hold the chain in one of the lower gears. Even though you will not be able to shift the rear gears, you won't be forced to ride home in high gear.

- Do not throw away frayed rear derailleur cables. The frayed end can be cut off and the cable can be used on the front derailleur.

CHAPTER EIGHT

THE WHEEL: HUBS, SPOKES, AND RIMS

Bicycle wheel building continues as one of the last remaining arts in cycling. Frame and wheel building require experience. Even if books were available to explain how to build frames and wheels, they could not replace the benefits of gaining the "feel" for how to do it right. This "feel" can only be developed by years of experience. Unfortunately, it is difficult, if not impossible, for the novice to visually determine an "acceptable" wheel from a well-built wheel, since both may include top-quality hubs, rims, and spokes. Although this chapter alone cannot teach cyclists to build wheels with the "master's touch," it will describe the components that are assembled to complete a wheel, the varying methods of assembly, and the advantages and disadvantages of each component and assembly procedure.

Before we begin the component-by-component breakdown, let's review the design philosophy behind a lightweight bicycle wheel. No other subject in cycling is surrounded with as much controversy as

proper wheel-building techniques. Although proper pedaling technique and saddle height seem to be highly controversial, the majority of coaches and experienced racers agree on the basic parameters described in chapter fourteen. Theories about wheel building, on the other hand, remain divergent even among top industry experts. However, there are some generalizations that are widely accepted.

A fundamental truth concerns weight reduction. The weight removed from the wheels is the most important weight reduction on the bicycle in terms of absolute cycling performance. This weight reduction is most noticeable under heavy acceleration or when riding uphill. Although properly built lightweight wheels are reliable, the performance benefits of ultralightweight wheels can create greatly reduced reliability. Far too many cyclists select wheel components and tires as though they were intending to ride on a smooth indoor track—free from sharp objects and chuckholes. How many cyclists ride under such desirable conditions? Yet, how many cyclists expect equipment that has been designed for smooth track riding to last when subjected to abuses such as chuckholes and increased loads caused by heavy touring packs?

SPOKING PATTERNS

Spoking patterns will not substantially affect the weight of the wheel but will influence the way the wheel feels. Although there are some individual building variations, there are four basic wheel-lacing patterns: radial spoke, two cross (2X), three cross (3X), and four cross (4X).

The radial spoke wheel is almost useless for the vast majority of the cycling public. In fact, it is probably used by less than 2 percent of the winning professional racers. The radially spoked wheel is easily identified among all other patterns—no spokes cross one another. The advantage of the radial spoke wheel is the minute weight reduction since the spokes are shorter than required by a wheel with lacing. The disadvantages are enormous, however. Any road shock is transmitted *directly* to the frame; shock absorption in the radial spoke wheel is the worst of all other lacing patterns since there is no supporting strength provided by the spokes as they cross. In addition, rim windup—the tendency for the rear driving hub to turn before the rim—is worse than for any other lacing pattern. This problem is severe enough that radial spoking is never used on rear wheels. The primary use for a

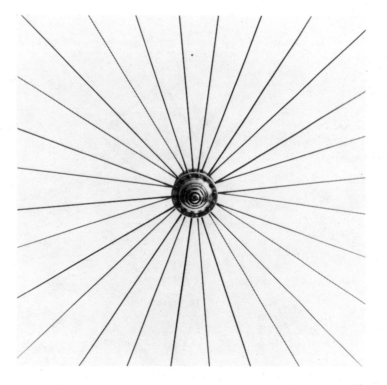

Photo 8–1: The radial-spoke wheel is easily identified. It is very light because it requires the shortest spokes of any spoking pattern. The radial wheel is weakest during cornering and it transmits the most road shock of all the lacing patterns.

radial wheel is in time-trial racing, where weight-conscious riders will go to great lengths for any weight reduction. Some cyclists prefer the unique appearance of the radial spoke wheel and select the wheel for appearance rather than function.

Two-cross wheels offer less weight-reduction advantages compared to the radial wheel with only marginal improvement in cornering stability or hub windup. Understandably, this lacing pattern is rarely used.

The 3X spoke-lacing pattern is probably the most popular pattern used. Many wheel builders believe it gives the optimum combination of strength, shock absorption, and hub windup. This pattern is virtually standard procedure on most stock bicycles. Although we spoke to many people on the subject of wheel building, we were unable to determine why most factories select the 3X pattern as the best wheel-building compromise. No one seems to know. This was especially confusing to us since many highly regarded custom wheel builders prefer the 4X pattern.

Although the spoke length of a 4X pattern is slightly longer than the 3X (which is slightly longer than the 2X), it provides the greatest amount of shock absorption of all of the patterns. The 4X pattern also provides the greatest cornering strength; the sharp angle at which the spokes cross over one another insures the greatest resistance to hub windup. So why doesn't everyone build wheels in the 4X pattern? We can't provide an answer to that, nor did we find anyone who could. Our personal wheel-building experience stems from the intuition of

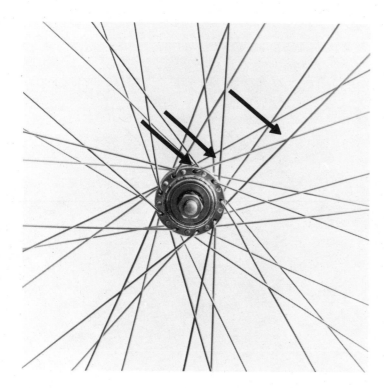

Photo 8–2A: Three-cross wheels.

Mike Walden, famous wheel builder.

Many people consider Walden one of the most knowledgeable cycling authorities in this country. Others refute his theories; some "alleged" authorities make flat statements that 4X wheels should never be built on high-flange hubs. We can only offer the results of our personal riding experience and the experience gained by actual use in real riding conditions varying from track and road races to transcontinental touring. We cannot back up our beliefs with tensile strength tests as some writers do, nor do we have the technical expertise to evaluate whether a stainless steel spoke will break under a greater load than a plain wire spoke. After selling hundreds of sets of custom wheels through our store and watching many champions like Sheila Young, Roger

Young, and Sue Novara ride on Walden-built wheels, we prefer to use experience as the determining factor—not some laboratory tests that may or may not duplicate actual riding conditions.

We believe that a spoke will not break in a properly built wheel. Spoke breakage is caused primarily by improper spoke tensioning and, in some cases, poor equipment. Two stories further illustrate our point.

One of our club racers, Kurt Bertz, was racing in the annual 50-mile Fred Cappy race in Chandler Park, Michigan, when one of the many park squirrels ran into the bicycle pack. Unfortunately for Kurt (and the squirrel), the squirrel ran right into the side of the front wheel while the bike was moving at 30 mph. Surprisingly, Kurt did not lose control of the bike. After the race, we found that

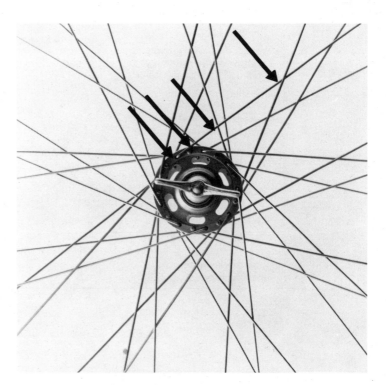

Photo 8–2B: Four-cross wheels.

Wheel Characteristics

	Advantages	Disadvantages	Recommended Use
Steel Low- or High-Flange Hub (nutted)	Low cost Durable Reliable	Heavy Requires a wrench to remove wheel Sloppy fits	Basic utility or recreational bicycles Commuting or recreational riding
Alloy/Steel Three-Piece High-Flange Hub (nutted)	Fairly inexpensive Fairly light weight Easy to repair Gives "appearance" of quality hub	Sloppy fits Lacks strength and reliability of one-piece alloy hub Quick-release hub skewer may break under stress	Recreational bicycles Can be used for commuting, recreational riding, or some sports riding
Alloy One-Piece High-Flange Hub (nutted)	Light weight Very strong hub requiring shorter spokes than a low-flange hub Improved appearance and attention to detail Solid axle (nutted) is stronger and more reliable than hollow (quick-release) axle	Requires a wrench to remove wheel	Track racing
Alloy One-Piece Low-Flange Hub with Nutted Axle	Very light weight Very strong More aerodynamic than high flange Good appearance and manufacturing standards	Requires a wrench to remove wheel	Some track events (This hub configuration is rarely used, since most riders prefer the additional wheel strength gained with high-flange hubs.)

	Advantages	Disadvantages	Recommended Use
Alloy One-Piece High-Flange Hubs (quick-release)	Light weight Very strong Does not require a wrench to remove wheel Good appearance and manufacturing quality	More expensive than a nutted hub Potential service or reliability problem from hollow axle or quick-release skewer	Recreational, sports, or performance riding. This hub has become the most popular choice of 10-speed cyclists.
Alloy One-Piece Low-Flange Hub (quick-release)	Very light weight Very strong Does not require a wrench to remove wheel Good appearance and manufacturing quality	More expensive than a nutted hub Potential service or reliability problem from hollow axle or quick-release skewer	Recreational, sports, performance, or touring over very rough roads. This hub is popular primarily with tourists.

although three spokes were badly bent, none had been broken! Incredibly, the front fork blades of the bicycle were bent back almost ½ inch as a result of the accident, yet no spokes were broken!

Another incident involved a group of club racers who were in a city-to-city road race in Ohio. They had broken away from the main group of riders and were desperately trying to maintain their lead. As the finish line came close, the pack gained on the small leading group. One of our best wheel builders (a Walden pupil), spotted a set of railroad tracks at the bottom of the long hill they were rapidly descending. He yelled to his teammates, "let's not brake—we will jump the tracks." Unfortunately, there were several sets of very rough tracks side by side. Although they managed to fly over the first set, they came down right on the rough

second set. The entire group crashed. Their wheels folded like pretzels—but there were no broken spokes! We would like to say that they went on to win the race because of their fabulous wheels, but the impact destroyed their rims and made further riding impossible. Even the best equipment won't make up for some errors in judgment!

Proper wheel-building technique is the vital ingredient for a well-finished product only if good-quality components are used. Bicycle hubs, spokes, and rims are very difficult to evaluate since their differences are very subtle. Unlike various derailleurs which may have drastically different shifting characteristics, all hubs roll but some wear out or break sooner than others. Some of the problems are difficult to diagnose, others are accepted because some cyclists simply don't know any better.

For instance, in a popular cycling magazine's article on bicycle road tests, a $500 Japanese bicycle was given complete approval by a test rider. It handled superbly, was light, shifted well, and was painted perfectly. In short, a great bike. We read the article with some amazement since we had previously tested the bike and elected not to offer it to our customers because of its poor quality. We were most amazed at the road tester's recommendation of the bike since he only experienced one "minor" problem—broken spokes on every ride. To us, broken spokes are inexcusable and present a major problem on a bicycle in the $500 price range. The broken spoke problem on that bicycle is a good example of how improperly matched, high-quality components can cause a problem without being defective.

In this case, the spoke hole in the hub was drilled for a larger gauge spoke than had been installed at the factory. Because of the sloppy fit, the spoke would move back and forth in the hole with each revolution of the wheel until it finally broke. Needless to say, 10, 20, or 100 wheel-truing jobs would not eliminate the problem.

Another example of the difficulty in selection on the part of the consumer is the lack of good information. Since there are so few cycling experts, most people rely on cycling advertisements as their whole input of knowledge. Many people were very misled recently by full-color ads by a new company which advertised a new line of lightweight bicycle hubs, jerseys, and tights. One would presume that if the quality of the ads were any indication, the product would be great. Physical examination of the product revealed a sealed bearing hub that was superbly finished at a price similar to Campagnolo hubs. Consequently, many cyclists bought them. Soon the bearing races developed a problem when the bearings loosened and

serious repairs were required. Unfortunately, the company is out of business and the owners of the hubs have no real recourse.

Cyclists often criticize the Campagnolo company because it does not produce dozens of exciting new ideas a year and because their products are expensive. But, their high price matches the high quality of their products. Take their hubs, for instance. For all practical purposes, they never break. Many individual hub manufacturers use Campagnolo quick-release skewers for their hubs. Frequently, skewers fail on the inexpensive Campagnolo look-alike hubs and Campagnolo skewers are then used as replacements.

HUBS

The bicycle hub is very simple in theory; it only becomes complex because of the usual need for light weight and convenience. Twenty years ago, hubs were either high flange or low flange. The hub-flange variation offered riders the option of a soft ride or a "performance" ride. Although the hubs perform exactly the same in terms of rolling resistance, reliability, and longevity, the larger flange helps create a stiffer wheel because the spoke length is substantially shorter on a wheel with a high-flange hub than on a low-flange hub. Although the high-flange hub provides substantially more cornering stability, the low-flange hub is popular in Europe because many of the roads are still pavé or cobblestones. Even the worst roads in the United States are a far cry from the European pavé. Consequently, most cyclists (including tourists) would be better off riding high-flange hubs unless extremely poor roads are commonplace.

The early hubs were attached to the bicycle with two nuts on the axle. To elimi-

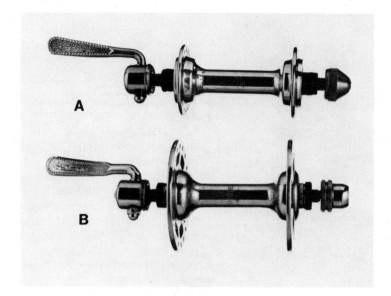

Photo 8–3: Low-flange hubs (A) use long spokes, which give a softer, less responsive ride. High-flange hubs (B) require shorter spokes and are usually used when a stiff, responsive ride is required.

The size of the hub flange is not an indicator of quality; it is a design variation for different ride characteristics.

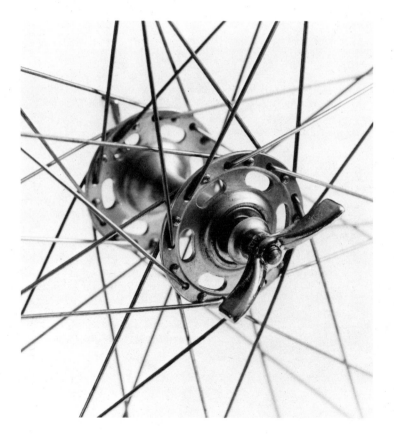

Photo 8–4: **Wing Nuts.** Before the introduction of the quick-release hub, most riders used wing nuts to secure the wheels to the bicycle. The wing nut is little more than the normal attachment nut with a lever to permit adequate leverage by hand instead of using a wrench. Wing nuts are not approved for racing bicycles because of the risk of catching a competitor's wheels.

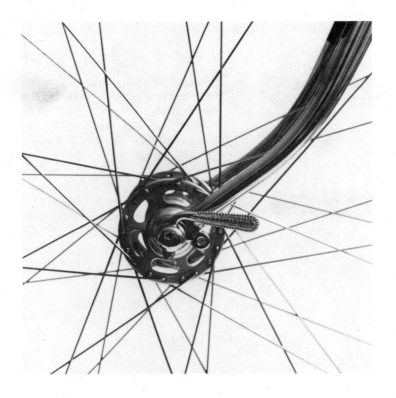

Photo 8–5: **Correct Position— Front Quick-Release Lever.** The front quick-release lever should point backwards on the bicycle. This position provides easy access to the lever. When releasing tension on the lever, the thumb can rest against the barrel to provide increased leverage. The lever should not run parallel to the fork blade since it does not leave adequate room for your finger underneath the lever.

Photo 8–6: **Correct Position— Rear Quick-Release Lever.** The safest position for the rear quick-release lever (in its tensioned position) is pointing down. This allows free access to the lever without creating the potential danger of catching the wheel of another rider.

Photo 8–7: **Adjusting the Quick-Release Skewer.** Hold the lever in one hand and rotate the "wing-nut" end clockwise to tighten or counterclockwise to loosen. Proper tension on the quick-release skewer is critical to insure safe riding without danger of the wheel slipping from its position in the frame. Too much tension can result in a broken skewer.

nate the need to carry a wrench for wheel removal, the nuts were often changed to wing nuts that could be loosened or tightened by hand. No tools were required.

In 1927 Tullio Campagnolo developed the first quick-release hub. The need for a hub that could be loosened without any tools and without the force required by wing nuts became obvious to Tullio while in a gruelling race held in a blizzard. Tullio's tire punctured in mid-race and his hands were too cold to loosen the wing nuts so he could repair it. His design for the quick-release skewer, which was prompted by this race experience, has remained the best method of positioning and holding bicycle wheels in the frame.

The quick-release wheel quickly became standard equipment on all quality bicycles. Unfortunately, many inexpensive bicycles also include cheap imitations of the quick-release mechanism that do not always provide enough holding power. Some quick-release skewers are made of inexpensive materials that will not withstand the stress of heavy acceleration or hill climbing.

A nutted hub uses a different axle than the quick-release hub. The nutted hub has a solid steel axle that can be made of inexpensive low-grade steel and still provide adequate strength and reliability. On the other hand, the quick-release axle is hollow and is made of high-quality steel. In addition to the higher cost of manufacturing a hollow axle with the same strength as a solid axle, the quick-release has a quality skewer that runs through the center of the hollow axle. This extra manufacturing cost limits the use of quick-release hubs to better-quality bicycles. The rider should recognize that a quick-release hub does not last longer, or go faster than a nutted hub. It is simply a convenience, a method of removing the wheel without tools.

The quick-release hub first appeared as a feature limited to racing bicycles. However, the popularity of the quick-release soon spread as tourists found that they could repair flats without carrying a heavy wrench which is needed when removing a nutted hub. The quick-release hub has advantages for the casual rider too. In addition to the easy repair advantages, it allows anyone to quickly remove the wheels so that the bicycle can be placed in the backseat or trunk of a car. Furthermore, the wheel can be removed so that the bicycle can be stored in a small area, such as in an office building where the bicycle may not be otherwise permitted. Owners of bicycles with quick-release hubs must remember to lock their wheels *as well* as the frame of their bicycle when leaving it unattended. It's just as easy for someone else to steal your wheels as it is for you to remove them!

Some racers become involved with special "drillings" of the hub. Many manufacturers offer hubs with an optional number of spoke holes for different uses. For instance, record attempts on smooth-surfaced tracks are often done on bicycles which have wheels with 24 or 28 spokes. Although the reduced number of spokes adversely affects the strength of the wheels, it also makes the wheels lighter.

Only the very serious competitor should consider wheels with less than the normal 36 spokes. Some riders over 200 pounds use 40-spoke wheels because of the extra strength benefits. Again, this option should be considered in only extraordinary circumstances since properly built wheels are more than adequate with 36 spokes. Because tandem wheels are subjected to far greater stress than a regular bicycle, tandemists would be wise to consider 40-spoke wheels (unless the 36-spoke wheels contain heavy-duty spokes).

Recently, some manufacturers have introduced hubs with sealed bearings. The advantage is that they are maintenance free. The disadvantage is inconsistent quality control. This is not to say that they are all bad—they aren't. The sealed-bearing bicycle hub is a relatively new concept and it has not been accepted by the cycling public as a whole.

If the right grease is used, relatively little maintenance is required to keep the normal ball bearing and cone hubs operating smoothly. Even when riding in racing conditions, the hubs should not need any more than cleaning and greasing once every 1,000 miles. The sealed bearing hubs do not require any maintenance in the first three or four years unless a defect develops.

SPOKES

At last, a simple component: the modern bicycle spoke is little more than a thick strand of wire that stretches between the hub and the wheel rim. Although all spokes are the same shape, they are available in many different sizes and compositions.

Spokes are manufactured in several sizes (for instance, 12, 12⅛, and 12¼ inches) to satisfy the varying lengths that fit varying hub-flange diameters, rims, and the selected lacing pattern. For these reasons, spokes are specifically selected to match components. To purchase a replacement spoke, either remove a spoke and take it to the bicycle store to match it or take the entire wheel in so they can match it for you.

The spoke is tensioned with a brass nut or, as it is properly called, "nipple." Some special nipples are available that are made

Spoke Characteristics

	Advantages	Disadvantages	Recommended Use
Plain Wire (without butted ends)	Inexpensive Reliable Strong Many sizes available Heavy	Corrode easily Not as attractive as other spokes	Utility and recreational bicycles where cost is an important consideration
Plain Wire (butted)	Fairly inexpensive Reliable Strong Slightly lighter than non-butted spokes	Corrode easily Not as attractive as other spokes	Utility, recreational, and sports bicycles
Plain Wire Chrome-Plated (butted)	Reliable Strong Attractive	Require some cleaning and waxing to eliminate corrosion Expensive	Sports and performance bicycles where overall quality and appearance are secondary to cost
Stainless Steel (butted)	Fairly reliable Strong Resist corrosion	Tensile strength less than plain wire spokes Not as attractive as chrome-plated spokes Expensive	Sports bicycles

of lightweight alloys. They are very expensive and should not be used unless the importance of the reduced weight outweighs the cost and potential thread-stripping problems of soft alloy.

Plain wire spokes are the best for both racing and recreational use. Many people praise stainless steel spokes, because of their resistance to rusting. However, this advantage is outweighed by a number of technical disadvantages. First, stainless steel is less flexible or malleable than plain steel. This lack of flexibility results in earlier stress fractures or breaks. Second, the stainless steel spoke has a lower tensile strength than the plain wire spoke. Our favorites are the chrome Berg Union spokes, which are hard to find but make up a very strong wheel.

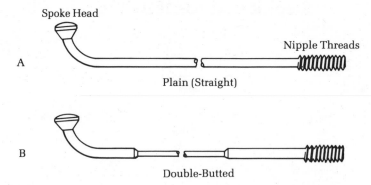

Figures 8–1A and 8–1B: **Spokes are available in two configurations:**
    • The plain-gauge spoke (A) has a consistent radius from the spoke head to the thread. These spokes are usually used for utility bicycles or in situations where strength is more important than weight.
    • The double-butted spoke (B) has a thicker diameter at each of its ends than in the center. Similar to double-butted tubing in the bicycle frame, this spoke provides the optimum concentration of strength and lightness. The manufacturing costs of a double-butted spoke are greater than a plain-gauge spoke. The double-butted spoke is usually used on only sports or racing bicycles.

RIMS

The alloy or steel hoop that the tire mounts on is the most maligned part of a bicycle. If the rider hits a chuckhole and the rim dents, it's the fault of the rim. If the wheel is out of true, it's the fault of the rim. To place the blame more fairly, answer this question: How many crooked rims have you seen *before* the wheel has been laced up? Before the wheel-building process begins, the rim is very close to a perfect circle. It goes out of true as the spokes are improperly tensioned.

Rims are made of steel on inexpensive bicycles and of lightweight alloys on better bicycles. One is not better than the other; they simply have different characteristics.

Steel rims are best on utility bicycles. They are inexpensive to manufacture and easy to repair. Because of the malleability of steel, many dents can be pounded out with a hammer! Alloy rims are more expensive because of increased materials and manufacturing costs. They have completely different characteristics from the steel rims. Generally, the alloy rim will spring farther than a steel rim, without a permanent bend. The steel rim can be bent back into position, however. The alloy rim, on the other hand, will buckle or kink on heavy impact. After the alloy rim has kinked, it must be replaced. It cannot be repaired.

Like tires, rims are manufactured to fit

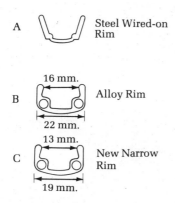

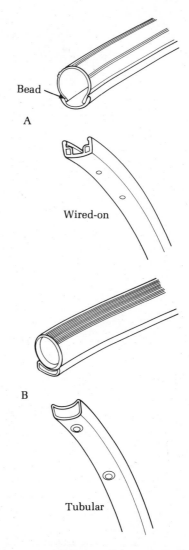

Figures 8–2A, 8–2B, and 8–2C: **Rim Sections —Cutaway Views.**

- Inexpensive steel wired-on (clincher) rims (A) are used with low-pressure tires on utility and lower-priced sports bicycles.
- Alloy rims (B) are used on high-pressure wired-on tires. Note the inward direction of the U-channel, which is necessary to keep the high-pressure tire bead from slipping over the rim.
- The 90- to 100-lb. wired-on tires use the new narrow rim (C). This tire/rim combination comes close to tubular tire performance with convenience of repair.

either tubular (sew-up tires) or wired-on (clincher*) tires. As covered in chapter nine, tubular/clincher tires are *not* interchangeable. Clincher tires require a U-shaped channel rim and tire pressure holds the wire bead inside the rim. The tubular tire has no tire bead and it sits on top of the rim, which has only a minor indentation or groove for the tire. Without glue, the tubular tire would slip off.

*Although the correct term is wired-on tire, most cyclists use the incorrect term "clincher." Since this misnomer has met such wide acceptance, we will use it interchangeably with the term "wired-on."

Figures 8–3A and 8–3B: **The Two Basic Types of Tire/Rim Construction.**

The wired-on tire (A) has a bead that is forced against the U-section of the rim and held in place by tire air pressure.

The tubular tire/rim combination (B) is completely different from the wired-on. The tubular tire is one piece. Its inner tube is sewn inside the tire casing. Unlike the wired-on, the tubular tire has no tire bead. It is held onto the relatively flat rim with glue.

Rim Characteristics

	Weight	Advantages	Disadvantages	Recommended Use
Steel Clincher	Not available	Durable; inexpensive	Heavy Unresponsive	Utility or commuting on rough roads
Alloy Clincher 16/22 mm.	480–500 gr.	Strong Large selection of tires are readily available Lighter and more responsive than steel	Not compatible with new lightweight high-pressure clinchers	General recreational, sports riding, and touring
Alloy Clincher 13/19 mm.	470–485 gr.	Strong More responsive ride than 16/22-mm. rims Lightweight ride approaches the performance of the tubular tire	Fewer bicycle stores stock the required narrow high-pressure tires Tires tend to "dig into" soft roads because of their narrow section	Performance-oriented touring and sports riding
Alloy Tubular Red Label*	300–375 gr.	Light weight Strong Provides practical optimum for performance-oriented rider	Increased attention needed to avoid dented rims from potholes	Performance-oriented touring and sports riding
Alloy Tubular Yellow Label*	260–300 gr.	Very light weight Responsive	Easily damaged Unsuitable for riders over 180 lbs.	Racing on smooth roads
Alloy Tubular "Record"	200 gr.	Ultralightweight Responsive	Expensive Difficult to keep in true Fragile	Record attempts on surfaced tracks

*Although there is no hard-and-fast rule, red-label rims are general all-purpose rims. The yellow-label rims (Super Champion Medaille d'Or or Fiamme Ergal) are racing rims.

WHEEL-BUILDING:
36-HOLE,
FOUR-CROSS
SPOKE PATTERN

Note: Manufacturer's label is on the joint opposite the valve hole.

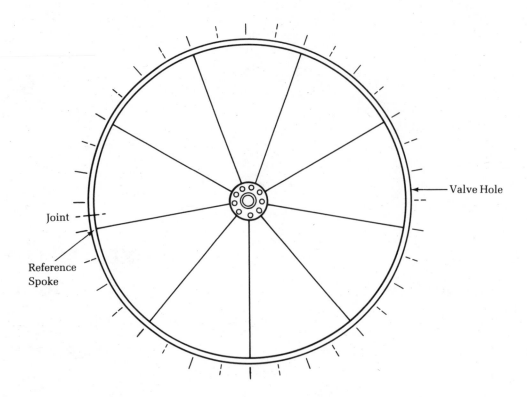

Figure 8–4: **Step 1.**

(A) Lay the rim on your lap. The rim should be positioned as in the illustration. You should have 36 identical spokes, a box of nipples, and a hub (front or rear—the lacing pattern is the same).

(B) Insert spokes from top into every other hole on the top flange. (Nine spokes are required.) *Note:* Remember to insert each spoke with the bend in the countersink, not in the spoke head (figure 8–7).

(C) Insert one of the spokes into the spoke hole adjacent to the joint (on the left side, or one hole counterclockwise from the joint). Install nipple; tighten two turns.

(D) Insert the remaining eight spokes (as illustrated); install nipples; tighten two turns.

Note: Contrary to what many "alleged" wheel-building experts claim, the first spoke should not be placed next to the valve hole. Although that method will provide the easiest access to the tire valve, it ignores the structural strength of the rim. Building a wheel with the above instructions will insure that two spokes pull the joint *together* from each side of the joint. This is critical for a well-built wheel.

In this particular case, the valve hole *will* be in the open spoke position, however, this will not occur in 24-, 28-, 32-, or 40-hole wheels.

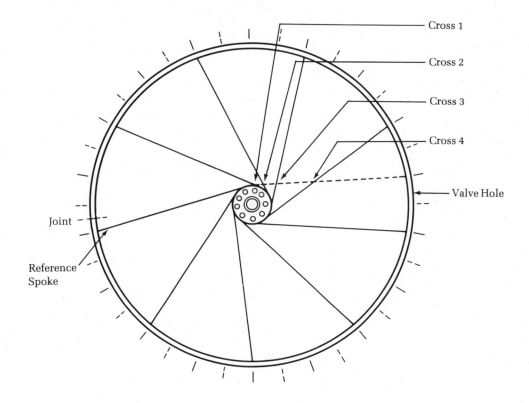

Figure 8–5: **Step 2.**

(A) Turn the hub clockwise until the spokes are taut.

(B) Install a spoke in the top flange from the *underside* of the flange into any open spoke hole on the top flange. In the illustration, the spoke is installed one spoke hole clockwise of spoke one. Run this spoke across three spokes and under the fourth. This spoke goes into the spoke hole midway between the spokes already installed. In this case, it is adjacent to the valve hole. Install nipple. Tighten two turns.

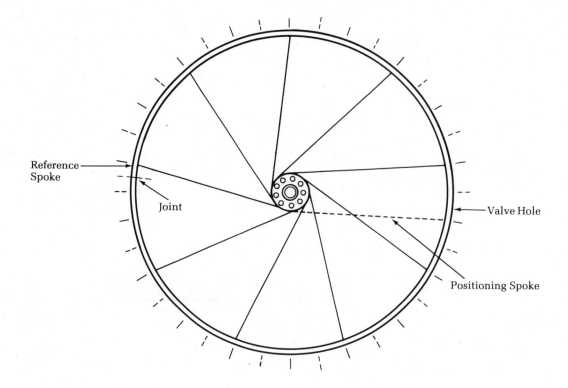

Reference Spoke

Joint

Valve Hole

Positioning Spoke

Figure 8–6: **Step 3.**

Do not install any more spokes from this side now. *Flip the wheel over.* By continuing the lacing pattern on the other side, there is less need to bend any spokes than if all spokes in the first side were installed and then the spokes on the second flange were started.

The wheel should look like the illustration.

DETERMINING LACING METHOD
(COUNTERSUNK VS. NONCOUNTERSUNK)

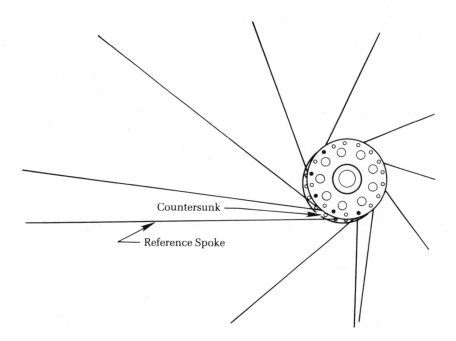

Countersunk

Reference Spoke

Figure 8–7: This is crucial for a properly built wheel. Since all hubs are *not* drilled alike, there are two alternative methods of lacing the next group of spokes. The proper lacing pattern is dictated by the way the hub manufacturer drilled the spoke holes in the hub flange. Quality manufacturers like Campagnolo usually countersink the spoke holes to allow the wheel to be built "in harmony" (figure 8–8). Some manufacturers countersink their hubs in a manner which requires the wheel to be built "out of harmony" (figure 8–12). There is no real structural advantage to either methods. However, you must know which direction to lace the next series of spokes based on your particular hub. This can be determined as follows:

Sight directly over the hub. Look at the spoke hole in the flange that is directly adjacent (clockwise) to the reference spoke. If that hole is *countersunk* go directly to the part of the wheel-building instructions for wheels that are built out of harmony. If the hole is *not* countersunk, the wheel will have to be built in harmony.

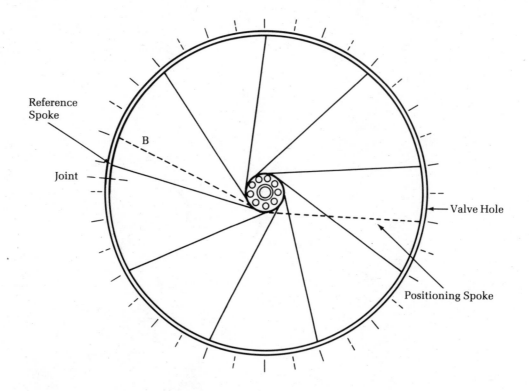

Reference
Spoke

B

Joint

Valve Hole

Positioning Spoke

Figure 8–8: **Step 4: Wheels in Harmony.**

(A) Insert nine spokes from the top of the top flange (again watching to properly insert the spoke in its correct position in the countersink).

(B) Sight directly over the hub and place the spoke (spoke B) that is positioned slightly clockwise of the reference spoke in the rim spoke hole directly clockwise of the reference spoke. Install nipple.

The wheel should now look like the illustration.

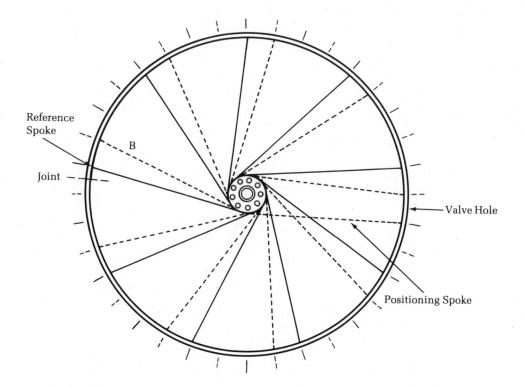

Reference Spoke

B

Joint

Valve Hole

Positioning Spoke

Figure 8–9: **Step 5: Wheels in Harmony.**

Place each of the remaining eight spokes, one spoke clockwise of the spoke already in the rim.

Note: Each of the spokes that you are now installing are four spoke holes apart. Some builders prefer to count the holes for each installation. Each method works the same. Install nipples and turn two revolutions. The wheel should now look like the illustration. (You may have to bend the spokes slightly to get them in place. Don't worry. As long as the bends are not near the hub, you should not encounter any problems.)

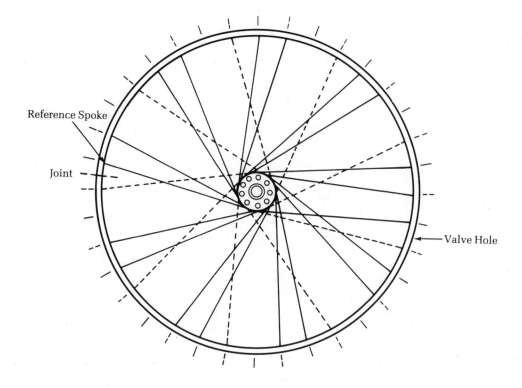

Reference Spoke

Joint

Valve Hole

Figure 8–10: **Step 6: Wheels in Harmony.**

(A) Insert nine spokes from the underside of the top flange.

(B) Take each spoke in turn and position it so that four spokes are crossed.

Note: As each spoke is installed, cross *under* the fourth spoke (the spoke crossing closest to the rim). These top spokes will be four spoke holes apart and they are located midway between the other spokes on the top flange. The wheel should now look like the illustration.

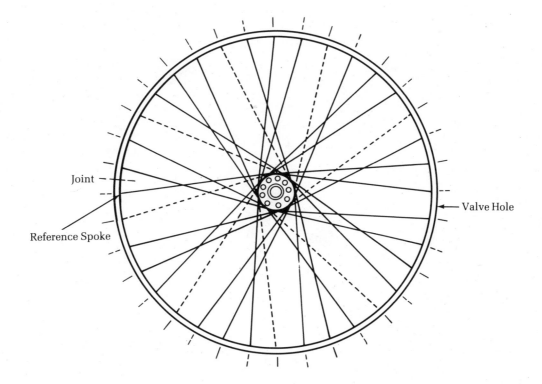

Joint

Reference Spoke

Valve Hole

Figure 8–11:   **Step 7: Wheels in Harmony.**

(A) Flip the wheel over. (You should have the wheel in the same position as Steps 1 and 2 at the beginning.) Insert the remaining eight spokes from the underside of the top flange.

(B) Place those spokes in the remaining spoke holes while crossing over four spokes. Don't forget to cross *under* the fourth spoke. Install nipples and turn two revolutions.

Your wheel is now complete! The easy part is over. Now you must true the wheel.

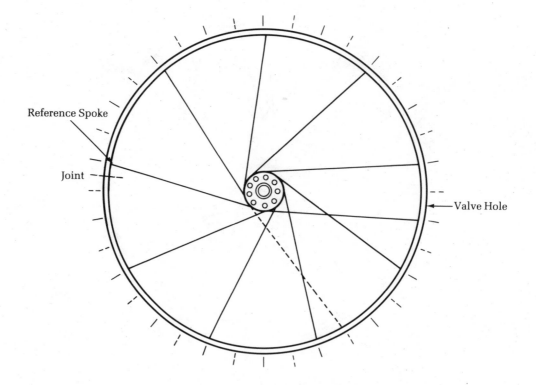

Reference Spoke

Joint

Valve Hole

Figure 8–12: **Step 4: Wheel Out of Harmony.**

Flip the wheel over. The wheel should be positioned as in the illustration. Install nine spokes in their proper flange holes from the top of the hub. Make sure you insert the spokes into holes that are *not* countersunk. The spokes installed in this flange will be parallel to the spokes already installed. To properly position the first spoke, sight over the top flange. Take the spoke adjacent to the reference spoke (one hole clockwise) and insert it where shown by the dotted line.

Note: The two spokes near the joint are pulling the joint together.

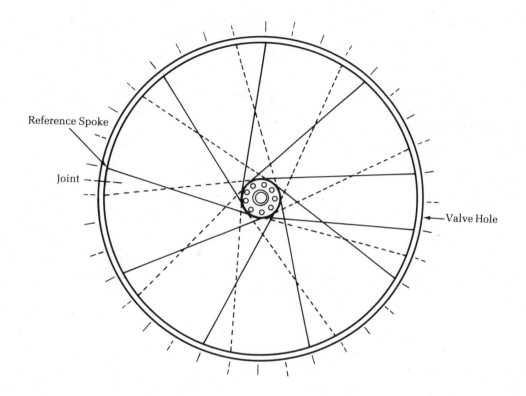

Figure 8–13:   **Step 5: Wheel Out of Harmony.**
     Place each of the remaining eight spokes, one spoke hole counterclockwise of the spoke already in the rim. Again, each of the spokes you install will be four spoke holes apart. Your wheel should look like the illustration.

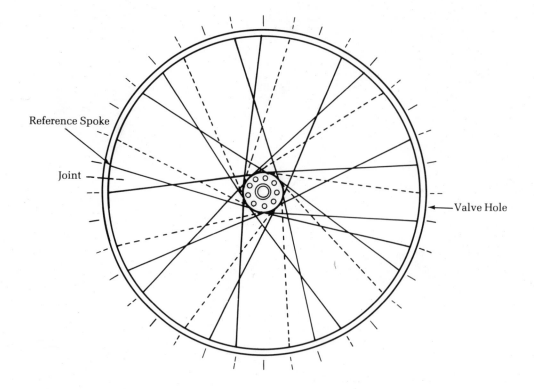

Reference Spoke

Joint

Valve Hole

Figure 8–14: **Step 6: Wheel Out of Harmony.**

(A) Insert nine spokes from the underside of the top flange.

(B) Take each spoke in turn and position it so that it crosses four spokes.

Note: As you install each spoke, cross *under* spoke four (the spoke crossing closest to the rim). These top spokes will be four spoke holes apart and they are located midway between the other spokes on the top flange. Be sure to cross under the fourth spoke each time. Your wheel should now look like the illustration.

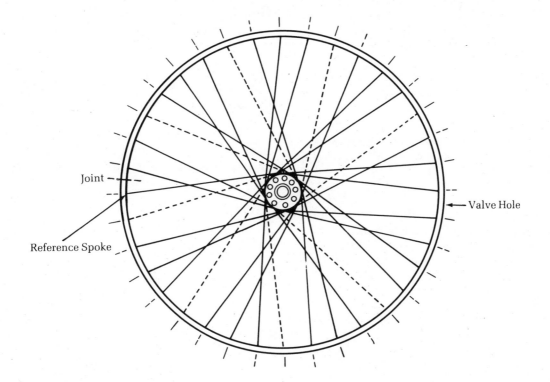

Figure 8−15: **Step 7: Wheel Out of Harmony.**

(A) Flip the wheel over again. (You should have the wheel in the same position as Steps 1 and 2 in the beginning.) Insert remaining eight spokes from the underside of the top flange.

(B) Place those spokes in the remaining spoke holes in the rim, while crossing over four spokes. Don't forget to cross under the fourth spoke. Tighten nipples two revolutions.

WHEEL TRUING

Building the wheel is far easier and less frustrating than truing the wheel. To properly true a wheel, you must tighten each spoke exactly the same amount to produce a wheel without any sideward wobble or hop (up-and-down movement). Our best word of advice for the wheel builder: patience.

Do not rush the job. A wheel can run straight and *still* be improperly tensioned! Presuming you have followed the previous steps for wheel building, you should be ready to true your wheel.

1. Tighten each spoke two turns. Start at a specific reference point (the valve hole, for instance) and tighten each spoke exactly two turns.

2. Once you have reached the valve hole, repeat the exercise: tighten each spoke two turns again.

3. Continue until the wheel has approximately 60 percent of the desired tension.

Note: See photos 8-13A and 8-13B for wheel *dishing* steps.

4. Tighten each spoke one turn at a time until 80 percent of the desired final tension is achieved. Since it is impossible to describe proper tension in a book, you should compare your wheel with a well-built wheel as a guide. Squeeze the spokes at their crossings for similarity between your wheel and the finished wheel.

Photo 8—8: The professional wheel-truing stand (or jig) is a handy aid for the individual who regularly trues wheels. A front fork from an old or damaged bicycle is equally effective for the casual, part-time mechanic. Many wheel-building experts do not use a "marker" to indicate the amount of wobble in a wheel. Instead, they use their thumb as an indicator. This method is more accurate because it indicates the amount of wobble by the force against the thumb.

Photo 8–9: To determine the proper spoke tension, squeeze the spokes (4X in this photograph) at their crossings on a finished wheel. Compare the amount of tension on the finished wheel to the tension in the wheel you are working on.

Rules of Thumb

- Do not (1) turn a spoke more than two revolutions at a time during the preliminary tensioning; (2) turn a spoke more than one turn at a time during the 60 to 80 percent tensioning; (3) turn a spoke more than one-fourth to one-half turn during the final truing.

- Novice wheel builders often presume that the final wheel-truing process involves one spoke at a time. This is not correct since tightening one side of the wheel *also* tightens the other side. Always think of the truing process in terms of groupings of spokes.

REMOVING "WOBBLE"

Using the guide on the truing jig (or your finger) locate the spot on the rim where it wobbles the most. This wobble can be either the right side or the left side, it makes no difference. Normally, the wobble covers an area of three, four, five, or more spokes. Determine the number of spokes that are included in the area of the "wobble." To pull the "wobble" out of the rim, tighten (one-quarter to one-half turn) the spokes that will pull the rim in the desired direction. You should notice that the direction of the pulling alternates with every other spoke. Presuming the wobble covers a six-spoke area, you would need to tighten three spokes. If

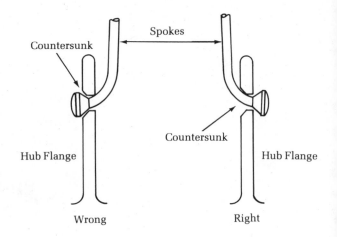

Photo 8–10: The manufacturer's label usually covers the seam in the rim. A well-built wheel must have the spokes adjacent to the seam pulling toward the seam, not away from it. Improper lacing can result in a spoke pattern that tends to separate the seam.

Figure 8–16: **Correct Installation of Spoke into Hub.**

The spoke should be inserted into the plain or *noncountersunk* hole in a hub. In this way, the bend in the spoke will occur at the countersunk part of the hole and spoke breakage will be reduced. If the spoke is improperly inserted with the spoke head in the countersink, the sharp corner of the hole will rest against the spoke and cause breakage.

you are reaching optimum spoke tension, you may wish to tighten three of the spokes by one-quarter turn and loosen the other three spokes one-quarter turn. You achieve the same effect.

Properly done, the amount of overall wobble decreases with each small variance that is reduced. Accordingly, you may need only one-eighth to one-quarter turns on each spoke to get the rim into its final alignment. Before you get the "wobble" corrected perfectly, you should tackle the "hop" in the rim since the wobble gets slightly worse as you remove the "hop."

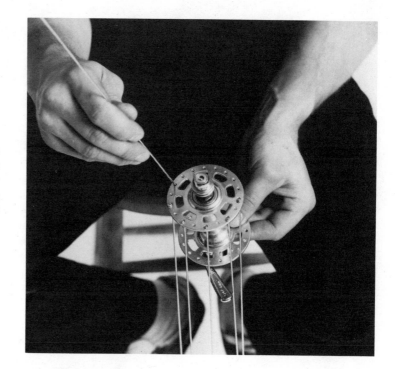

Photo 8–11: Always work from the top of the hub when building a wheel. Install the spokes in every other hole from the top flange. Remember, do not install the spokes in the holes that are countersunk.

Photo 8–12: The easiest way to keep the rim, hub, and spokes in the proper relationship is to build the wheel with the rim on your lap.

REMOVING "HOP"

To remove a "hop" you must tighten or loosen spokes to remove the up-and-down (hop) motion of the rim. Most people find that removing a hop is more difficult than correcting the rim "wobble," although there is no real reason why this should be true. Understanding how the spoke tension affects the rim helps you to remove hop without too much trouble.

First, concentrate on the largest amount of hop or high spot. Again, use the wheel-jig fixture or your thumb as a guide. Assuming you have isolated the area that creates the biggest bump or hop, correct the spokes in the problem area.

Assume there are six spokes, for example. If you tighten all six spokes, the rim will be pulled *in* . . . and the bump will be reduced. *Do not tighten all six spokes equally.* If you tighten them equally you will tend to create a flat spot on the rim. Adjust the spokes as shown in figure 8-18. If the wheel is stubborn and the hop is severe enough so that it's difficult to tighten the bump down sufficiently, you can loosen spokes on the opposite side of the rim. This brings the rim out slightly.

After the hop has been eliminated, you can touch up the rim wobble and your wheel is almost done! Now, you should firmly grip

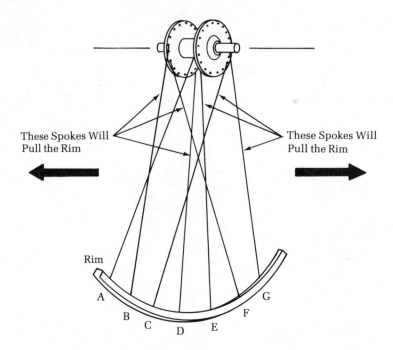

Figure 8–17:
To move the rim to the *left*, tighten spokes B, D, F or loosen spokes A, C, E, G. To move the rim to the *right*, tighten spokes A, C, E, G or loosen spokes B, D, F.

Photos 8–13A and 8–13B:
Dishing the Wheel.

The wheel builder must be careful to properly align the rim in relation to the hub. The front wheel has a hub that is designed for the rim to run in the center of the hub flanges (A). The front wheel is *not* dished. The rear wheel hub is designed for a freewheel (B). The rim does *not* align with the midpoint between the hub flanges. The wheel is offset or "dished" as it is more frequently called. Special tools to assist the wheel builder in dishing a wheel are available; however, they are probably too expensive for anyone who plans to build only one or two sets of wheels.

If you do not have a dishing tool, you can determine the proper amount of dish in a wheel by installing the wheel on the bicycle frame. Presuming the brakes have been adjusted for a set of wheels that have been properly dished, the rim should be equidistant from the brake blocks.

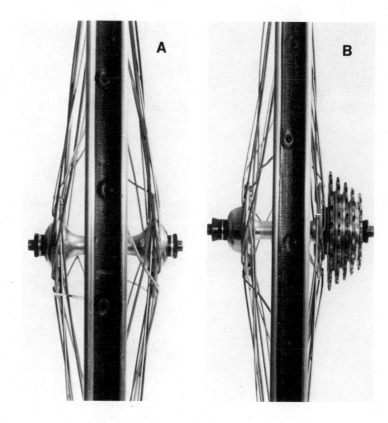

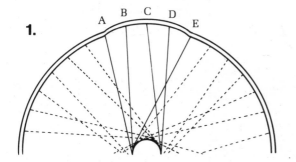

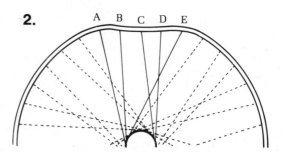

Figure 8–18: **Removing Rim Hop.**
Two methods:

1. Tighten spoke A—⅛ turn; spoke B—¼ turn; spoke C—½ turn; spoke D—¼ turn; spoke E—⅛ turn.

2. Loosen spoke A—⅛ turn; spoke B—¼ turn; spoke C—½ turn; spoke D—¼ turn; spoke E—⅛ turn.

Troubleshooting Guide: Wheels

Problem	Probable Cause	How to Repair
Repeated spoke breakage	Wheel is improperly built	Rebuild wheel with all new spokes
	Spokes are the incorrect gauge (too small) for hub spoke holes	Replace with spokes of proper gauge
	Improper loading of bicycle (too much weight over one wheel—weight not distributed properly)	Distribute weight of rider and weight of packs 45 percent front and 55 percent rear
	Spoke gauge too light for loads	Rebuild wheel with heavier gauge spokes. This should be done as a last resort, since improper match between spoke/hub or incorrect wheel-building procedures are probably the difficulty.
Hub drags—wheel does not roll freely	Bearings are dirty	Disassemble hub, clean bearings, pack with grease, and reassemble
	Bearing cones are too tight	Readjust as required
Rim "wobbles" from side to side	Hub cones are too loose	Readjust as required
	Wheel out of true	True wheel as needed
Wheel goes out of "true" frequently	Wheel is improperly built or tensioned	Rebuild wheel with new spokes

the spoke crossings as shown in photo 8-9 and squeeze. Again, it is hard to describe how hard to squeeze. As a rule, you should squeeze hard enough that the spokes cause some pain in your hand as you squeeze. Perform this squeezing exercise on every group of spokes in the wheel. Examine the wheel for trueness once again. Touch up the truing as required. This squeezing of the spokes helps to "seat" them and results in wheels that stay trued longer. In any case, you should slightly tighten and retrue the wheels after the first 10 to 15 hours of riding. If you have built and trued the wheels properly, you should get years of reliable service from them with only one truing a year.

Rules of Thumb

- Keep a couple of spare spokes inside your handlebar in case of emergencies. The bend required to get the spoke in will not hurt it and will also reduce any rattling.

- Never rebuild a wheel with spokes that have been used before. Use only new spokes that have not been fatigued, stretched, bent, or corroded.

- The front and rear quick-release levers should be on the same (left) side of the bicycle for aesthetics.

- Always position the rear quick-release lever on the left side of the bicycle. This reduces interference with the rear derailleur.

CHAPTER NINE

TIRES

Most bicycle components are fairly simple. If the component has been properly matched with its intended use, few problems are experienced. Tires, on the other hand, should be grouped with wheels and frames in their complexity and in the relative scarcity of available information that explains how to properly select, use, and maintain them.

WIRED-ON TIRES

Although this tire is frequently called a clincher, its true name is a wired-on. It is named for the wire bead that physically holds the tire on the rim. This type of tire is very similar to the design of a car tire except that most car tires are now tubeless. Bicycle tires can't share the same tubeless design since the air would leak through the holes in the rim where the spokes join.

Proper selection of tires depends on two important factors: (1) what type (size) of rim your bicycle has; and (2) what type of riding you do.

The rider should seek competent technical advice before attempting to change brands and/or tire sizes. Some sizes are totally incompatible and mounting them is impossible. Others will fit, but incompatibility may cause part of the tire to slip off the rim under pressure and cause a potentially dangerous blowout. It is impossible for us to list tire/rim compatibility within the scope of this book because of the constantly changing specifications—you should check for compatibility as you make your next tire purchase. Our intentions are to try to explain the design variations (and their characteristics) that exist so you can make an informed decision based on your individual needs.

As previously covered, revolving weight affects bicycle performance to a much greater degree than stationary weight. Bicycle tire designs vary to take advantage of the importance of light weight. Specifically, tread design, size, and the composition of materials used affects the way the tire performs.

Presuming the same wheels are used, the most noticeable characteristic in tires is their rolling resistance. Some tires seem to roll forever while others seem "dead." What causes this difference and more important, why would a manufacturer offer a "dead" tire to the public? The way a tire feels is affected primarily by its air pressure. Within reason, as the tire pressure increases so does the lively feeling. Tire pressure capabilities are designed with appropriate performance characteristics in mind. For instance, how important is performance to the paperboy with 50 pounds of cargo on his bicycle? Obviously, the paperboy is more interested in the ability of a tire to handle heavy loads than he is with how responsive the tire is.

As a rule, large-section balloon tires (as found on the heavyweight newspaper bicycle) do not require the same pressure as the tires on a lightweight 10-speed. In order for a large-section tire to handle high tire pressures, the overall weight of the tire would also increase, thereby reducing responsiveness. The large-section tire provides a greater carrying capacity and increased traction, particularly on gravel roads. The low tire pressure, when combined with the natural flexibility of the large tire section, results in a very comfortable and stable ride. This is particularly important for the bicycle that is used for transportation rather than performance.

Tread design also affects the performance of the tire. As the tire pressure increases (and the tire section decreases), the tread design plays a proportionately greater share in the overall performance. That's why balloon tires are available in few tread designs and high-performance tires are offered in several tread designs.

TUBULAR TIRES

Tubular tires which are often called sew-ups, have a completely different design than wired-on tires. The tire consists of an inner tube with the tire casing sewn around it. Even though there is considerable variation in the sectional diameter of tubular tires, the largest is approximately the same size as the smallest wired-on. Unlike the wired-on tire that fits inside the wheel rim, the tubular is glued on the rim surface. The chief design criterion for the tubular tire is performance. Until recently, tubular tires were designed primarily for racing applications. However, with the bicycle boom, more riders became aware of the benefits of tubulars for fast recreational riding.

Tread patterns for tubular tires vary from slick rubber without any tread to small motorcycle-like tires for races held through muddy fields. For normal riding, the cyclist should be aware of two recommended tread patterns: the ribbed and the mixed tread. The ribbed tread is a fast design with acceptable traction under most conditions. The mixed tread is not quite as fast but has better gripping power. When riding on tubulars, you should approach corners with caution until you learn the characteristics of the tire.

In addition to choosing the specific tread design, the rider must decide what casing is appropriate. Understanding tubular-tire construction is the most important part of knowing which tire to select. For each type of construction, prices, the recommended use, and maintenance vary considerably.

Tubulars are manufactured by one of two processes, either vulcanized or cold-processed by hand. The vulcanizing process requires machinery that joins the tread and the casing by using heat. The process is far less time consuming than the hand-built method and consequently, the tire is less expensive. The casing is always made of cotton. A characteristic of the vulcanized tire is its stiff construction.

Cold-process tubulars are glued together by hand. The major difference between the two processes is the type of casing used. Silk is offered only in cold-process tires, since heat would damage the delicate silk. Moreover, high-grade cotton tubulars are made by hand with the cold-process method. Although many riders treat cotton and silk tires the same, their use and maintenance requirements are quite different.

Cotton casings are quite tough and can withstand more handling and abuse than the silk casings. Silk casings are more resilient and responsive, but all silk casings are not alike. The quality of the silk tire is determined by the number of threads per inch. Cotton has relatively coarse threads with comparatively fewer threads per inch than standard silk tires. The best lightweight silk tubulars are made of fine-quality silk that has more threads per inch than the standard silk tire.

Tubular tires are also available with either latex or Butyl rubber inner tubes. The latex tube is more puncture resistant and more responsive. Unfortunately, it is also more porous and it will lose a substantial proportion of its air pressure over a period as short as 12 hours. Butyl, on the other hand, is not as responsive but it will maintain its tire pressure for days.

Although the silk tire is more responsive than the cotton tire, the former is also less durable. Since many cyclists experience problems with tubulars, we will provide information that is applicable to both silk and cotton tires. Hard as it is to believe, the care a tubular gets *before* it is ridden is as important as the care it receives during actual use.

The quality among tubular tires varies dramatically. Although there are riders who will disagree, most experts recommend Clement tubulars. (Barum, Canetti, Continental, D'Allesandro, Hutchinson, and Wolber are all close runners-up.) In selecting tires remember one important fact: nothing stops a bicycle as effectively or frequently as a flat tire.

Before you buy the tire, ask the dealer to mount it on a wheel and inflate it. This will accomplish two things: (1) it will determine if the tire will hold air (most stores will not refund money for tires that have punctures as determining the cause of the puncture is usually impossible) and (2) by sighting down the length of the tire as the wheel spins slowly, you can determine if the tread has been put on straight (usually more of a problem with vulcanized tires where the tread is put on by machine) or if there are any bulges or lumps. Look carefully near the valve for bulges. Less-expensive tires frequently have this problem. Although it won't usually affect reliability, a bulge in the tire will cause an annoying bump when riding. Larger bulges may indicate weaknesses in the casing.

Next, check to determine the age of the tire. The age of the tire (or the hardness of the rubber) is directly related to its resistance to punctures. Optimally, a tire should be at least six months old before use. Ideally, a year is preferred. You can tell the degree of hardness (or age) of the tire by two simple tests. Press your thumbnail into the tread of the tire, *not the sidewall*. If the indentation caused by your nail disappears quickly, the tire is fairly hard and it will resist glass and other sharp objects that would cut a green (unaged) tire. Second, with moderate pressure, rub your thumb over the tread. If your thumb slides easily over the rubber, this is an indication that the tread is fairly well aged. If

Tire Characteristics

	Wired-on		Tubular	
	70-lb. Tires	90- to 100-lb. Tires	Cotton	Silk
Responsiveness	Good	Very good	Excellent	Excellent
Ability to Withstand Abuse to Sidewall	Very good	Good	Fair	Poor
Cost	Inexpensive to moderate	Moderate	Expensive	Very expensive
Advantages	Easy to repair Inexpensive Unaffected by poor weather (rain, sleet, snow) Relatively puncture resistant Last longer Less likely to roll off rim Better traction		Easy to carry on bicycle Easy to change along the road without any tools Very fast and responsive	
Disadvantages	Difficult to carry spare on bicycle Less responsive than tubulars		Time-consuming to repair Frequent punctures (if not aged) Require aging	

your thumb does not slide easily and it lifts small particles of rubber as it moves, like an eraser, the tire might need more aging. These tests have no real value for vulcanized tires since the heating process hardens the rubber as it is bonded. To insure an adequate aging period, serious cyclists often purchase their tires well in advance of actual use.

The way you age your tires is as important as the way you treat your tires when riding. If you age the tires improperly, you have done more damage than good. To eliminate problems, you should mount each individual tire on its own rim. This accomplishes several things: it eliminates damage caused by folding the tires where a permanent crease will result; it reduces the danger of scuffing the delicate sidewalls; and it prestretches the tire making it easier to mount. You can usually obtain damaged rims that have been removed from repaired bicycles. Clean off the glue, use a hammer to straighten any large dents, and you have a rim for tire storage.

The tires should be stored in a cool, dark, airy space. Check tires periodically to keep enough air in them to maintain their round section. They should not be pumped up to riding pressure. Also check to see that the sidewall is aging consistently. A change in sidewall color in only part of the tire indicates that sunlight or dampness is affecting the aging process. Rotating the position of the rim is required. If you store your tires for an extremely long period of time, you should coat the sidewalls with liquid latex to reduce the possibility of drying out and cracking.

MOUNTING TIRES

To mount wired-on and tubular tires, follow the suggestions given below.

Wired-on Tires

To mount a wired-on tire you will need a wheel, tire, inner tube, and a rubber rim strip.

The rim strip is designed to reduce punctures caused by abrasion of the inner tube against the rim and spoke nipples. This problem is particularly common on new bicycles or on bicycles which recently have had the wheels trued. Sometimes tightening the spokes will cause the end of the spoke to stick up high enough to puncture the tube. *Before* you mount the rim strip, run your finger over all the nipples and along the inside of the rim. Any sharp edges or rough spots should be filed smooth. After making certain that the rim is absolutely smooth, position the rim strip in the center channel of the rim. Don't forget to line up the valve hole in the strip with the valve hole in the rim.

Without using any tools, gently force one side of the tire onto the rim. Inflate the inner tube just enough to give it shape and insert the side of the inner tube with the valve first. Make sure the valve is inserted properly before placing the rest of the inner tube in the tire. Put the remainder of the inner tube in the tire. Be certain that there are no wrinkles in the inner tube. Without using any tools, carefully force the other side of the tire on the rim. This will be fairly easy until the last 12 to 18 inches of the tire remain. Do not use any tools to push the tire on the rim because it increases the likelihood of pinching the tube against the rim (which will cause the tube to leak air and you will have to take the tire back off the rim and patch the tube).

After the tire is fully mounted, work the tire around forcing it down deep into the rim. Push the valve stem in halfway and pull it back out again to insure that it is not hung up against the bead of the tire. Check to make sure the valve stem is still straight. If it is, inflate the tire to normal pressure.

Tubular Tires

Proper mounting of tubular tires is considerably more complex and in general, is poorly understood by most cyclists. Before starting to mount the tire, the rim must be prepared. Since the curved surface of the tubular tire rim is practically flat, poor preparation of the rim can result in a tire that rolls off while cornering. Unfortunately, this happens with alarming regularity.

Before you apply the smallest amount of rim cement, check the rim to insure that there are no sharp surfaces that will chafe the underside of the tire. These should be filed smooth as previously described. After you have checked the entire rim, take a sharp-

(continued on page 186)

Photos 9–1 to 9–10: **Installing the Wired-on Tire.**

Photo 9–1:   Check the rim strip for tears. Adjust it to cover all spoke heads.

Photo 9–2:   Begin the installation of the tire by starting one of the tire beads in the rim.

Photo 9–3: Using your hands, push the bead onto the rim.

A

B

Photos 9–4A and 9–4B: Most tires require considerable leverage to "pop" the bead onto the rim. If you are unable to accomplish this with your bare hands (A), you could as a last resort use a tire iron (again, remembering to use the curved part of the "spoon" down) to force the bead onto the rim (B).

Photo 9–5: Once you have mounted one side of the tire, install the inner tube. Before you attempt to install the tube, inflate it just enough to give it a round shape. This will reduce the tendency for the tube to fold over which can cause chafing and leaks. Carefully insert the valve into the valve hole in the rim.

Photo 9–6: Use your fingers to position the tube inside the tire—all the way around the rim.

Photo 9—7: Be careful to tuck the tube inside the tire. This reduces the possibility of the tire bead pinching the tube against the rim.

Photo 9–8: Check the valve to make sure it is installed properly—at a 90-degree angle to the rim. Adjust as required. Starting at the valve, insert the other tire bead onto the rim and, using both hands, work the tire bead in place.

Photo 9–9: Continue pushing the tire onto the rim until you reach the last (and most stubborn) few inches of tire.

Photo 9–10: Make sure the inner tube is safely nestled inside the tire before you complete the last step. If it is OK, force the remaining portions of the tire onto the rim *with your bare hands.* Do not use tire irons because it is very easy to pinch (i.e., puncture) the tube during this step. If you pinch the tube, you have to remove and patch it, so be careful! Inflate the tire with 20 pounds of air and check to see that the tire is properly seated on the rim. Adjust as required. The tire should sit evenly on both sides around the entire rim. If so, inflate to recommended pressure.

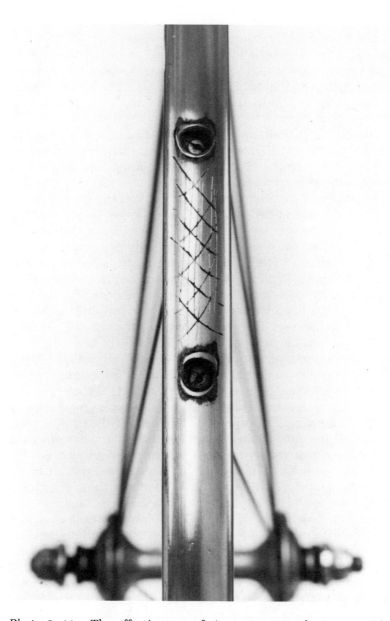

Photo 9–11: The effectiveness of rim cement can be improved by "scoring" the rim prior to application of the cement. The score marks should be just deep enough to "rough-up" the smooth curved surface of the rim.

edged tool and make several grooves in the soft metal between spoke ferrules. Do not dig too deeply; the grooves are only intended to provide a receptacle for additional glue.

Again, before applying any glue, practice mounting the tire once (figures 9-13 to 9-16). If the tire is difficult to mount, you should stretch it. It's better to discover it *before* applying the glue. With the tire on the rim, pump it up hard and let it sit for a few hours to stretch. Lightweight (or silk) tires stretch far easier than the heavier tires (especially vulcanized). Take the time to properly stretch the tire before applying any glue.

The most critical step in the tire-mounting procedure is applying the glue. Most problems occur in the selection and application of the glue. We have mounted hundreds of tires and used several different types of glue. In our opinion, Clement mastice "Gutta" strada is the best. If applied correctly, this glue is effective in any temperature. It is available in small tubes or large cans. If you intend to mount a large quantity of tires, by all means, get the can. It is easier to use since the glue must be mixed before it is applied to the rim. If you use this glue you will see two distinctly different-colored liquids in the tube (or can). The clear liquid is the preservative which keeps the glue from drying out. The dark brown liquid is the glue itself. The effectiveness of the bond is severely reduced if the two substances are not mixed prior to application to the rim. If you use the tube, squeeze the tube (with the cap on) at least 50 times to guarantee that the glue is properly mixed. The can has a wide mouth and can be stirred easily.

Do not use Clement mastice pista for normal riding—it is designed to be used for track racing and it has completely different properties than the road cement.

Once the glue has been mixed, a very thin coating should be applied to the rim. If you elect to use glue from tubes you will be forced to spread the glue with your fingers, which is one of the reasons why we use the can. Using a small artist's brush, you can easily apply the glue straight from the can. Allow the first coat of glue to harden.

After the first coat has dried, apply another thin coat of glue evenly over the rim. You should also apply a very thin coat of glue on the cloth tape on the underside of the tire. When the glue is tacky, mount the tire. (Don't forget to first wash off any glue that you have on your hands.)

After the tire is mounted, check to insure that the valve stem is properly positioned. If it is, put about 40 to 50 pounds of air into the tire. Check to make sure that the tire is mounted accurately, using your thumbs to push the tire into place. Spin the wheel slowly to see if the tire wobbles. If it does, keep adjusting; if not, pump up the tire to normal riding pressure and allow it to dry for 24 hours. Before the wheel is remounted on the bicycle you should clean off any glue that gets on the rim to prevent braking problems. If glue oozes out from under the tire, too much glue was used. There is nothing to do except wait until it is dry and peel it off. Remember how much glue you used and try to use less next time.

Should you decide to change a tire in the future, it will not be necessary to put two coats on the rim—one thin coat should be adequate. If you change tires regularly, you will need to remove the glue that accumulates after 10 to 12 tire changes.

Track cement requires several coats to be effective and dries out quickly. Therefore, you should check your track-bike tires regularly because the cement can dry out in a matter of days and lose all effectiveness. Since several coats are required for proper adhesion, all of the glue on the rim should be removed before applying a new coat.

(continued on page 193)

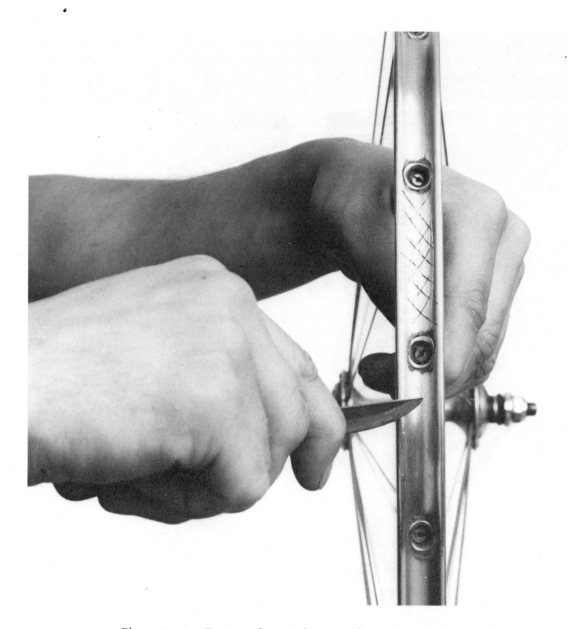

Photo 9–12: To "rough-up" the smooth surface of the rim for improved tire adhesion with tubular tires, grasp the wheel firmly and scratch the rim with a sharp object. You should also use a file to "rough-up" each spoke ferrule. This will dull any sharp edges and provide a more adhesive surface for the cement.

Photos 9–13 to 9–17: **Mounting a Tubular Tire.**

Presuming that the rim has been properly prepared and glued, and the tire has been inflated just enough to make its casing round (this reduces glue on the sidewalls), the tire is installed as follows:

Photo 9–13: **Step 1.**

Start with the rim positioned so that the valve hole is at the top. Insert the valve squarely in the valve hole and carefully spread the inner strip of the tire on the rim.

Photo 9–14: **Step 2.**
 Keep the tire under tension as you place it on the rim because the tire circumference is always smaller than the circumference of the wheel to insure a tight fit.

Photo 9–15: **Step 3.**
 Keep stretching the tire and be sure to place the inner strip squarely on the wet glue.

Photo 9–16: **Step 4.**

The Hard Part—Force the remaining portion over the rim into position. This usually requires considerable leverage. This method is the most frequently recommended procedure. We have found an alternate way of completing Step 4 which seems easier.

Photo 9–17: **Alternate Step 4.**

When you have reached the hard part (the last few inches), turn the wheel around. The valve should be on the floor now. Hold the rim in position with your toes and *pull* the tire up and over the rim. Be careful not to step too hard on the rim. Spin the wheel to check for proper tire alignment on the rim. If it's OK, inflate the tire to full pressure and let it sit for 24 hours to let the glue dry thoroughly.

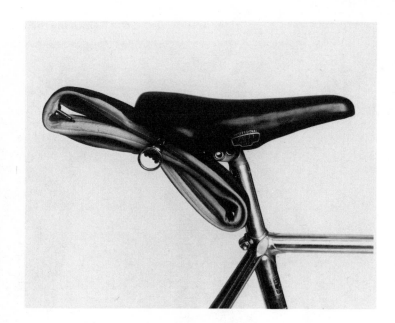

Photo 9–18: A tubular tire can be easily folded and stored under the saddle. Most riders use an old toe strap to attach the tire to the saddle support wires. Some use a special enclosed carrier while others use special spare tire clamps that attach to the saddle. Whichever you use, always fold the tire with the valve at the fold—not in the center.

FIXING PUNCTURES

Sooner or later every cyclist will have a flat tire. Usually, a flat occurs at the worst possible time. For most of us it occurs when we ride without a patch kit or pump. While it isn't fun to patch a tire, it really isn't difficult. The following is a summary of the necessary steps to repair a flat with both a wired-on tire and tubular tire.

Wired-on Tires

Before you take the tire off the rim, check to see that the valve core is tight. If it is, make sure you have the necessary materials to complete the patch job:

- Two or three tire irons;
- Patch kit containing rubber cement, patches, and emery paper.

The next thing to do is to carefully inspect the tire. Try to find the piece of glass, nail, or wire that caused the puncture. This object should be extracted and thrown away (after marking its location on the tire). Many riders have fixed a puncture and found that the tire still leaks air since they never removed the sharp object which caused the flat in the first place.

If you are unable to find the leak, inflate the tire to riding pressure and dip sections of the tire into a tub filled with water. Look for air bubbles escaping from the area of the tire that is punctured. Mark the spot and dry off the rim and tire.

Removal of the tire is the same as installing the tire as previously outlined; however, it is sometimes difficult to get the first section of the tire off of the rim. *Do not* use a screwdriver to pry up the bead of the tire.

(continued on page 202)

Photos 9–19 to 9–26: **Removing the Wired-on Tire.**

Photo 9–19: Remove air from the inner tube by depressing the valve core.

Place the valve at the bottom and start working at the top, opposite the valve stem.

Carefully insert the tire iron under the tire bead with the curved part of the tire iron pointing down.

Photo 9–20:   Hook the tire iron onto a spoke.

Photo 9–21: Insert the second tire iron under the tire bead approximately two spokes away from the original tire iron. Hook it onto a spoke.

Photo 9–22: Insert the third tire iron under the tire bead two spokes away from the second tire iron. Hook it onto a spoke.

Photo 9–23:   Slide your fingers under the bead between the tire irons.
(Tire irons will fall off the wheel once the bead is loosened.)

Photo 9–24:   Slide your hand along the circumference of the tire until the bead is completely off the rim.

Photo 9–25: Gently pull out the inner tube (except for the area near the valve).

Photo 9–26:   Using your bare hands, force the remaining bead off of the rim. Gently remove the tire and the inner tube *together* at the valve.

This procedure can damage the tube and will give you more holes to patch. Tire irons are designed without sharp edges to reduce the possibility of cutting the inner tube. Yes, they are still capable of pinching the tube. Do not allow the tube to get pinched between the tire iron and the rim or bead of the tire. Once you get a few inches of tire bead over the edge of the rim, it is easy to slide your hand under the tire and pull the tire over the rim. *Do not* remove the tire from the rim. Only one side of the tire must be off to patch the tube.

Push the valve through the valve hole and remove the inner tube. If you have already located the puncture, do not lose track of its position. If you were unable to locate the hole previously, inflate the inner tube (it will expand a great deal without bursting, but to be safe do not inflate it more than two to three times its normal size) and dip it into a tub of water.

Carefully check to see if the puncture went through both sides of the tube. It is very frustrating to patch one hole and realize, after reassembling the bicycle, that you still have a leak. If the tube is punctured on only the inside surface, you have a sharp object on the inside of the rim. Fixing the tire will not stop the problem from happening again. Check the rim strip and rim for any sharp projecting surfaces.

Use the emery paper to roughen up the area around the puncture hole. The rough area should be approximately one inch in diameter. Apply a thin coat of rubber cement to the roughed-up area of the tube and to the patch. (Make sure that you have very thin patches if you are riding high-pressure tires; otherwise, you will feel an annoying bump with each revolution of the wheel. The best patch material is a small piece of the rubber inner tube from a discarded tubular tire.)

Wait until the glue appears to be dry and

then apply the patch and hold firmly for one minute. The patching process is now complete and you can follow the same procedures previously explained indicating how to mount a tube and tire.

Tubular Tires

Repairing a tubular tire is not nearly as difficult as it sounds, but it is time-consuming. To make the job easier, purchase a patch kit designed for tubular tires. The complete kit will include needle and thread, a thimble, patches, and glue, and should cost less than $2. All you need to add to this kit is a razor blade.

Remove the tire without using any tools. This is best accomplished by using the combined force of two thumbs to loosen a little of the tire at a time. Some riders choose not to ride a tubular that has been patched and relegate patched tires to duty as spares. If you decide to adopt this practice, you can simply glue a new tire on the rim. Many riders put punctured tires away until they accumulate several that require patching. In any case, the patching process remains the same whenever you decide to perform the repairs.

Visually inspect the tire. Look for the object that caused the puncture. Remove it and mark the spot or perform the water test. The test is the same as for the wired-on tire but it may be more difficult to locate the hole since the tire and tube are one sealed unit. Frequently you will find that the only bubbles that appear are around the valve stem. Check to see if the valve is tight and undamaged—many tubulars have replaceable valves that can work themselves loose. The bubbles may appear at the valve because the air is escaping from a hole in the tube and traveling along the inside of the tire until

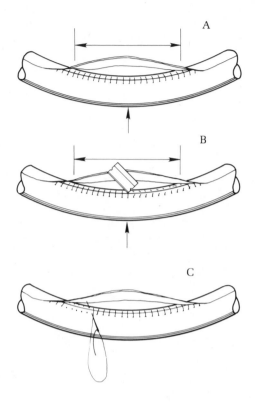

A

B

C

Figures 9–1 to 9–3: **Tubular Tire Repair.**

After determining where the air leak is, through the water test or visual inspection:

(A) Remove the glued-on rim tape for approximately two inches on each side of the puncture.

(B) Cut the stitches (under the cloth strip) over the same two inches on each side of the puncture.

(C) After the inner tube is repaired (following the same procedure as for a wired-on tire), and the tube and cloth chafing tape have been inserted in the tire casing, restitch the tire through the same holes using a circular (overhand) stitch.

it escapes at the unsealed area at the valve stem. Pump up the tire a little harder and carefully examine the tire for telltale air bubbles when submerged.

After locating the puncture, turn the tire over and remove the glued-on rim tape approximately two inches on each side of the puncture. Be very careful when removing this strip not to puncture the sidewall of the tire. Under the cloth strip you will see the stitches that hold the tire together. Cut the stitches over the same two inches on each side of the puncture and throw away the pieces of thread. Open the tire casing, push aside the cloth chafing tape (inside the casing), and carefully pull out a section of the inner tube.

The inner tube should be patched exactly the same way as described for wired-on tires. After the patch is in place, spread a small amount of talcum powder around the inner tube and reposition it inside the casing. The talcum powder will reduce the likelihood that any excess glue on the inner tube will cause it to stick to the inner tire casing. Carefully reposition the inner tube and inner cloth chafing tape so that they are not kinked or twisted. Use double-thickness thread (insert thread into the eye of the needle and tie the ends in a knot; the knot will keep the thread from pulling through the first hole in the casing) and *using the same casing holes*, restitch the tire using an overhand (circular) stitch.

After the stitching is completed, apply a thin coating of rubber cement to the stitches and the base tape. Reposition the base tape carefully to eliminate any wrinkles.

Troubleshooting Guide:
Tires

Problem	Probable Cause	How to Repair
Cut sidewall; broken cord in tire	Riding underinflated tire	Replace tire—small sidewall ruptures can sometimes be repaired with an internal patch; however, when using high-pressure tires, it is best to replace the tire if *any* damage is noted.
Abraded sidewalls	Brake block touching tire	Actuate brake lever and observe position of brake block. Adjust as required.
	Tire has been scuffed against curbs or buildings	Replace tire if required. The only cure for this is to avoid letting anything touch the sidewalls.
Tire has a large bulge	Overinflation	Check tire pressure; adjust as required.
	Broken cord(s) in tire	Replace tire.
	Incorrect tire-to-rim compatibility (wired-on only)	Check compatibility at local bicycle shop.
Tire is developing small cracks in the rubber	Tire is drying out from age	Always keep the bicycle hanging up when not in use.
		Tubular tires should not be stored at full tire pressure (except vulcanized tires or ones with Butyl tubes).
		Apply Armor-All to wired-on tires per instructions included on label.
Tire makes squeaking or clicking noises going around corners or under heavy acceleration (tubular only)	Glue has hardened and tire is moving on rim	Check to see if tire is firmly cemented into position. Reglue as required.

Rules of Thumb

- Do not use the washers or caps that come with the valve. If the tire (or tube, in the case of a wired-on) creeps on the rim, the creeping action will remain undiscovered until the valve is pulled from the tube and the air leaks out. It is better to permit the tire to creep and be able to see the position of the valve. This is the only way you can take preventative action before the damage is done. In the case of the tubular tire, if the tire rolls off the rim and you have the valve bolted to the rim, the valve will be ripped out of the tire. Similarly don't leave the valve adapter on the valve. Keep it somewhere else on the bicycle. (We have found that brake center bolts and front-derailleur mounting bolts often have the same threads as the adapter.)

- Check your tire pressure regularly. Too much tire pressure can cause blowouts and possible traction problems. Too little pressure can cause flats as the tube is pinched against the rim when hitting bumps.

- The rear tire should be inflated five to ten pounds more than the front tire for proper handling (remember the 45 percent—55 percent weight rule).

- Always clean off your tires after riding through glass or sharp objects that accumulate along roads. This task should become routine since it significantly reduces the likelihood of getting a puncture.

Photo 9–27: **Cleaning the Rear Tire while Riding.** Although you do not need to look at the rear tire while you clean it, you must be careful not to stick your hand into the wheel as it revolves. Place your thumb on the rearstays and using the stays as a guide, slide your hand down until your fingertips make contact with the tire. With a little practice this becomes easy.

Caution: Do not allow your fingers to make contact with the spokes and do not let your hand follow the tire as it can become wedged between the tire and the seat tube.

Photo 9–28: Cleaning the front tire while riding is easy. Place your fingertips lightly on the top of the revolving tire. This will force debris off of the tire and it will decrease your chances of getting a flat.

• Be careful when inflating your tires with a gas-station air pump. Many riders have learned the hard way that it is all too easy to blow out the tire. Remember that the pumps are designed for car tires (large volume—low pressure). When you pump the air into your tire use short bursts of air and check the pressure frequently. Do not rely on the gauge that is built into the air compressor.

• Do not scuff the sidewalls of the tires on curbs, buildings, or other objects. The sidewalls are designed to be thin in order to reduce revolving weight and to provide elasticity. This is particularly important with tubular tires—do not handle the sidewalls at all!

• Always inflate your tires to the manufacturer's specifications which are usually printed on the sidewalls of most wired-on tires.

• Do not use double-sided rim tape to secure sew-up tires onto the rims. This tape is adequate for emergencies; however, it cannot secure a tire as effectively as properly applied cement.

• Use a rubber preservative like Armor-All on rubber brake hoods and all rubber clincher tires (not silk or cotton tubular tires). This prevents cracking.

• Do not leave the valve cap (or adapter) on the tire valve of tubular tires. If the tire should roll off the rim as a result of poor gluing practices, the valve cap will not pass through the valve hole in the rim and the valve will probably be ripped from the tube.

Photos 9–29A and 9–29B: Using the two different pump ends:

• The press-on end (A) fits directly over the Presta valve.

• The thumb-lock pump end (B) is inserted on the Schrader valve and then locked in position by locking the lever in the down position.

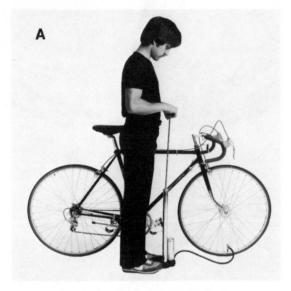

Photo 9–30: Do not twist or pull the pump from the valve after the tire has been inflated. This can damage the valve and the pump end.

Instead, strike the top side of the pump sharply downward.

Photos 9–31A and 9–31B: **Proper Use of a Foot Pump.** The valve should always be at the bottom of the wheel to reduce the tendency for the pump end to "pop" off under pressure (A). *Do not* pump air into the tire if it is completely flat since the air pressure can burn a hole in the inner tube. If the tire is completely flat, pump air slowly into the tire until the tire resumes its normal shape.

Always raise the pump handle to the top of its stroke (A) to maximize the quantity of air injected into the tire. Push the handle all of the way down its stroke (B) to obtain maximum volume and pressure.

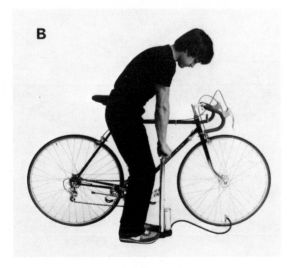

Photo 9–32:   The Schrader valve is found on all American tubes and most American utility bicycles. This valve is the same size as valves found on car tires and will fit standard air pumps.

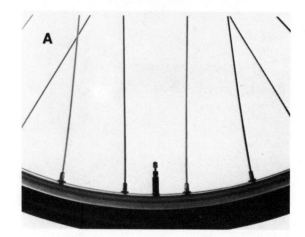

Photos 9–33A and 9–33B: The Presta valve is found on European tubular tires and inner tubes. It consists of the outer valve body and a screw stop to keep the air from escaping. (A) This valve is shown in its open position ready for injection of air into the tire. The air will escape from the tire only when the adjustable stop is pressed down. The bicycle should not be ridden with the valve open. (B) Valve is closed—air cannot escape.

Note: The valve should always be perfectly perpendicular to the rim.

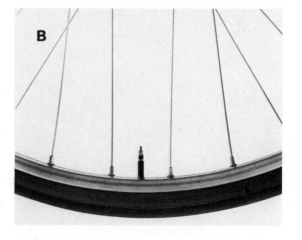

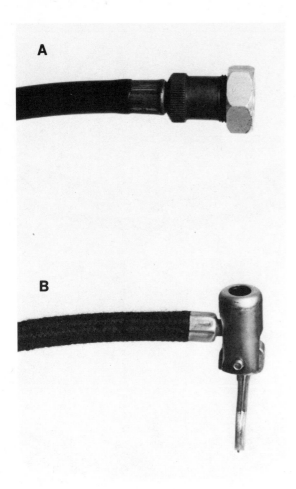

Photo 9–34: Bicycle foot pumps are available with two different connectors for the tire valves:

(A) Push-on. This type is used on Presta valves only.

(B) Thumb-lock. This type is used on Schrader valves or Presta valves with an adapter. The connector is very effective since it conveniently is locked into place on the valve (to reduce leaking and blowing off) by the thumb-lock lever.

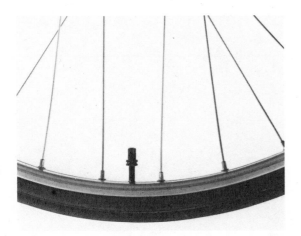

Photo 9–35: The Presta valve requires an adapter to permit inflation with the most common air pumps found at gas stations.

CHAPTER TEN

CLOTHING

Just about any kind of clothing can be adapted for cycling. What you wear, however, should provide riding comfort and safety. For example, it doesn't make sense to wear a wide-brimmed hat which shades your eyes from the sun but invites disaster as the brim flaps in the wind. Remember you can be vulnerable on a bicycle and you don't want to compound your vulnerability by the clothing you wear.

Cycling clothes are designed to aid the cyclist in the pursuit of his or her cycling goals. To the novice, cycling clothes may look peculiar but each article of attire is designed and manufactured to improve comfort, safety, and efficiency of the rider.

In our bicycle store, we often had trouble convincing women who were experiencing problems with saddle soreness to try a pair of bicycle shorts. The expensive, chamois-lined black shorts are certainly not a fashion item; and at first, it is difficult for a newcomer to the sport to understand the advantages of sitting on a chamois rather than on a piece of material. Although cycling shorts are not the cure-all for saddle sores, they do help to decrease discomfort much of the time.

Cycling clothes are designed to provide protection from the elements. Being properly designed, the clothing helps to maintain normal body temperatures. Many times during hot summer days it is common to see men cycling with no shirts and women cycling in small halter tops. These cyclists are apparently unaware of the potential hazards created by exposing their bare torsos. First, while it is a nice way to get a fast tan, it is also the fastest way to get a painful sunburn on the back and shoulders. Because of the infrequent change in upper body position when cycling, the back and shoulders are directly exposed to the sun. Due to the cooling effect created by the wind, the rider may not feel the actual effects of the sun. Severe burns are common and second-degree burns or sun poisoning occur far too frequently.

Another problem with riding shirtless is

the lack of protection in the event of an accident. Most crashes result in minor road burns on elbows, knees, hips, and ankles, but a rider without a jersey sustains more serious road burns on his or her back and chest. Riders without shirts quickly learn of the degree of protection afforded by a shirt. A minor crash can cause extremely painful burns that can ruin the remainder of the ride (and make life generally miserable for several days). The danger of infection can be serious during an extended trip, so why take chances?

If you ride in the cooler seasons, you will find that you have to protect yourself from the wind as well as the cold. An actual air temperature of 30°F. with a wind of 10 mph will create a windchill factor of 16°F. Couple that with your velocity on the bicycle and your body is exposed to temperatures that are equivalent to below 0°F.

Properly designed bicycle clothing allows for warmth and ease of movement. Therefore, cycling clothes should be close fitting. The material should cling comfortably to the rider's body without binding or restricting mobility. Close-fitting clothes are more aerodynamic since baggy clothing that "flaps in the breeze" works against the rider.

In order to provide warmth in cold weather and relief in hot weather, cycling clothes need to transmit water vapor (permeability) and air (breathability). Clothing must provide ventilation, enabling air to circulate between the clothing and the skin. This air space creates warmth in the cool weather and coolness in the heat. The air trapped next to the rider's skin is kept warm by the rider's body temperature. On the other hand, the permeability of the material allows perspiration to evaporate, thus cooling the rider when riding in the heat.

Since they are elastic and resilient, knit fabrics are used for most cycling clothes. Woven fabrics are best used for cycling outer garments. They are more restricting and less comfortable than knit materials.

Knit cycling clothes are strong, permeable, and hygenically safe. Natural fibers provide optimum ventilation and moisture absorption. Although cotton, wool, and silk are all natural fibers, wool best satisfies the cyclist's needs.

Wool is an appropriate material for cycling clothes as it is light, comfortable, and durable. Furthermore, it offers superior insulation from rain and cold. Its properties of elasticity are unequaled by any other fiber. Wool fibers can be stretched more than 30 percent of their original length yet recover and return to their natural shape within minutes.

JERSEYS

Specially made bicycle shirts are called jerseys. Jerseys should be breathable, permeable, light weight, and soft. They should be form fitting and should enhance freedom of movement. Jerseys should not bind in the neck area, shoulders, or arms. A good jersey will be long enough to insure that the rider's back is completely covered while riding down on the drops. A jersey should fit in such a way that it does not chafe.

Jerseys are made in two different styles: road and track. Although these jerseys may look the same, there are major differences between them. The road jersey is designed for long events in changing climatic conditions. Track jerseys, on the other hand, are designed for short, fast events in fairly stable temperatures.

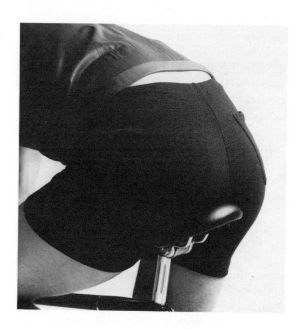

Photo 10–2: If the bicycle jersey is too short, it will ride up the back and leave a space between the jersey and the shorts. Good cycling clothes are designed for the bent-over position.

Road Jerseys

Generally, road jerseys are made out of wool, acrylic, cotton, or polyester. The best are those made out of either cotton or wool. Most cotton jerseys are a blend of 50 percent cotton/50 percent polyester which adds strength and provides resistance to wrinkling. Moisture absorption and permeability increase as the percentage of cotton increases. Cotton is ideal for summer use where bicycle riding is done at temperatures above 70°F.

Many riders wear cotton jerseys while riding at temperatures below 70°F. because they see runners who wear cotton shirts at

Photo 10–1: Jerseys and shorts should fit snugly, without constricting. Loose-fitting clothing creates unnecessary bulk and may prove to be an abrasive irritant.

The zipper on the jersey should operate smoothly and should not constrict when fully closed.

temperatures far below 70°F. That is a mistake for the cyclist. Body heat loss is far greater for the cyclist than the runner because of the windchill factor caused by the greater speeds. Wool jerseys help retain body temperature more effectively than cotton and, consequently, they are usually the first choice of cyclists.

Interestingly, wool is well suited to bicycling in the summer as well as in winter. Many riders incorrectly assume that the warmth of wool makes it a fabric limited to winter wear. Wool works better than other materials in both cold and hot weather. Why do the Bedouins, the nomadic Arabs, use wool for their undergarments and burnooses? It is the only fabric that gives them adequate protection from both the very hot temperatures of the desert days and the cold nights. In other words, it helps stabilize and maintain body temperature. This is why a wool jersey is just as well suited to 90°F. temperatures as it is in 40°F.

Another characteristic of wool is its ability to repel rain, yet absorb perspiration. Wool fiber absorbs up to 30 percent of its weight before it begins to "feel" wet. Wool fibers, made up of cells of complex proteins, maintain a balance with the surrounding moisture conditions. This characteristic of wool creates a warm feeling even when riding in the rain.

There are some manufacturers who make jerseys using wool blends. The main advantage of a wool blend is cost; it's more economical to use wool blends such as wool/acrylic, wool/nylon, and wool/polyester, than it is to use 100 percent wool. Although clothing manufacturers who use wool blends advertise their products as "having the advantages of wool and the toughness of synthetics," when cycling you start losing wool's advantages with any blend of less than 60 percent wool. We would recommend choosing wool cycling clothes containing at least 70 percent wool.

The best-fitting jerseys are knit. A knit fabric will "give" whereas a woven fabric can bind and restrict movement. There are also variations within knits. The fabric count (the number of threads per inch) provides some indication of the relative strength among knit jerseys. More threads per inch means increased fabric strength. You should examine the number of rows of knitting per inch to compare strength. The same applies to seams. When comparing jerseys, turn the garments inside out to inspect the seam stitching. The jersey with the greatest number of stitches per inch probably has the strongest seam. Ideally, all seams should be "overcast" (to reduce fraying) and stitched flat on one side with a reinforced locking stitch to prevent them from chafing. Sergal, an Italian manufacturer which has set the standard for quality jerseys in this country, only overcasts the seams but doesn't stitch them over. Under normal use, this creates no problem.

Most quality bicycle jerseys are made with as few seams as possible. They are made from tubular knits which allow for a better fit and the elimination of body seams. Any horizontal contrasting stripes are always knitted into the fabric rather than sewn in, eliminating the need for horizontal body seams.

All jerseys should have a ribbed neck and cuffs. The ribbing holds the material in place and prevents it from sliding and chafing. Ribbing helps maintain the shape of the material. Otherwise, the jersey might stretch out of shape after a number of wearings and washings.

The closures used on jerseys are chosen primarily for their ease of operation. Zippers are always used on the front neckline so the rider can easily adjust the amount of opening while riding. Zippers used are steel or nylon. Steel zippers, which can be corroded by sweat, are the most common and are stronger than nylon. Nylon, however, is not affected by perspiration. Consequently, if you do perspire a lot, you might want to consider a jersey with a nylon zipper rather than a steel one.

Buttons are used on jerseys to keep the pockets closed. The buttons are important since the contents of the pockets may fall out without a closure and the buttons ensure a flat aerodynamic profile. Open pockets act like miniature parachutes which can affect cycling efficiency.

We have indicated the various features of all road jerseys (breathability, fit, and comfort) but there is one feature in particular which distinguishes a road jersey from a track jersey—a place to carry food.

Most road jerseys have three pockets in the rear and two pockets in the front. It is safer to use the rear pockets since there is less likelihood of anything falling out. The front pockets are generally reserved for foodstuffs like raisins since the front pockets are far easier to reach when riding. Good jerseys will have double stitching at the bottom of each pocket to ensure strength. If, however, you find a jersey which is ideal except for the stitching on the pockets, just run a solid stitch one-half inch from the bottom of the pocket along the entire width of the pocket. This will provide greatly increased strength with minimal effort.

Road jerseys have either short sleeves or long sleeves. Short-sleeved jerseys are all-purpose jerseys. With the addition of a long-sleeved cotton turtleneck, you can quickly approximate the warmth provided by a jersey with long sleeves. (More on this in the Cold-Weather Riding section.) Long-sleeved jerseys are usually called winter jerseys. Although they are most appropriate for

temperature ranges between 40° to 60°F., long-sleeved jerseys are appropriate for far cooler temperatures.

Track Jerseys

Track jerseys often are as brightly colored as the road jerseys, but their similarity ends there. While the shape of the jersey is basically the same, the track jersey is made from fabrics which improve the rider's aerodynamic efficiency.

Not surprisingly, track jerseys don't have pockets because most track events are short; speed is of primary importance. In jersey design, little concern is given to characteristics like breathability and moisture absorption. Consequently, a man-made fabric such as rayon is generally used. Some professional riders use silk track jerseys which are expensive and not generally available.

Similar to road jerseys, track jerseys are sewn to stretch more horizontally than vertically. This feature allows the material to expand freely as the rider's chest expands and contracts with each breath. Track jerseys have body seams and if there is an addition of a contrasting stripe or two, it is always sewn in—not woven or knitted. Normally, this isn't a problem since track races are usually short which minimizes potential abrasion problems caused by seams.

Track jerseys look similar to road jerseys except that they appear to be silky smooth. The neck and cuffs are ribbed, and the front neckline has a zippered closure. The only obvious difference is the lack of pockets. *Don't* purchase a track jersey instead of a road jersey. They are not designed to help maintain body temperature in hot or cool weather. In fact when wet, they feel clammy and uncomfortable like most synthetics.

Clothing Fabric Characteristics

	Advantages	Disadvantages	Cost	Comfort Range
Cotton	Good at absorbing and dissipating moisture; comfortable; static free; nonirritating; keeps body cool since fiber and fabric breathe; readily accepts dye; machine washable	Doesn't resist mold and mildew; poor elasticity and resiliency; stretches somewhat with wear; decomposes under strong sunlight	Moderate	Fairly wide when used with wool garment
Wool	Excellent moisture absorption; insulates from rain and cold; comfortable; excellent elasticity and resiliency; static resistant; readily accepts dye	Special handling in washing; decomposes under strong sunlight; prone to damage by moths if not treated; sometimes coarser fibers are irritating to skin	Expensive	Wide
Nylon	Excellent elasticity and resiliency; accepts dye fairly well; machine washable; resistant to mold and mildew	Poor moisture absorption; accumulates static; deteriorates in sunlight	Moderate	Narrow
Polyester	Excellent elasticity and resiliency; machine washable; resistant to mold and mildew; does not deteriorate in sunlight	Poor moisture absorption; static prone; does not readily accept dyes	Inexpensive	Narrow
Acrylic	Fair elasticity and resiliency; accepts dye fairly well; machine washable; resistant to mold and mildew; does not deteriorate in sunlight	Poor moisture absorption; static prone	Inexpensive	Narrow
Silk	Good absorption and breathability; good elasticity and resiliency; accepts dye fairly well	Special handling in cleaning; deteriorates in sunlight	Very expensive	Moderate

SHORTS

Bicycle shorts make cycling more efficient and comfortable over long distances. High-quality, properly sized shorts can eliminate discomfort such as saddle soreness. A good pair of cycling shorts gives you just the right amount of padding without unnecessary bulk.

Cycling shorts should fit tightly. They are designed to be form fitting in order to prevent wrinkling, which can cause severe chafing. The body of the shorts must be long enough to reach slightly past your waist since bending over will tend to pull them down. Like jerseys, shorts stretch in primar-

Photo 10–3: If you choose to ride in long pants, but you don't want to use a pants clip, roll up your pants high enough to clear the chain, chainwheel, and front derailleur.

Photo 10–4: Always wrap your trousers toward the outside of your leg when using pants clips. This will reduce the possibility of catching a loose fold of cloth in the chain.

ily one direction—horizontally. This feature allows the expansion and contraction of the powerful thigh muscles to go unhindered. (This is the prime reason why form-fitting denims are not recommended for cycling.)

Regular cycling shorts are made with double-knit fabrics. Most are made from wool, although some manufacturers use various wool blends, acrylics, nylons, or polyesters. The synthetic fabrics are somewhat stronger than wool, but their ability to absorb perspiration and to "breathe" is less than wool.

Like jerseys, the best-quality shorts are made from wool. Although we have heard a number of people complain that they are allergic to wool, few riders experience problems with the treated wool in shorts and jerseys. More riders experience chafing problems from coarse materials than from actual allergic reactions.

When choosing bicycle clothing, make sure that they are soft and feel good against your skin. If you are allergic to all animal hair, you may not be able to wear wool. In that case, stick to cotton blends and acrylics. Nylon shorts will retain their shape better than acrylic shorts, yet they are uncomfortable when wet.

There is some variation in the design of cycling shorts. For instance, special shorts are designed for six-day or Madison races. They have a special inside pocket designed for a "jamming tool" or wadding. The jamming tool is inserted into this pocket to create a bulge on the rider's left rear. This "lump" is used as a "handle" to provide a means to push the rider into the race. Since the backs of the shorts are constantly being stretched, they have an additional layer of material that is quilted for extra strength.

The waistbands on shorts use either an elastic band or a drawstring. Many riders remove the drawstring or elastic waistband because it can cause chafing. Instead, they use suspenders to hold the shorts in position. Many manufacturers include buttons on the front and rear of the shorts for this purpose.

The most important feature of cycling shorts is the chamois lining. These shorts are meant to be worn without undergarments so that the rider's crotch is in direct contact with the chamois. The purpose of the chamois is to act as a cushion, reduce friction, and help absorb perspiration. A good-quality chamois will prevent abrasion far better than any fabric. Some manufacturers use high-quality wool for their shorts, but skimp on the chamois. Inspect shorts carefully before you buy. Turn the shorts inside out. Feel the chamois. Rub it against your face for comparison purposes since the tender skin on your face is a better judge of softness. Choose the pair of shorts that combines good quality with a soft chamois.

Now is the time to inspect the construction of the chamois lining, which should be equally soft throughout. It should be the same color and thickness all over. Make sure that there are as few seams as possible. The less the better to reduce the possibility of chafing. Seams are essential, however, since they keep the chamois from wrinkling. The seams must be flattened. Rub your hand along the seams. Do they feel bulky or rough? Holding the chamois taut, rub your face back and forth along the seams. A good chamois will pass visual inspection as well as the facial test.

Turn the shorts right side out and inspect the outside. Cycling shorts should have side seams or seams on the inside through the crotch area. They should not be in both places. Again, fewer seams are better. As in all cycling clothing that is worn directly against the body, all of the seams should be overcast and stitched over. Some

Photo 10–5: It is important to have a good-quality chamois in your bicycle shorts. The chamois reduces saddle friction and helps prevent saddle soreness.

manufacturers reinforce their wool shorts in the crotch area with a synthetic fabric to give this area extra strength.

If you decide to ride without cycling shorts, it is best to wear shorts or pants that are a dark color. This is particularly important if you have a leather saddle. Only plastic saddles will not stain clothing. Some plastic saddles that have been covered with leather also stain. If you're not sure, wear dark shorts or use a plastic saddle cover.

Some manufacturers offer nicely tailored street clothes for bicycle riding: culottes, fleece-lined shorts, and khaki-type pants are now available. Although they are more fashionable, they are not as comfortable as regular cycling clothes. The choice, however, is yours. Wear whatever feels comfortable and works best for you!

TIGHTS

Tights are cycling shorts with long legs. They are available with or without chamois crotches. Tights without chamois crotches are more versatile in colder climates because regular cycling shorts and long underwear can be worn underneath for additional warmth. If you live in an area where the low temperatures average about 40°F., a well-fitting chamois-lined pair of tights is ideal. However, they are usually expensive and hard to find. Obtaining a proper fit can be difficult since the length of the legs must be considered as well as the waist size. Tights that are too short can be a problem since the normal cycling motion tends to pull the tights downward, creating a baggy fit in the important crotch area. If you are unsure of the fit, consider tights without a chamois. Since these are used with cycling shorts underneath, there is a lot more latitude in the fit.

All tights should have ribbed ankle cuffs to prevent riding up on the leg. In addition to the ribbing, there should be small zippers on the bottom of each leg to insure a close fit for the life of the tights. Without zippers you are destroying the staying power of the ribbing every time you put on the tights.

Frequently, manufacturers use a coarser, bulkier wool for their tights than for their shorts. This is usually for warmth. Bulky wool ski sweaters are good examples of this. The bulk of the sweater keeps the athlete warmer since it provides a thicker layer of "dead air space." The additional bulk should not restrict movement nor create saddle soreness.

LEG WARMERS AND ARM WARMERS

Both leg and arm warmers come in 100 percent wool or in wool blends. They are worn when the temperature drops and you need something to keep the bare flesh on your legs and arms from cooling down. Leg warmers are held in place by an elastic band placed over the bottoms of cycling shorts. Arm warmers, also held in place by an elastic band, slightly overlap the ribbed sleeves of a regular jersey. Some people buy warmers in lieu of a pair of tights or a long-sleeved jersey. We feel that this is a mistake since they are not designed for long-distance, casual riding. Warmers can be very bothersome as they tend to slip while riding and require constant adjustment. Arm and leg warmers are used primarily by racers who need some extra warmth at the start of a race

that is held in cold conditions. As the race progresses and their body temperatures rise, they can easily shed the unnecessary insulation. Obviously, it is easier to remove arm and leg warmers while riding than it is to remove long tights and a long-sleeved jersey.

As with tights, leg warmers should have ankle zippers for ease in dressing and long life. The bottoms and tops of both arm and leg warmers should have elasticized ribbing. Be careful to avoid leg warmers that are too tight since the elastic will work against the contraction and expansion of your thigh muscles.

CYCLING HATS

Cycling hats look a little like small-brimmed painter's hats. They are made of 100 percent cotton. Elastic is inserted along the back to hold them securely on your head. The visors are small, about two inches in depth, but large enough to properly shade your eyes from the sun without interfering with your vision. Cycling hats keep your head cool as the perspiration absorbed by the hat evaporates. They also keep hair and perspiration out of your eyes.

Cycling hats do not come "sized"; they are advertised as "one size fits all." Yet, a cycling hat must fit properly. A hat that is too loose can be forced off your head by the wind. One that is too tight can stop circulation and give you a headache. There are size differences among manufacturers. The only way to tell how a cycling hat will fit is to try it on.

Some manufacturers make hats that are designed to be worn over a leather "hairnet" helmet, but most are designed to be worn directly on the head. There is no valid reason to wear a cycling hat over a helmet. Some

A

B

C

Photos 10–6A, 10–6B, and 10–6C: **Use of Cycling Hat.** Most cyclists ride with the brim of the cycling hat in its "up" position (A). When riding into the sun, the brim can be lowered to shade your eyes (B). On hot, sunny days, the hat can be reversed (C) and the brim will protect the back of the neck from sunburn.

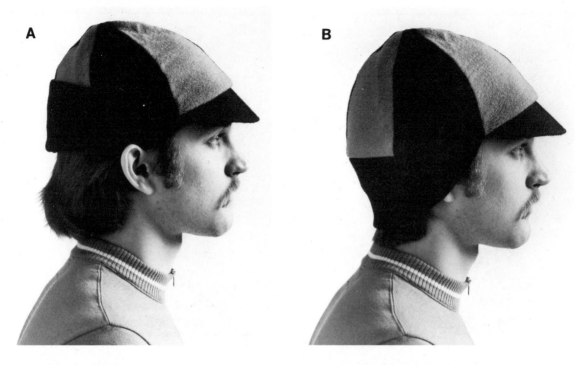

Photos 10–7A and 10–7B: Cold-weather wool cycling hats can be used with the rider's ears exposed (A) or with the earflaps folded down to give more protection (B).

racers do; probably because they feel that they can disguise the fact that they are wearing a helmet. Wearing a cycling hat over a helmet reduces many of its advantages. First, the hat cannot absorb your sweat when it is sitting on a helmet. Second, the cooling effect of the hat is reduced because of the large air pocket between head and hat.

The best cycling hats for summer use are white. They absorb the least amount of heat from the sun. Dark hats, on the other hand, absorb heat. As a rule, wear a light-colored hat (preferably white) on a really hot summer day. This helps your body's efforts to maintain normal temperature. Probably the most bizarre, though sensible reason for wearing a

cycling hat in the heat is stated in *Cycling* (Rome: F.I.A.C., 1972), a book published by the Italian Cycling Federation:

> Above all in the summer season, the head should be protected . . . in days of blazing sun, the head should be further protected either with a cabbage leaf placed under the cap or by moving back the visor of the latter to create a large area of shadow on the most exposed and delicate part of the head, namely the cerebellum.

Bicycling hats for winter use are made with double-thickness wool knits. The wool-knit cycling hat provides a snug, contoured fit. The snug fit minimizes cold air reaching your head; and furthermore, the thick wool provides adequate insulation for temperatures approaching 0°F. Unlike many winter hats which slide up on the head leaving ears exposed, a well-designed winter cycling hat stays in place without restricting movement or constricting circulation.

GLOVES

Gloves cushion the hands against road shock and protect them in the event of a fall. Many riders have learned (the hard way) that road burns on the palms of the hands are very painful and, unlike road burns on elbows, knees, and hips, severely restrict cycling activity.

While gloves are strongly recommended for the road rider, they are a must for the track racer. There are two basic methods of stopping a track bicycle (which operates on a direct-drive system)—apply pedal pressure counterclockwise or "grab" the front wheel. In emergency stopping situations, the "hand" brake may be the only way to stop.

Steve Savageau, one of our good (and fearless) friends, learned this lesson the hard way. Although he normally used gloves whenever riding his track bike, he was in a hurry one day and forgot. Everything went fine until riding at top speed downhill, he approached a traffic light which quickly changed from amber to red. "Backpedaling" furiously, Steve knew he would be able to stop within the narrowest of margins. Unfortunately, his chain snapped and he was virtually brakeless. "I knew I had only one choice," Steve said, "and that was to use my hand just as if I were wearing a glove. I knew it would hurt and was I right!" His hand was completely raw before he had the bike

slowed enough to negotiate the corner between the traffic and the curb. We've noticed that Steve now leaves his gloves on the handlebars when he stops riding.

Gloves are a real advantage in touring or long-distance riding. They provide a cushion between the hands and the handlebars. Many riders who develop numb hands during long rides may find that gloves help alleviate the problem. Don't forget, however, that gloves cannot compensate for too much of the rider's weight on the handlebars as a result of improper bicycle setup.

Only leather is used in the manufacture of cycling gloves. The palms are reinforced with extra leather for strength and additional cushioning. Some gloves actually have small foam cushions sewn into the palms. These provide the maximum amount of shock absorption and are recommended for riders who suffer from numb fingers.

The backs of cycling gloves are fitted with a fishnet mesh for ventilation. The fingers of the glove cover only one-half of the rider's fingers, which permits better ventilation and finger mobility. Velcro fasteners or snap closures are used at the wrist. To insure a tight fit, we prefer gloves with Velcro fasteners because they provide optimum fit for any size wrist.

Leather tends to stretch with wear; therefore, it is necessary to buy gloves that are a little tight. It is not advisable to buy gloves that must be stretched a lot to be comfortable since the seams and the stitching are the weakest parts in a pair of gloves. Too much stretching causes ripped seams. Most often this split occurs in the glove between the area joining the thumb to the palm. When selecting gloves, look for a pair that fits snugly without constricting. This is especially true of the glove fingers. Many times a glove fits nicely across the palm but feels as if five separate rubber bands are attached to the fingers and thumb. Don't buy a pair of gloves on the premise that the fingers will stretch. Usually you will end up with poor circulation in your fingers.

SHOES, CLEATS, AND SOCKS

Shoes come in many varieties and styles and are made by some of the world's most famous manufacturers of quality athletic shoes—Puma and Adidas. Incidentally, Puma and Adidas shoes are independently manufactured by two brothers. Their careful attention to the demands of the world's top athletes have resulted in virtual dominance of the enormous sports shoe industry. The previous standard of the industry, Detto Pietro, has been hard pressed to meet the successful promotion efforts of the two brothers.

All cycling shoes made by Puma, Adidas, and Detto Pietro are designed to be used with special cleats which firmly secure the rider's foot to the pedal, increasing pedaling efficiency. Unfortunately for the everyday rider, all these shoes have been designed with the racer and long-distance rider in mind. (Any kind of shoe designed for cycling presumes the use of toe clips and straps.)

Shoes

The popular bicycle shoes share several common features: a soft, supple leather top with dozens of perforations to aid in ventilation, a rigid sole (Detto Pietro uses a steel insert, Adidas uses a rigid plastic in-

sert, and Puma uses a thick plastic sole), and light weight. (They are *not* designed for walking.) The soles are curved to a shape similar to track (running) shoes which keeps the heel above the toe. These shoes are very impractical for the casual rider because the stiff sole doesn't allow the amount of flex required in a normal walking step and the shoe wears out very quickly if it is used for anything else other than cycling.

Consequently, a number of manufacturers, notably the Bata Shoe Company in Mary-

Photo 10–8: Bicycle shoes are shaped somewhat like running shoes. Their supple leather tops are perforated for coolness. The soles usually include a stiff liner to support the foot while pedaling and they also have holes for ventilation. Shoe cleats are mounted on the shoes to maintain the proper position on the pedals. The cleats, in conjunction with the toe straps, hold the feet on the pedals enabling the cyclist to pull *up* on the pedals as well as pushing down.

land and Avocet, Inc., in California, have offered riders an alternative bicycle shoe. These have been designed along the lines of a regular "tennis" or athletic shoe using canvas, suede, or leather uppers (for breathability and coolness) with rubber soles for walking. Steel shanks have been inserted in the soles to help distribute pedaling force and support the rider's arch. Although these shoes are designed with both cycling and walking in mind, the outcome is somewhat of a compromise. When used for cycling, some slippage on the pedal results even though nonslip soles have been used. It's just not the same as "locking" the foot into position with a shoe cleat. You *are* able to walk in these shoes, but generally not for great distances. Still this shoe is ideal for the casual rider or the tourist who places comfort and adaptability above speed and efficiency.

Most casual riders make the same mistake when selecting noncycling shoes for bicycle use. They presume that the soft, rubber-soled casual or jogging shoes are best. Unfortunately, the soft sole permits the heel to sag below the toe when pedaling and the sharp edges of the rattrap pedals dig painfully into the rider's feet on long rides.

The traditional black cycling shoe* has been designed with an eye to pedaling efficiency. Proper selection is somewhat of an art since the shoe should fit like a glove. There should be no room for movement, yet your toes should not be cramped or doubled over. There's an old bicycle racing adage that says, "if you can get the shoe on, it fits." You

*These shoes are available only in men's sizes. Women must adapt. However, the smallest size available is generally about 36 which is a men's size 4–4½ (women's size 6–6½).

should seek a shoe that restricts movement of the foot but allows movement of the toes (like a good downhill ski boot).

There are many different types of cycling shoes made in many different countries. Ironically, cycling shoes only come in only one width and that width depends primarily on the country of manufacture. For instance, Belgian shoes are very wide and Italian shoes are very narrow. For this reason alone, we do not recommend buying shoes through mail-order houses. It's impossible to know which size is best for you unless you try on different sizes and models by different manufacturers.

A cycling shoe should feel like part of your foot. There should be no forward or backward movement. The back of the shoe should be shaped to mold to the back of your foot. Proper fit at the heels reduces the tendency to pull your feet out of the shoes when sprinting or hill climbing.

Before trying on cycling shoes, you should decide whether you intend to ride with, or without, socks. If you decide to ride without socks, try the shoes with a pair of very thin socks. If the shoe feels slightly too narrow, then it's probably the right size. If your toes feel cramped, it's too small. If the shoe feels comfortable, like a walking shoe, it's definitely too big. Since the shoes will stretch a lot (especially if they get wet), you are advised to start out with a tight fit. A well-fitting shoe will be hard to remove even with the laces loose because of the curve on the back of the shoe. As the shoes stretch you can continually change the thickness of your socks.

Years ago, the best cycling shoes were made of kangaroo hide because it was lighter and more flexible than cowhide. With the depletion of the kangaroos came a sharp reduction of the availability of kangaroo leather and, as a result, cycling shoe manufacturers switched to cowhide. Good cycling shoes are made of leather and like other leather products, the grades of leather will vary.

Leather is used for several reasons: breathability, suppleness, strength, long wear, and lightness. Breathability is important to the cyclist whose feet perspire, especially on a very hot day. To insure comfort, cycling shoes have holes in the leather tops and in the soles. This helps circulate air, cooling the rider's feet.

The holes that are drilled in the sole allow the passage of water during wet-weather cycling. Cycling shoes that do not have perforations are designed for cold-weather riding. Frequently, these shoes come with a wool-fleece lining for extra warmth. Unlike summer cycling shoes, winter shoes should be fitted to the heaviest sock you plan to wear. The shoes should feel comfortable; they should not constrict as this will reduce circulation and make your feet more susceptible to frostbite.

Cycling shoes come in a large array of sole variations. There are single-soled, double-, and triple-soled leather varieties. Recently, manufacturers have tried various plastics either as an alternative to, or in combination with, leather for the soles. The disadvantage with synthetics, of course, is breathability. Their advantage is less weight with a small penalty in flexibility.

Spring steel plates are inserted in most leather-soled shoes to keep the arch from "wrapping around the pedal." Steel plates help concentrate the rider's energy on the ball of the foot instead of losing it in the motion of a flexing arch. Single-soled shoes have the thinnest steel plates because manufacturers try to design these shoes for walking as well as riding. These single-soled

shoes may also have small heels which simulate the feel of a walking shoe.

You shouldn't purchase racing-type cycling shoes with heels in the belief that you will be able to walk in them for the following reasons:

- The heels are soft leather and will wear out quickly.
- Without cleats, the shoe is slippery and will slide back and forth on the pedal—it's better to use the rubber-soled shoes we covered in the beginning of this section. With cleats it is very difficult to walk.
- The soles and heels are too thin and stiff to walk comfortably.
- Walking will cause pressure on the leather tops of the shoes which results in stretching the shoes in all the wrong places.

Double-soled shoes are stiff and can be used for racing or touring. Triple-soled shoes are strictly for sprint racing: they are so stiff that walking is virtually impossible.

Cleats

The shoe cleats help to position the shoe on the pedal yet they allow the rider to disengage quickly, if necessary. Except for a leather cleat produced by the French company, TA, all cleats are made out of either alloy, steel, or plastic. The leather TA cleat is designed for touring. It is flexible enough to permit walking for short distances. Most cleats have grooves which fit over the rear section of the pedal cage. The groove is narrow enough to permit very little side-to-side wiggling of the foot while pedaling.

Well-designed cleats serve two primary functions. First, they keep the foot properly positioned on the pedal (the ball of the foot over the pedal axle). Second, the cleats keep

Photo 10–9: **Shoe Cleats.** Shoe cleats help the rider keep his or her feet in a fixed position on the pedals. Shoe cleat A is designed for the recreational rider. It has a fairly shallow slot for the pedal, which enables the rider to remove his or her feet easily. Riders interested in performance generally prefer a cleat with a deep slot (B or C) to reduce the chances of the foot sliding off the pedal when pulling up with the leg. The long shoe cleat (C) is designed to provide additional stiffness to the sole of the shoe.

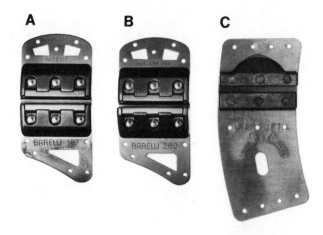

the foot in its proper position as the leg is pulled on the upstroke of the crank arc, when you use the toe straps and clips. Without cleats, powerful riders would tend to pull their foot out of the toe strap.

Most shoe cleats look the same and all perform the same function. The only real exception is the Cinelli Uni-bloc cleat. It fits over the pedal-axle housing instead of the pedal cage like most cleats. This design fits only Campagnolo or Campagnolo-copy pedals.

There are no real advantages or disadvantages between alloy or plastic shoe cleats. The plastic cleats may be somewhat lighter but they usually wear a little faster. You should use only plastic cleats with the super-lightweight, black alloy pedals. Alloy cleats cause premature wear or damage to the lightweight alloy pedal cages.

MOUNTING SHOE CLEATS – Some shoes, like Puma, come with premounted cleats. These shoes only need to be adjusted to your pedal and toe-clip size. When mount-

ing cleats on other shoes, great care has to be taken to get the correct placement. Incorrect cleat placement hinders pedaling style and can cause knee problems.

Before you attempt to mount the cleats, you must fit the proper size toe clip (see chapter six). Riding without toe clips and straps is not recommended with bike shoes since the slippery sole does not maintain proper position on the pedal unless it has a toe clip and strap to hold it. If you do not want to use toe clips and straps you should use regular sports shoes.

Some experts advise using the shoes for 50 to 100 miles to create indentations on the sole to help act as a positioning guide. If you choose this method, remember that you must position the cleat so the slot in the cleat is slightly ahead of the rear line on the sole. This will ensure that the toe of the shoe does not touch the front of the toe clip. Ideally, it should be $1/16$ to $1/8$ inch from the toe clip.

When the toe clip and shoe cleat are properly attached, the rider's feet will be slightly "pigeon-toed." This results in a nat-

Photos 10–10 to 10–12: **Positioning Shoe Cleats and Toe Clips.** The proper position for shoe cleat placement is best illustrated away from the bicycle. The cleats and toe clips should be mounted in such a way that the rider's knees remain close to the top tube when pedaling.

Photo 10–10: If the feet of a rider are pointed straight ahead, the knees will also point straight ahead. This position, however, does not encourage the "knees to the bar" aerodynamic position.

Photo 10–11: If the feet of a rider are pointed out, the knees will also point out. Obviously incorrect.

ural tendency to keep the knees close to the top tube which assures an efficient pedaling motion and the least wind resistance. Moreover, this foot position will reduce the tendency for the rider's ankles to strike the crankarms with each pedal revolution.

Socks

Cycling socks should be thin, breathable, and low cut. Although many bike riders do not wear socks in the summertime, it is healthier for your feet to do so. The dye that the shoes release when your foot perspires, or when it rains, can cause skin problems. The socks also reduce the effects of any abrasion that occurs as the feet move inside the shoes or in the unconscious flexing and relaxation of the toes.

Although most bicycle stores do not carry cycling socks, thin wool, cotton, or even silk socks can be purchased from backpacking stores. Usually these socks are meant to be used as liners, worn under thick socks in hiking boots, but they can be used for cycling.

The traditional sports sock (or sweat sock) can be used but is not very popular with serious cyclists because cycling does not require a heavy wool sock. The heavy sock is necessary for a leather or canvas sports shoe because the shoe does not breathe very well and the mass of the sock will absorb a great deal of perspiration. The holes in the cycling shoe provide efficient ventilation and with thin socks the shoes are both adequate and comfortable.

Most women cyclists tend to use the tennis "footlets," and find them to be acceptable. Racers should be reminded that socks are required for all road-racing events. The United States Cycling Federation (the governing body of bicycle racing in the

Photo 10–12:   If the feet are pointed in, the knees will point in. Although this is an exaggeration of the correct position, the cleats should be mounted to position the foot with the toes pointed *slightly* inward. The cycling shoe should *not* make actual contact with the front of the toe clip. It should be positioned ¼ inch behind the clip.

Clothing Characteristics

	Composition	Advantages	Disadvantages	Recommended Use
Road Jersey (with pockets)	At least 70 percent wool	Absorbs perspiration Warm in cool weather Cool in hot weather	Very expensive Easily damaged in spills Must be carefully laundered	All road riding, racing, or touring
Road Jersey (with pockets)	Synthetics (acrylic, polyester, nylon, rayon)	Tough (durable) Resistant to crashes Easily laundered Fairly inexpensive	Cold in cool weather Hot in hot weather Poor moisture absorption	Road riding when cost is a consideration
Track Jersey (without pockets)	Synthetics (acetate, rayon)	Aerodynamic Attractive Fairly inexpensive	Cold in cool weather Hot in hot weather Poor moisture absorption	Track racing
Shorts (with chamois crotch)	Wool or wool blends	Freedom of movement (legs are long enough to reach past edge of saddle) Best protection against saddle sores	Very expensive Must be carefully laundered	All road riding, racing, or touring
Tights (with chamois crotch)	Wool or wool blends	Freedom of movement Tight fit reduces flapping and chance of catching material on chain Good protection against saddle sores	Very expensive Must be carefully laundered	Cold-weather riding for the serious cyclist
Warm-up Suit	Wool, wool blends, cotton, synthetics	Freedom of movement Tight fit Can be used for cycling, jogging, and tennis	Moderate to expensive depending on material Will wear quickly in the seat area unless reinforced for cycling	Casual or recreational riding

United States) does not accept the tennis "footlets." Although this rule is not widely enforced, racers should always bring a pair of white socks to any road event. Track racing, on the other hand, does not require the use of socks. Interestingly, very few track riders choose to wear socks whether racing on the track or training on the road. For nonracers, the use of socks is simply a matter of personal preference.

HELMETS

Most cyclists are oblivious to the need for head protection. They cycle miles upon miles thinking that they are immune to head injuries. The statistics prove otherwise. In 1974, there were 989 cyclists killed while riding. Of that number, 90 percent were involved in collisions with motor vehicles. In 75 percent of the crashes, death was attributed to head injuries.

Although everyone agrees that the head should be protected from injury, few manufacturers have stepped up to the problem. Most cycling helmets provide limited protection at best. The British Standards Institution's publication *Specification of Protective Helmets for Pedal Cyclists* (London: BS 4544, 1970) suggests:

> The protection given by any helmet cannot ensure full immunity in severe accidents, but can go far towards mitigating the effects of a blow which could otherwise cause severe injury.

Adequate head protection for cyclists can only be presumed since most helmet manufacturers are unwilling to divulge the capabilities of their helmets. We are only aware of two countries, England and Australia, that have adopted standards for bicycle

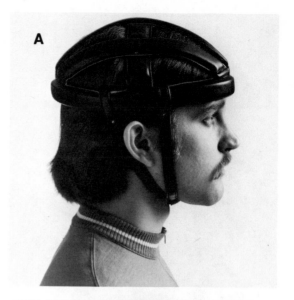

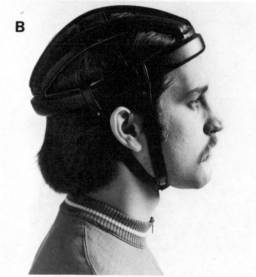

Photos 10–13A and 10–13B: Even the best cycling helmet can be poor protection if you don't wear it properly. Always fasten the chin strap tight enough to assist in holding the helmet in its proper position (A). *Do not* wear the helmet on the back of your head (B). It does not provide adequate protection and probably will fall off your head in an accident.

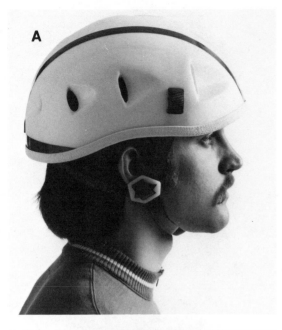

Photos 10–14A and 10–14B: The hard-shell helmet (A) offers superior protection but it is heavier, hotter, and more expensive than the leather hair-net type (B).

helmets. All helmets sold in these countries are certified accordingly.

In the United States, a number of organizations have set uniform standards of performance for helmets. The Snell Memorial Foundation, the American National Standards Institute, and the United States Government Department of Transportation have all developed their own helmet standards, yet no manufacturer is required to adhere to any standard nor will the manufacturer indicate what standards the helmet actually meets. Consequently, when purchasing a helmet the consumer is left to his or her own discretion and can only hope that he or she is making the right choice.

When selecting a helmet, you should consider some of the prerequisites of a good helmet:

- Protection from impact, penetration, and abrasion;
- Adequate ventilation;
- Uninterrupted peripheral vision;
- Good, solid retention system;
- Light weight.

All helmets protect against penetration, abrasion, and impact to some degree. The leather racing helmet (sometimes referred to as a hairnet), offers very little protection from direct blows. At best, leather helmets offer some protection from abrasion and limited shock absorption. Hard-shell helmets with foam liners are a better choice for most people since they provide both penetration protection and good shock absorption.

The hard-shell helmets are constructed on the premise that the force of a severe blow is absorbed by a large section of the helmet rather than just the area receiving the blow. The ability of the helmet to absorb impact is paramount in head protection. Top-quality motorcycle and car-racing helmets have a hard exterior shell and a foam lining. This liner crumbles upon sharp impact; therefore, most manufacturers recommend that the helmet be returned to them for inspection after hard crashes. Other hard-shell helmets have soft foam liners which do not destruct under impact, but do not provide quite the level of protection.

A fully covered helmet initially provides maximum protection from penetration and abrasion. We stress initially, since the less rigid the outer shell the more penetrable it becomes. In addition, as the number and the size of the ventilating holes in a helmet increase, the less protection it affords.

Ventilation is very important in cycling helmets since cycling is a high-intensity activity which generates a lot of body heat. Much of this heat escapes through the top of your head (see Cold-Weather Riding section). If your head is "plugged" with a poorly ventilated helmet, body temperatures can approach heat stroke levels. At the same time, too many ventilation holes can markedly decrease the helmet's ability to effectively distribute force and increase the possibility of injury by penetration.

A good solid retention system is mandatory for any helmet. What's the point of having the "best" helmet if it slides off your head when you crash? The retention system of any helmet must securely keep the helmet on your head in a relatively fixed position. It must allow free head movement without restricting your vision.

Because most riders value safety as secondary to comfort, the weight of the helmet is important. Increased weight on the head increases the load on the neck. Unfortunately, there is not adequate head protection with helmets weighing less than 16 ounces. Before buying a helmet decide on *how much* head protection you desire, then try on the types that offer the desired level of safety. The best method is to try it on and spend 15 to 30 minutes walking around in the store, moving your head around in different positions. Try out the helmet while sitting on your bike. Vary handlebar positions to ensure that the helmet is not uncomfortable and that it does not limit visibility. If it feels too heavy, try on a lighter helmet. If you find that your neck hurts even with the lighter helmets, it's time to perform some exercises designed to strengthen your neck muscles.

In our opinion, only two cycling helmets, the Bell and the Pro-tec, provide really adequate protection. Most other helmets offer approximately the same level of protection as the widely accepted leather "hairnet" style.

COLD-WEATHER RIDING

Properly dressed for the cold weather, you can enjoy bicycle riding all year around. We do not recommend riding your bicycle in ice or snow, unless you are a superb bicycle handler. One moment of indecision on a small patch of ice could send you careening into traffic. Be careful when riding in the winter because to motorists you are less visible in rain and snow.

When preparing for cold-weather riding, the best place to start is at your local skiing or backpacking stores. The cotton turtlenecks that skiers use under their sweaters are ideal for cold-weather cycling. The turtleneck traps body heat and keeps it from escaping through the neckline.

Skiers also use long underwear both on top and on the bottom. Long underwear is generally made of wool, wool blends, or cotton blends. The underwear is soft, form fitting, and suited to sports where unrestricted movement is important. It gives you warmth without a lot of bulk to hinder movement. For the upper body the underwear should be worn next to the skin, forming a thermal layer between body and turtleneck. Although turtlenecks are generally made from cotton, there are some that are thin, light weight, and made from wool. If you need the additional insulation, wool turtlenecks provide more warmth than cotton.

Turtlenecks should be worn underneath the wool cycling jersey. Depending on the outside temperature and the number of layers of clothing you plan on wearing, you may be able to use a short-sleeved jersey. In colder temperatures, a wool sweater can be substituted for the cycling jersey. However, you should not wear one that is overly bulky as this will have a tendency to interfere with your movements on the bicycle and it will tend to "bunch up" when riding. Wear two thin sweaters, rather than one heavy sweater, as this gives you the option of removing one if you become too hot. Remember you're always going to be coldest at the beginning of the ride.

The outside garment on your torso should be some type of wind-resistant jacket. Although a Windbreaker is not fully suited for cycling, it does provide the important function of "stopping" the wind from lowering your body temperature. Windbreakers are great on days when large temperature changes occur since they can be easily stored in either a front handlebar pack or a small seat pack until they are needed.

As an emergency aid to keep warm, use a trick of the famous Tour de France riders: stuff some newspaper under the front of your jersey. This technique is almost standard practice for mountain racers since the temperature changes between the top of the mountain and the bottom of the mountain are so great. At the bottom, the temperatures may be 100°F. and the rider is perspiring freely. As they reach the top of the climb, the temperatures may have fallen to the freezing mark. The descent to the bottom would be absolutely bone-chilling with the combination of the cold temperature and large windchill factor caused by a high-speed descent. The riders solve the problem by accepting newspapers from the spectators. They stuff the newspapers under their jerseys to shield the flow of cold air from their chests. The paper is discarded when the bottom of the mountain is reached.

You should use cycling shorts under whatever insulation you have chosen for your lower body. This is especially important for winter riding since additional layers of clothing will increase the tendency for chafing in the saddle area. If you plan to use long underwear, be sure to get them large enough to fit over your shorts. A good pair of cycling tights over shorts and long underwear will usually keep you warm enough in all but the coldest areas of the United States.

Warm-up pants can be substituted for tights and warm-up tops for Windbreakers. Generally, warm-up pants are not reinforced in the seat area which causes premature wear on the pants. Smart riders eliminate this problem by reinforcing the seat of the warm-up pants with a sewn-in piece of strong material such as nylon. The best warm-ups for cycling are wool. The pants should be form fitting around the ankles with zippers on each leg to ensure a snug fit.

Another alternative is cross-country ski outfits, especially those that utilize knickers. Combined with a pair of knicker socks, a cyclist should be warm enough to ride in very cold temperatures with no restriction in pedal action.

It is difficult to predict what is going to be comfortable for all riders. Common sense must be used. The rider must recognize the effects of a strong wind. Clothing that seems comfortable at 20°F. one day, may be too light the next day because of a strong wind.

When it is cold outside, wear a hat. The top of your head acts as a chimney and severe loss of body temperature cannot be controlled without a hat. By keeping your head and torso warm, you improve circulation to your feet and hands and they will be able to withstand cold temperatures longer.

A thin wool hat will satisfactorily retain body heat. If you use the hat in combination with a hard-shell helmet, the helmet probably will have to be readjusted to accommodate the hat. The winter cycling hat is ideal for cold-weather riding. Unlike regular wool caps, it does not have the tendency to move upon your head, exposing your ears to the cold.

The rider's feet and hands are most vulnerable in cold weather. If your head and torso are even slightly cold, your body shuts off the blood supply to the outer extremities.

Keeping your hands warm is far easier than keeping your feet warm. Ski gloves generally provide sufficient warmth for most riders. In extremely cold weather, down-filled mittens provide unparalleled insulation. Whether you use mittens or gloves, be sure that the palms are leather lined; leather gives you a good grip on the handlebars.

The cyclist's feet are the most difficult part of the body to keep warm in the winter. Even the slightest tightening of the toe straps can create enough pressure to reduce proper blood circulation in the foot. Ideally, thick Arctic boots would keep the feet warm; however, the large boots simply will not fit in the toe clip and strap and they interfere with the cycling motion.

Some riders use hiking boots for cold-weather riding, but even the hiking boot is usually too bulky. Some insulated après-ski boots provide enough insulation without too much bulk. The best alternative is to have a pair of wool-lined cycling shoes.

Proper choice of socks helps solve many cold feet problems. Again multilayers are helpful. A thin liner of 100 percent silk or wool under a thick heavy wool sock works well. The silk sock is worn directly next to the foot to reduce friction. We have heard of cyclists using electric socks, but don't recommend anything that relies on batteries for its source of heat.

If cold feet persist, there are two other solutions. First, an external shoe covering will help keep cold air from reaching the foot. Some riders use a heavy wool sock over the entire shoe. It should be cut out on the bottom, however, to allow for the proper seating of shoe cleats on the pedal. In addition, regular shoe covers are commercially available from bicycle clothing manufacturers. These are usually made from waterproof stretch material and are available in different sizes.

The second solution is to increase the wind-stopping ability of the toe clips. Toe clip covers are difficult to find in the United States, but they are easily constructed out of canvas. Canvas covers should fit around the toe clip itself to eliminate looseness.

RIDING IN THE RAIN

Riding in the rain on a hot summer day can be refreshing but can be chilling, uncomfortable, and dangerous when temperatures drop below the comfort range. There are two basic types of cycling rain gear: the rain jacket and trousers, and the rain cape.

The rain jacket and trouser combination

provides excellent protection from the rain at a reasonable cost. Unfortunately, they are made of a nonbreathing waterproof plastic which does not vent perspiration. This lack of breathability creates a virtual sauna for the hard-working cyclist which results in the rider getting just as wet from perspiration as from the rain.

A better alternative is the rain cape. Some manufacturers have done a good job in designing a cape that matches the shape of the cyclist when riding the bicycle. The cape covers the rider's arms and hands, upper legs, and body. Although there is some problem with loose material flapping in the wind, the large opening of the cape permits enough air flow to counteract the effects of the nonbreathing material.

Recently, a new breakthrough in rainwear has changed the entire situation. This product is called Gore-Tex, named after its inventor, W. L. Gore. It is a textile which allows gaseous water molecules to pass through it while shedding liquid water (rain) molecules. Unfortunately, at this time, cost is prohibitive. Jacket and pants will cost more than $100.

If you can afford it, a Gore-Tex outfit makes riding in the rain tolerable in most temperatures. Gore-Tex jackets and pants can be used in any kind of rainy outdoor activity; their use is not limited to just cycling.

When choosing rainwear, be sure to decide what type of clothing you'll be wearing underneath. Rainwear should fit without constriction over the heaviest and bulkiest garments. Be sure that there are no gaping separations between pants and jacket or jacket and neckline. Rainwear, like all clothing worn for cycling should not impair vision, restrict movement, nor interfere with the safe operation of the bicycle.

CARE OF BICYCLE CLOTHING

Most wool cycling clothing must be hand washed in cool water with a mild detergent. Because of wool's naturally built-in soil-releasing properties, it is not necessary to scrub garments clean. When washing or rinsing wool garments, it is best to turn them inside out, and not to wring them out. Allowing a wool garment to dry by "blocking" it on a towel prolongs its life. It is ill-advised to hang up a wool garment when it is soaking wet. Since wool has such great water-absorbing properties, the retained water acts as a weight, stretching and distorting the garment. Drying wool garments is accomplished by laying them flat between towels on a rack where air is able to circulate around them, speeding up the drying process.

It is important to keep shorts clean for proper hygiene and the prevention of saddle sores. After many washings the chamois "hardens." To soften the texture, rub a small quantity of oil into the chamois. Any kind of natural oil works. We have heard of riders using Crisco vegetable oil, but if you don't feel right about using a salad oil on your shorts, Johnson's baby oil works well. Before using the shorts again, spread a small amount of baby powder or antiseptic powder (such as Caldesene) on the chamois to absorb the remaining oil. Depending on how much you perspire, it may be a good idea to "disinfect" the chamois after each ride. To do this, use a cotton ball dabbed in some rubbing alcohol. This removes the salt that accumulates from your body perspiration and it will reduce the threat of saddle sores.

Many wool garments need not be washed by hand. Such garments will always say "machine-washable wools." These fabrics have been specially treated to permit the longer immersion times required in a washing-machine cycle as opposed to hand washing. Although machine washing is more convenient, wool garments will last longer and look better when washed by hand. Machine-washable wools can also be tumbled dry, but make sure to read the specific instructions for each machine-washable garment.

Nonwool jerseys, warm-ups, and tights are usually machine washable. It's best to wash cycling clothes in short washing cycles and dry them in warm or cool drying cycles.

Regular bicycling shoes should be polished regularly. Polishing protects and strengthens the staying power of the leather. If shoes become soaked, stuff them with newspapers to help retain their shape as they dry. Do not place them near any heat sources as this will cause them to distort. Dried out, distorted shoes cause blisters and foot fungi.

Rules of Thumb

- When mounting shoe cleats yourself, do not use the nails supplied with the cleats. They are generally too small to hold the cleat on the shoe. Replace the nails with sturdy tacks or have a shoe repairman install the cleats.

- Clothing should not be loose and allowed to blow around. This includes scarves, coats, skirts, pants, and dresses. A loose garment can easily find its way into the spokes and cause an accident.

- If long pants are worn, be sure that the right pant leg is either partially rolled up, or securely fastened so that it cannot come in contact with the chain and chainwheel. If the pant legs are extremely wide on the bottom, it is a good idea to roll up or fasten both the left and right pant leg.

- The easiest way to remove cycling gloves without damaging or stretching them is to *peel* the glove off your hand.

- Clothing should not encumber you in any way from properly operating the bicycle. For example, if it's cold and you're wearing gloves, be sure your gloves allow you to effectively use your hand brakes.

- If you decide to carry something with you (grocery bag, purse, or tennis racket), *don't* hold it with one hand while steering, shifting, and stopping the bicycle with the other hand. This is very dangerous.

- Always wear a helmet.

- *Do not* wear short shorts when riding since the tender skin on the inside of your legs will chafe against the saddle as you pedal.

- When checking the quality of cycling clothes, stretch the seams in various directions. A properly tensioned seam should stretch the same as the rest of the material. Extreme tautness indicates a likelihood of splitting.

CHAPTER ELEVEN

TOURING EQUIPMENT

Like racing, touring requires thorough preparation in order to achieve satisfaction and enjoyment. For long-distance tourists, choosing the right equipment is as important as choosing the proper bicycle. In many cases, riders spend as much for their add-on touring equipment as they paid for the bicycle!

If you like to ride at a fast pace, your needs are different than someone who rides slowly. The slower cyclist enjoys stopping more often and takes great pleasure taking pictures, hiking, and exploring. The "high-speed" cyclist thinks in terms of miles and pushes every day to achieve mileage objectives. Obviously, the slower cyclist is going to need different equipment to be able to enjoy the various diversions along the road, while the faster cyclist needs to carry a minimum amount of gear to permit riding 100, 125, or 150 miles a day.

Whichever way you like to travel, one important thing holds true for everyone: travel light. An overloaded or improperly loaded bicycle can be unstable and difficult to handle. Unlike a rider's weight which can be controlled, the attached equipment is deadweight.

Bicycle setup relationships of seat height, handlebar height, and stem length remain basically unchanged when setting up a bicycle for touring. The important difference between the problems encountered by the tourist vs. the racer is the additional equipment that the tourist carries. The handling of the bicycle can be drastically affected by improper mounting of packs.

If a bicycle is designed properly, it will be stable up to very high speeds. The frame design complements the suggested weight distribution of the rider (45 percent of the weight on the front wheel, 55 percent on the rear). In fact, the bicycle rolls easier and handles best when the weight is distributed 45 percent front—55 percent rear. Therefore, any equipment that is added to the bicycle should be distributed in such a way that it complements the design criteria of the bicycle. For that reason, a bicycle will handle considerably better with 18 pounds of equipment over the front wheel and 22 pounds of equipment over the back wheel than it will with the same total weight of 40 pounds over the back wheel alone. In addition to the unbalanced condition, the rear tire, rim, and spokes will take much greater punishment if all of the weight is over the rear wheel of the bicycle.

A bicycle loaded down with 60 pounds of gear will handle differently than it does with 40 pounds. It will also handle differently depending on where the weight is distributed—whether it is high or low, front or rear. Furthermore, how you pack the equipment can mean constantly fighting the handlebars because of bicycle shimmy or the tendency to weave to the right or left because of unbalanced loads.

The problem of stability is not totally solved by the proper distribution of weight. Loosely mounted racks or packs can create unexpected forces on the bicycle that can lead to a serious accident. This is most evident in the situation where a loosely secured handlebar pack contains a heavy object; it is virtually impossible to steer the bicycle without overcorrecting.

Bicycle touring is a unique experience in some ways comparable to backpacking in that everything you will need must be carried. Consequently, backpacking gear and cyclo-touring gear must have the same general inherent qualities: easy to operate, weather resistant, durable, and light weight. While shopping, you must be aware of the features of each product before you make a decision. A good example is the difference between lightweight camp stoves. Some work best at high altitudes but must be primed at lower levels. If a piece of backpacking equipment is not totally suitable to your cycling needs, you must deter-

mine if it can be adapted or an alternative should be explored. Although most camping/backpacking equipment can be used for cyclo-touring, certain items may be more utilitarian and convenient than others.

In our example of proper weight distribution of a 40-pound load, we selected 40 pounds as an arbitrary example. In certain extreme situations, you might decide to carry 60 pounds, while in other situations you might be able to get by with just 20 pounds. There is no set recommendation on the optimum touring load. It's a personal decision. Remember, on your first trip pack as light as possible. Weigh and log everything that you pack including the racks and bags. This exercise helps you to decide what to include or exclude. In addition, this weight-log system makes it easy to include just the "essentials." In touring, experience is the best teacher. After each tour you should take an inventory of the items you didn't use (excluding emergency repair items). This gives you a better idea of what you'll need on subsequent trips.

BICYCLE TOURING BAGS

The world's best bicycle bags are made in the United States. Nowhere else in the world have manufacturers responded so enthusiastically in providing refined touring equipment. In fact, many foreign manufacturers are unable to understand the American cyclist's demand for good-quality touring equipment because, traditionally, cyclo-touring needs have been preempted by the demands of the racer.

Touring bags are made out of nylon or canvas. Nylon is used by the American manufacturers because of its light weight and ease of cleaning. Originally, canvas was the first choice of tourists because it was more water repellent than untreated nylon, since the cotton fibers expand when wet and seal out water. Canvas is heavier than nylon, but less expensive. The modern nylon packs are treated with vinyls, polymers, or polyurethane which creates a virtually waterproof material that is both light weight and durable.

Nylon specifications are described by weight in ounces and the density of the weave. The fabric density is expressed in denier. The lower the denier, the more tightly woven and less permeable the fabric. Since there is very little consistency among manufacturers, it becomes difficult to make comparisons among touring bags based on fabric (type of nylon, denier, and waterproofing used) alone. You can make some choices based on the quality of workmanship.

Seams are a good place to start. The straightness of the stitching is a good indicator of overall workmanship. Thread tension should be consistent. The closer the stitches, the stronger the seam. Seam puckering indicates weakness. Comparisons can be made of the number of rows of stitching among products. The more rows the better. Attention should also be directed to stress areas. They should be reinforced with extra stitching.

Zipper quality is also important. Bags should have zippers that are strong and work with ease. Double zippers in some instances are convenient because they can be opened from either end. Zippers that turn sharp corners might prove inconvenient as they jam and stick when rounding the corners. Provided there is a small protective flap over the zipper, zippers are better at keeping out water than most other closures including Velcro fasteners. Check for ease of operation, reinforcement of stress points, and quality of stitching before purchasing a bag with zippers. Test the zipper by opening and closing

it with the bag in various positions to make sure the protective flaps don't get caught in the opening and thus jam the zipper.

When using equipment that has been labeled "waterproof," remember that there is no such thing as a 100 percent waterproof stitched product unless the seams have been sealed. Anytime you have a needle piercing a fabric, you have an increased possibility of water seepage. As a pack ages, the seams stretch and eventually become less waterproof. Some pack manufacturers, like Eclipse and Cannondale, use cotton-wrapped polyester threads. The polyester provides strength while the cotton swells when wet and makes the pack more waterproof. Your safest bet is to buy a tube of seam sealer from a backpacking store and seal all the seams. In this way you can be assured that your "waterproof" equipment indeed is 100 percent waterproof.

Panniers

Panniers is a French word for bags and refers to the saddlebags that are mounted on a rack and hang down on both sides of the bicycle wheel. All panniers must be used in pairs. That is, both right and left sides are required. Unless a pair is used, the bicycle will be unbalanced. The panniers should be loaded with the heaviest items at the bottom. You should take the effects of riding into consideration; otherwise, the contents tend to move around inside the pack. One way to protect your equipment is to pack it in individual plastic bags. This accomplishes three goals: it prevents wear and abrasion on the inside of the pack, helps distribute weight, and protects the articles from rain.

Another way to help eliminate movement is to use a pannier that is not cut square on the bottom. A triangular bottom will force

A

B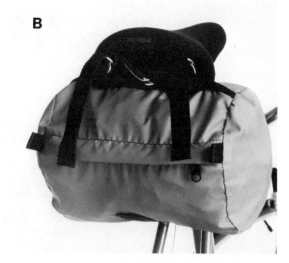

Photos 11−1A and 11−1B: For reasons of convenience, a bag with a larger opening (A) is generally preferable to one with a small opening (B). It is easier to get large items into the bag (A) and it is easier to pack. For reasons of security as well as convenience, a bag with a three-sided opening (A) should always have a double zipper (two tabs), an important consideration as it will permit you to open partial sections of the bag. This feature is of considerable importance to the touring cyclist who carries a sizable load.

all weight to the point of the triangle. This assists in convenient, solid placement of heavy objects. If properly packed, box-shaped panniers are also acceptable; however, greater care must be taken to securely pack heavy objects since the box-shaped panniers lack the convenience of the triangular-shaped panniers.

Sufficient gear must be packed to fill the compartments to eliminate bouncing around. In addition, the load must be equally distributed between the two sides. Heavy objects should be packed close to the centerline of the bicycle. When attaching the panniers to the racks, try to keep the packs as close to the center of the bicycle as possible.

The front panniers should be attached as far toward the back of the bicycle as possible and the rear panniers should be attached as far forward as possible.

Proper bag placement is important to maintain correct riding technique and position. You should not have to alter your riding position because of the placement of bags. This becomes very crucial if you have large feet, long crankarms, or short chainstays. Before you buy a set of rear panniers check to see if you have adequate heel-to-pannier clearance and if you are able to pedal freely without the bag hitting the undersides of your thighs with each pedal stroke.

Photo 11–2: Good-quality panniers use stiffeners to help the bags retain their shape and keep from bending into the wheel. The Kirtland bag uses an aluminum stiffener to which the spring-mounting system is riveted.

The use of front panniers is a controversial issue because the slightest overweighting of the front wheel can cause shimmying and instability. On the other hand, the use of front panniers helps to provide proper bicycle balance and reduces the tension on an overloaded handlebar pack. You shouldn't carry much weight in a handlebar pack because the steering stability is reduced as the weight of the load is increased.

Great care must be taken in choosing front panniers. In theory, rear panniers will work on the front wheel. Some manufacturers like Eclipse, Touring Cyclist, and Kirtland, make a smaller, narrower set of panniers to fit on the front of the bicycle. These packs can also double as rear panniers when a small load is being carried. Again, we must

stress that front loading can accentuate a high-speed shimmy to dangerous limits. Never start on a tour packed front and back without taking a test run. Reposition and retest the equipment until you feel comfortable and safe. Only then should you attempt an extended trip.

Pannier stability many times depends more on the rack or carrier than on the bags. Panniers must fit securely and not shift on the rack when riding under normal conditions.

Panniers attach to each other and the rack by various methods. Some manufacturers use sophisticated variadjustable spring-suspension systems. Others use combinations of buckles, snaps, elastic loops, and Velcro fasteners. Which is better? In most

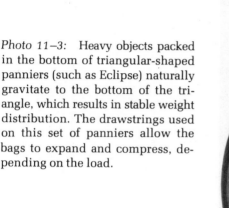

Photo 11–3: Heavy objects packed in the bottom of triangular-shaped panniers (such as Eclipse) naturally gravitate to the bottom of the triangle, which results in stable weight distribution. The drawstrings used on this set of panniers allow the bags to expand and compress, depending on the load.

cases, the spring-suspension systems are more secure and less likely to move around, but simple systems are more readily reparable on the road in the event of a malfunction. Whichever pack you choose, the mounting hardware must be durable, weather resistant (able to withstand the scorching sun as well as torrential downpours), easy to mount, and fasten securely.

It is more convenient and more functional for panniers to attach directly to the rack, leaving the top of the panniers clear for placement of light, bulky items such as tents and sleeping bags. Panniers that snap together are convenient when using planes or trains on a tour. Your panniers can be carried as luggage. Be sure that the handle on the panniers for off-bike use is strong and comfortable enough to haul the loaded panniers.

Some panniers convert into backpacks. Make sure the conversion is comfortable, otherwise it's not worth the additional price.

Many manufacturers compartmentalize their panniers for easy access, better organization, and the separation of clothes and food from fuel and greasy tools. Although compartments are nice, too many can complicate packing. Separate compartments are good for organization; however, one compartment is the best for bulky items.

Thought should also be given to additional uses of the panniers. If you travel a lot, panniers with many compartments are best for organization of toiletries, clothes, and books. If, however, you use panniers to carry groceries, it's easier and less time consuming to stuff the entire grocery bag into a separate compartment.

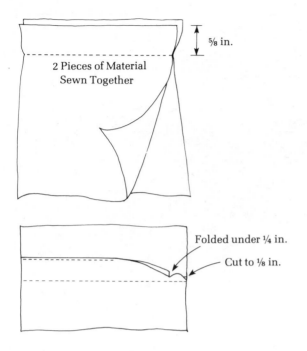

2 Pieces of Material
Sewn Together

⅝ in.

Folded under ¼ in.

Cut to ⅛ in.

Figure 11–1: A flat-fell seam is used by many touring bag manufacturers. It is strong, free of bulk, and does not leave any raw edges exposed. Two pieces of material are sewn together and then pressed to one side. The lower seam allowance is cut to ⅛ inch. The edge of the top seam allowance is folded under (¼ inch) and stitched very close to the folded edge.

Handlebar Packs

Nothing less than the best handlebar packs should be considered. What constitutes the best? Like all other packs, they are nylon coated with a waterproofing substance, but more importantly, they must be entirely stable on the handlebars. Although it is difficult to place values on safety, panniers may cause shuddering and instability but generally only at high speeds, whereas an unstable handlebar pack can create adverse steering at any speeds.

Most good handlebar bags have some kind of support. Otherwise it would be impossible to keep a handlebar bag stable. The support system should securely fasten to the bicycle and in turn, the bag should securely fasten to the support. There should be no movement between handlebars and support or support and bag once everything is se-

cured. Some bags use a shock-cord suspension system which gives additional stability. Test-ride it. The importance of a properly mounted handlebar pack cannot be overemphasized—it is extremely difficult to control the bicycle with a poorly mounted bag. In emergency situations, a marginally designed bag can drastically reduce the chances of escaping a crash.

Handlebar bags are sometimes difficult to mount and may be incompatible if the front end of the bicycle is cluttered with reflectors, lights, stem shifters, or safety brake levers. In such cases, it's best to modify the bicycle by removing the safety levers (or whatever else is in the way), rather than trying to make do and squeeze everything together. The riding position is a vital safety concern and the position of the bag should

Photos 11–4A, 11–4B, and 11–4C: Front handlebar bags must be well supported from the top *and* the bottom to insure stability. The Eclipse bag (A) uses elastic cords to secure itself to the fork ·dropouts (B) while the Kirtland bag loops around the bottom head tube lug (C). Both bags are rear-entry handlebar bags, which facilitate easy access while riding.

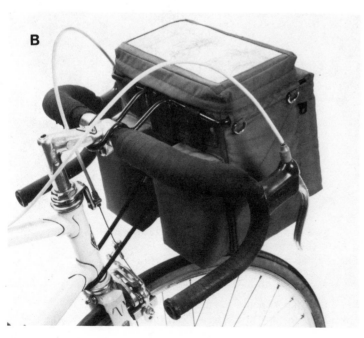

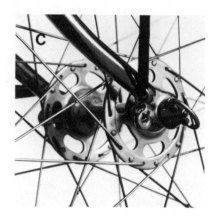

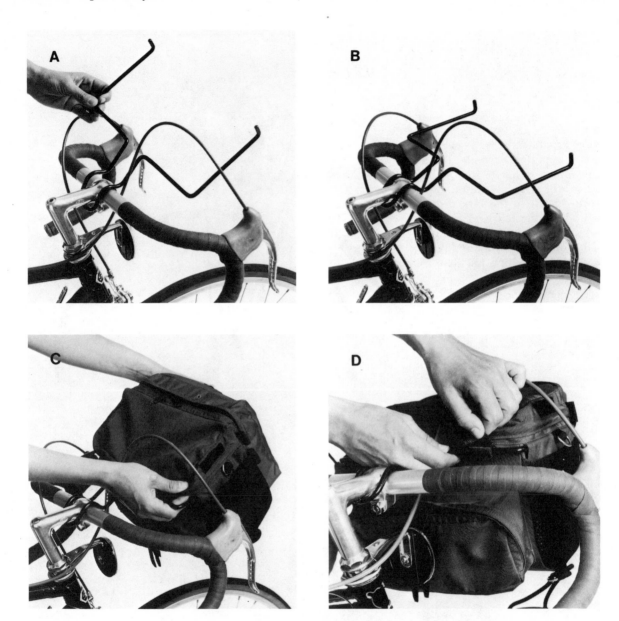

Photos 11–5A, 11–5B, 11–5C, and 11–5D: Front handlebar bags must be well supported from the top as well as from the bottom to insure stability. A number of quality bags use an uplift support rack. This rack must first be attached to the handlebars and stem as shown (A and B).

Then the rack is slipped through a special sewed-on casing on the bag (C). Finally, Velcro fasteners are used to firmly secure the bag to the rack (D).

Photo 11–6: If you need to carry a heavy load in your handlebar pack, you might want to consider attaching it to the rear of your bicycle. Eclipse makes a special seatpost attachment which allows you to mount a front handlebar bag on the rear.

Note: you must have proper clearance between the bottom of the pack and the tire.

Photo 11–7: Many front handlebar bags are available with shoulder straps, which make them ideal for off-the-bike use.

allow your usual placement of hands in all the various handlebar positions. The bag should not interfere with braking nor should it sag on the front wheel.

Although handlebar bags should fasten securely to the bicycle, they should also detach quickly for convenient off-the-bike use. Some have attachable shoulder straps and can double as carryalls. For extended off-the-bicycle use, check to make sure that the carrying strap securely attaches to the bag and hangs comfortably from your shoulder.

The handlebar pack is the most easily accessible storage area on the bicycle. Consequently, most quality bags are constructed with a number of pockets, dividers to assist in organization, and rear-entry openings for convenient use while riding. Some packs also include transparent map cases to protect maps from sun and rain. Map cases are found on almost all handlebar bags, but unless securely fastened they will distort and curl up. A map case on the inside of the pack is more waterproof.

Touring Bag Characteristics

	Capacity	Cost	Recommended Features
Handlebar Bag	Varies between 325–750 cubic inches	Moderate to very expensive	Good, sturdy support system
			Easily accessible while riding
			Waterproof map case
			Double zipper
			Three-sided opening
			Carrying strap for off-the-bike use
Seat Pack	Varies between 130–250 cubic inches	Moderate	Long straps for secure fit on saddle
			Strong buckles
			Well supported from the bottom
			Double zipper
			Three-sided opening
Front Panniers	Varies between 900–1,100 cubic inches	Expensive	Double zipper
			Secure mounting system
			Narrow, wedge-shape design
			Easily adapted as rear panniers
Rear Panniers	Varies between 900–2,500 cubic inches	Expensive to very expensive	Double zippers
			Compartmentalization
			Secure mounting system
			Carrying straps for off-the-bike use

Seat Packs

Seat packs have traditionally been used to carry tools and tire-repair materials. When originally conceived, these tool bags were small and compact—large enough only for the required tools. Fashion soon started dictating larger bags, and the original tool bag became a seat bag with room for tools and more.

Since most seat bags bounce and sway, it is best to stay away from seat bags for serious use. A properly supported seat bag can be functional. Unfortunately, this little bag has been usually slighted in the design phase and becomes annoying in use. Unless the bag is firmly attached at the bottom as well as at the top, it has a tendency to bounce around. An alternative is to buy a bag that is the same size as the vertical area between the saddle and the rear rack. This reduces movement since the top of the bag is fixed to the saddle and the bottom of the bag rests on the rack. For many bicycle riders this is an impractical solution since this measurement on individual bicycles can vary greatly.

If you're convinced that a seat pack is the most practical and appropriate bag for your riding style, be sure that the straps securing it to the saddle are long enough and placed correctly to attach to your saddle. Many times, manufacturers do not make the straps long enough to wrap around saddle wires (which is necessary with better-quality saddles that do not have bag loops).

A

Photos 11–8A and 11–8B: The Pletscher alloy rack (A) is inexpensive and great for light loads. Its single-strut support system cannot support very heavy loads. The rack attaches to the rearstays, with the struts attaching to the eyelets on the dropouts. Purchasers of the Pletscher rack should consider buying a vinyl-coated rack support (B). It eliminates slippage and protects the bike's paint finish.

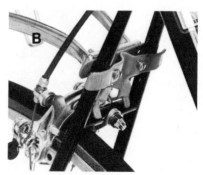

B

249

Miscellaneous Bicycle Packs

For riders requiring additional carrying capacity, other types of packs are available, including frame packs and a wide assortment of add-on rack-mounted packs.

Before you purchase any additional capacity packs, reevaluate your requirements. Many experts believe that if you cannot fit all your gear in front and back panniers, a front handlebar pack, and seat pack (allowing room for tent, sleeping bag, and foam pad on the rack), then you are carrying too much equipment. Some rack-mounted packs are useful for holding a sleeping bag; however, you can achieve the same results for less money by using waterproof stuff bags and elasticized cords.

Mid-frame packs are made to attach within the main triangle, the most stable section of the bicycle. The width of mid-frame packs is extremely limited because they must allow unrestricted pedaling motion. Obviously, the thin pack does not accommodate a wide variety of contents.

Proper Care of Bicycle Bags.

As suggested earlier, all seams on bicycle bags should be sealed. The nylon packs are all hand washable with a mild detergent. Don't use strong detergents because they can weaken the waterproofing of the bag. Before you wash your bags, check the manufacturer's instructions. Some bags are machine washable! If your bag does not include any specific washing instructions, wash it by hand with a mild detergent.

Before washing bags, remove all detachable stiffeners. If there are permanent stiffeners in the bag, you must check to see if they will hold up when immersed in water. Aluminum supports will; cardboard will not. If they are not immersible, the bag must be dry cleaned.

If your touring bag is old and has lost its original shape, you don't have to throw it away. A number of manufacturers make racks (excluding racks for panniers) that keep bags from sagging. For instance, both the Park Tool Company and TA of France produce front racks that will keep a handlebar bag from rubbing on the front wheel. By attaching some Velcro fasteners to secure the bag to the rack, a sagging bag can be made ready for another 10,000 miles.

Bicycle Racks

Bicycle racks must securely fasten to the bicycle. Racks that attach to a brake bolt or braze-on frame fittings are the most stable. Some manufacturers have developed excellent racks that clamp onto the seatstays. With racks, it's important to be especially critical. We have seen many racks that looked secure but slid down during a ride and required repairs on the road.

Double-support rods will increase the strength of a rack under heavy loads, as they help distribute the weight between both supports. We have seen many racks with single supports bend because too much weight was carried. Racks with single supports are designed for carrying light loads for the casual rider. If used according to the manufacturer's instructions, a $7 Pletscher aluminum rear rack will last and perform admirably provided an adapter is purchased to keep the rack from sliding down the framestays.

For the serious tourist, a $20 double-

A

Photos 11–9A and 11–9B: **Front Handlebar Bag Supports.** Front handlebar racks are made to keep the front bag from riding on the front wheel. Support A, made by TA, attaches without any trouble to a Mafac centerpull brake, but must be altered for use with other brakes.

Support B, made by the Park Tool Company, fits around the handlebars and can be used with most bags provided there is enough clearance between the rack and the tire.

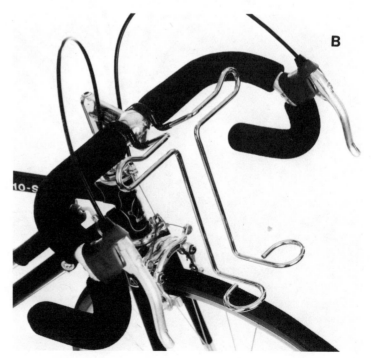

B

support rack is a necessity. Remember to match the rack with the intended panniers. The world's best rack may not provide the support required for your pannier selection. Your bicycle shop is the place to get recommendations and trial tests.

Photo 11–10: **Bungee Cords.** Bungee cords are stretch cords with a vinyl-coated hook on each end. These cords come in various sizes and are ideal for strapping down tents, sleeping bags, and other camping equipment on touring racks.

Photos 11–11A and 11–11B: The strongest and most durable touring racks incorporate a double- or triple-strut support system.

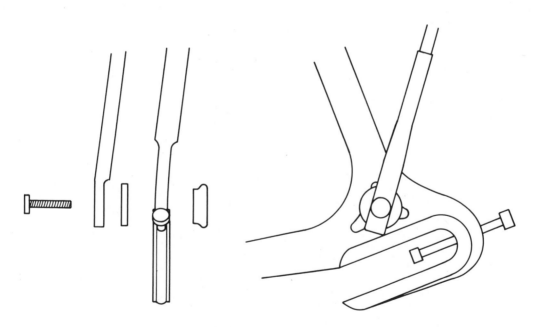

Figure 11–2: **Custom Eyelets.** Jim Blackburn offers "custom eyelets" which can be used to attach a rack or fenders to bicycles without eyelets on the dropouts.

Rules of Thumb

- Using a knapsack or small backpack for short distances is acceptable as long as it is securely fastened to your back. On longer rides, it is best to secure your gear to the bicycle. Carrying a load on your back in the bent-over position strains the back, shoulders, and arms. In addition, it can drastically affect your balance on the bicycle if the load shifts.

- Always select bicycle panniers that provide a low center of gravity and can be mounted as far toward the center of the bicycle as possible without interfering with your pedaling.

- Maximum load weight for handlebar bags should not exceed 10 pounds.

- Always load heavy items at the bottom of touring bags to keep the center of gravity low.

CHAPTER TWELVE

BICYCLE ACCESSORIES

A wide assortment of bicycle accessories is available at bicycle stores. Often it is difficult to sift through the piles of equipment to determine what is really useful or necessary. The difficulty is compounded by an influx of constantly changing products, cheaper versions of successful products, and antiquated products that would be best appreciated as memorabilia.

In the preceding chapters, we have pinpointed the advantages and disadvantages of various components and how they relate to their intended use. Since accessories are not mechanically complicated, in this chapter we provide brief descriptions and recommendations of some useful accessories.

Except for lights and locks, all the other accessories that are examined here are incidental to cycling. Nonetheless, they make life on the road more enjoyable. Lights, however, are mandatory if you intend to ride at night. Similarly, locks are required if you plan to leave your bicycle unguarded.

LIGHTS

There are basically two types of lights: battery and generator. Although there are many companies that produce bicycle lights, the best-quality lights are made in France. During the bicycle boom in the early 1970s, the Wonder Lite became a generic term for the arm/leg light. This French company (the Wonder Corporation) set the standard for quality arm lights. Although there are many other arm lights on the market, the Wonder Lite still reigns supreme. The Wonder Corporation has expanded and now produces a series of battery-operated bicycle headlights and taillights which are widely available. These lights are durable, light weight, and powered by French 4.5-volt sealed batteries.

Although there are many other battery-powered bicycle lights, few provide the reliability, visibility, light weight, and durability of the Wonder Lites. They are made of impact-resistant plastic and consequently do

Bicycle Light Characteristics

	Advantages	Disadvantages	Recommended Use
Arm/Leg Light	Light weight Noncorrosive Visible to motorists, especially when placed on the left leg Stays on when stopped Inexpensive	Easily misplaced if not attached to bicycle Does not provide light on the road Light gradually fades as a result of battery weakening Frequent need to replace batteries Not bright enough for off-bike use Adjustable strap loosens while riding	In conjunction with battery- or generator-operated headlight and taillight
Battery Light (plastic)	Can be used off the bike Easily detachable Durable Noncorrosive Stays on when stopped	Easily misplaced if not attached to bicycle Easily stolen Light gradually fades as a result of battery weakening Frequent need to replace batteries	For short commuting rides
Battery Light (chromed steel)	Always ready to use since permanently attached to bicycle Difficult to steal Inexpensive	Highly prone to corrosion Light gradually fades as a result of battery weakening Frequent need to replace batteries Added permanent weight to bicycle	For short commuting rides
Generator Light (plastic)	Noncorrosive Always ready to use since permanently attached to bicycle Difficult to steal Light is bright while riding Inexpensive to operate	Tire wear as a result of generator riding on tire Increased pedal resistance Wires can break or detach Lights go out when not riding Bulbs burn out when riding downhill at high speeds Added permanent weight to bicycle Expensive	Touring

	Advantages	Disadvantages	Recommended Use
Generator Light (chromed steel)	Always ready to use since permanently attached to bicycle Difficult to steal Light is bright while riding Inexpensive to operate	Same as plastic generator light plus highly prone to corrosion Expensive	Touring
Belt Beacon	Light weight Extremely visible to motorists	Easily misplaced if not attached to bicycle Does not provide light on the road Frequent need to replace batteries Light gradually fades as a result of battery weakening	In conjunction with battery- or generator-operated headlight and taillight

not rust; their enclosed battery is protected from corrosion; and they are easily mounted on the bicycle.

Generator lights provide improved visibility, but like battery-operated lights, they do not provide totally adequate lighting for safe, night riding. In the past, generator lights were made of chromed steel and like the chrome-steel, battery-operated lights, they tended to rust quickly. Today, Marchal (producer of the French Soubitez generator lights) manufactures the best lightweight generator sets. Use of chromed plastic eliminates rust and corrosion. Improvements have been made on the reflection and projection of the light beams by simulating the optical systems used for car headlights.

What follows are a few observations on types of lights currently on the market:

• The Belt Beacon is a battery-operated light that can be attached to the bicycle or the bicyclist. Models are available that flash between 40 to 60 times per minute. This blinking action draws the motorist's attention to the cyclist's presence. The Belt Beacon does not, however, provide any assistance in helping you to see the road.

• The Wonder Head Lite and Tail Lite are easily adjustable to provide the maximum lighting for the wattage. The only difference between the two is the color of the lens—white on the front and red on the rear. Both provide good lighting for off-bike use in cyclo-touring.

• The arm/leg light is easily attached and operates on two C batteries. There is a red lens for the rear and a clear lens for the front. Be sure the adjustable strap has a good buckle. Otherwise, the light will have a tendency to slip and slide around while riding.

LOCKS

Along with the tremendous growth in cycling has come an increase in bicycle thefts. Many unsuspecting cyclists have fallen prey to the bicycle thief. We constantly reminded our customers to lock up their bicycles at all times. Many would say, "it'll be alright; I'm watching it." Watching it? It only takes a split second to ride off on an unlocked bicycle and it happened in front of our store at least two or three times a year. We cannot overstress the importance of locking your bicycle. But remember: the best lock you can buy is only a deterrent.

For maximum protection with either a cable or chain, loop it through both wheels and the frame. Many cyclists have returned to their bicycles to find one wheel missing. You are only inviting trouble when you leave a wheel unlocked. It is too easy for someone to take your wheel. Although wheels that use quick-release hubs are a target for such a theft, wheels with nutted hubs are not immune—all it takes is a small four-inch crescent wrench to relieve a bicycle of its wheels.

When locking your bicycle, be sure that your locking system is as high off the ground as possible. This makes it more difficult for the thief to use the ground as leverage for bolt cutters or to use a hammer to smash your lock against the ground.

A cable is a more practical security device for bicycle use than a chain. The heavyweight characteristics of chains make them incompatible with the lightweight 10-speed. Be sure your cable is long enough to lock the entire bicycle. Usually 6 feet is required. Cables are encased in a thin vinyl coating which protects the bicycle against scratches. A cable that has a diameter of $7/16$ inch will provide adequate protection from the novice bicycle thief.

The self-coiling cable is light and easy to use. Its six-foot length can be easily carried and stored under the bicycle seat. To retain its self-recoiling properties, the cable thickness must be kept below one-half inch. Consequently, this cable, in combination with a lock, provides only a moderate amount of protection.

The horseshoe-type Citadel and Kryptonite locks offer maximum protection, yet limited parking options. The bicycle must be locked to a pole the size of a parking meter, that is long enough to prevent the thief from lifting the entire bicycle up, and over, the pole. These locks usually come with an anti-theft guarantee which pays you up to $200 toward the purchase price of your bicycle if it is stolen. Read the guarantee carefully as they differ between manufacturers.

PUMPS

There are two types of pumps for bicycles: the hand pump and the foot pump. Good-quality hand pumps are designed to be carried on the bicycle frame in case of emergency. They are not designed for everyday use. The thrust of the pump is too short to be able to consistently inflate the high-pressure tires used on almost all 10-speed bicycles today. We have, on numerous occasions, listened to cyclists complain because their pump could not get 90 pounds of pressure in their tires. Usually they were trying to pump air into tires that already had 80 pounds of pressure. Unfortunately, the last 10 pounds of pressure are the hardest on a pump since the tire is at its maximum expansion and the largest amount of air must be compressed.

Foot pumps, on the other hand, are made for daily use. A good foot pump is durable and reliable. It can afford to be since weight is not a consideration. Foot pumps are made of heavy-gauge steel.

Both hand and foot pumps are available with either Presta or Schrader valves. Although it is possible to use a Schrader pump on a Presta valve with the use of an adapter, there is less air loss when the Presta pump is used with the Presta valve.

SPEEDOMETERS AND ODOMETERS

Traditionally, speedometers and odometers have been unpopular with serious cyclists. Although it is nice to know how far and how fast you have traveled, most mechanical speedometers create a small amount of friction, make it difficult to remove the front wheel, and speeds in excess of 8 mph can be incorrect. Usually, speedometers are accurate within a given range, but you never know what the range of accuracy is.

In June 1976, Chester Kyle reported his results on speedometer accuracy in *Bicycling!* magazine. Kyle found that certain mechanical speedometers were only accurate between 14 and 19 mph, others between 15 and 25 mph. The most accurate was the Schwinn–Huret speedometer which was accurate within 1 mph between 5 and 25 mph. All of the tested mechanical speedometers were grossly inaccurate over 30 mph.

Odometers are also inaccurate and most are unable to adequately function at speeds in excess of 15 mph. For many cyclists, the odometer is an annoyance because of the ticking noise as the striker contacts the recording mechanism.*

*Huret produces a totally silent odometer—the Multito. There is not a striker to disrupt the tranquility of your ride. It gives you two readouts, one with the cumulative mileage total and one with the individual trip total.

For the casual cyclist, speedometers and odometers can be used to measure progress toward a mileage or speed goal. The readings, however, have to be taken with a grain of salt because they are not 100 percent accurate.

WATER BOTTLES AND HOLDERS

Most water bottles are made of plastic, and they usually hold about one pint of liquid. These bottles usually come with a snap-on plastic cap and pouring spout in the center. A few come with a second cap attached. This perforated cap is used for spraying yourself while riding on really hot days.

The flask is another type of water bottle. The flask's capacity varies from one-quarter to one-half pint and it is usually tucked away in the rider's rear jersey pocket.

Water-bottle holders (or cages) attach to the down tubes or seat tubes or the handlebars. Since the method of attachment is different, down tube and seat tube bottle cages cannot be fitted on the handlebars and handlebar bottle cages cannot be attached to the down tube or seat tube.

Frames with braze-on fittings use bottle cages that are bolted into the fitting. Frames without the braze-on fittings require mounting clamps.

Water-bottle cages are made from spring steel, plastic, or light alloys. The plastic cages can break easily and do not retain their shape. The light alloys are great for weight reduction but we have found that they do not hold the water bottle as firmly as the steel cages. The spring-steel cages, especially those made by TA of France, are the most reliable, functional, and durable.

TIRE PATCH KITS

Tire patch kits for sew-up tires are different from those used for clincher tires. The clincher-tire patch kit includes patches, glue, and a sander while the sew-up tire kit has all the aforementioned articles plus a thimble, needle, and thread.

To fix a flat on a clincher tire on the road, you'll need a patch kit, a hand pump, tire levers, and a six-inch adjustable wrench to take off the wheel if you don't have quick-release hubs. If you don't want to be bothered patching a tube on the road, then carry a spare tube instead of a patch kit.

To fix a flat on a sew-up tire, all you need to do is to use the spare tire folded under your saddle. It is too time consuming to sit and repair a sew-up tire during a ride. You'll also need a pump.

TIRE-PRESSURE GAUGES

Tire gauges are available with ends to fit either the Presta valve or the Schrader valve. (They are not interchangeable.) Two types of pressure gauges are available—the dial and the pencil.

The dial gauge is expensive but it is easier to operate and more accurate. The pencil gauge is cheaper but requires a little bit of expertise to be able to read it without letting air out of the tire.

Although we have listed a number of accessories that you might find useful, we don't recommend that you clutter your bicycle with all of them, especially the handlebars. If you were to mount a water bottle, a light, a speedometer, a horn, and a rearview mirror on your handlebars, you would find that you literally would have no room for your hands.

Examine the advantages and disadvantages of each item you plan on attaching to your bicycle. If the disadvantages outweigh the advantages, then the answer is simple. Remember the bicycle is a beautiful, simple machine. Keep it that way.

Rules of Thumb

- Use extreme caution when riding at night. Most lights that are suitable for bicycle use are designed only to allow others to see you. The projected beam from a front bicycle light is usually not bright enough for you to see enough of the road ahead to prevent riding into chuckholes.

- When using a hand pump, the bicycle should be leaned against something solid to eliminate any movement. The rubber washer in the pump end (where the valve goes) should be wetted with saliva and then pushed on the valve. To reduce damage to the valve (excess pumping force can break off the valve), the pump should be held into position by wrapping one or two fingers around a spoke and a thumb around the tire.

- Not all "eyeglass" mirrors fit all eyeglass frames. Always check for compatibility. Be sure that the frame of the eyeglass mirror is flexible. This reduces the chances of the wire injuring the cyclist in the event of an accident.

- Whenever you leave your bicycle unattended, lock it. If you have to leave your bicycle for any extended period, use the U-shaped locks that provide maximum security. If these locks are not adaptable to the parking facilities that you use, make sure that your cable or chain is long enough to lock the entire bicycle to a strong, immovable object.

- Generator use on most sew-up tires is not recommended. The outer casing is generally too thin to sustain the frictional wear caused by a generator.

- When using the horseshoe-shaped lock, the front wheel must be removed to secure it. The lock is slipped around a stationary pole, around the seat tube, and through the wheels.

- If riding frequently at night, use of reflective tape on the bicycle, clothing, bicycle bags, and helmet adds greatly to your visibility with minimal additional weight.

- To remove the stale taste from your water bottle, put in some lemon juice with your next water refill.

- When testing the quality of arm/leg lights, insert the batteries, turn the light on, and shake it. Many lights have bad connections and do not stay on when you are riding over rough terrain.

- Whether or not you ride at night, the bicycle should be equipped with front, rear, pedal, and wheel reflectors for better visibility at dawn and dusk, or on dark, rainy days.

- Always check to see that your water bottle fits tight inside its holder. Frequently, riders lose their water bottles on bumpy roads and, in addition to losing the water, a crash can result. Bend the top of the water-bottle holder in slightly to increase its hold on the water bottle.

- Many cyclists who regularly commute leave a large heavy chain and lock permanently attached to a bicycle rack. This enables the cyclist to ride unencumbered by heavy locking devices, yet provides him or her with security at the final destination.

SETTING UP YOUR NEW BICYCLE

Many riders wind up purchasing bicycles from sources other than their local bicycle shops. This can cause problems since the bicycle may be partially, or incorrectly, assembled. You should take time to consider the advantages and disadvantages of purchasing your bicycle from a friend, a department store, or your local bicycle shop. Generally, most good bicycle shops are price competitive, model for model, with the major retail chains. *Frequently, the major chains revise their equipment specifications from the manufacturers' and you must be careful to compare the potential bicycle purchase on a component-by-component basis.* For instance, as we discussed in chapter five, all cranksets are not equal; check to see which cotterless crank is being offered.

The bicycle shop owner usually makes his living selling and servicing bicycles. Therefore, he must be willing to stand behind his product. On the other hand, the large department stores sell many products. Few of their other products require special expertise. The major retail stores will have trained technicians available to repair their dishwashers, clothes dryers, and television sets. But who do they have to assemble and repair their bicycles? If many bicycle stores lack qualifications to properly handle the lightweight 10-speed, what can you expect from the large department stores?

To illustrate two types of problems that are common, we would like to relate our personal experiences. To help get through the cold Michigan winters, our bicycle shop obtained a service contract with two large retail stores in our area. Specifically, we assembled the bicycles for sale and handled warranty work after the sale. We learned amazing things that we would never have known without the service contracts. For instance, we had to repair one bicycle that had a broken 3-speed hub. We were unable to locate any parts for the hub through any of our distributors. Our efforts led us back to the retail store where we discovered that their 3-speed hub had been manufactured to their individual specifications and that the parts were only available through their store! Six months later we were still waiting for the parts. Finally, we had to tell the customer to take the bicycle back to the department store and try to get their help in obtaining the parts. The point of this story is simple: the successful bicycle shop will not sell a product that it cannot stand behind because they know that they will be required to repair the bicycle if there are any problems. The large department store, on the other hand, usually does not perform repairs on their own bicycles.

Since we performed all of the initial assembly and setup for one major department store, we learned another interesting fact. Department stores generally offer bicycles that are not really price competitive with those offered by good bicycle shops. The department-store bicycle does not measure up, component for component. Consequently, in the department store, bicycle sales at the recommended retail price are relatively small. On a regular basis, however, the department store offers major "special sales" that are widely advertised. The sale price reflects the store's true acquisition cost of the bicycle (which will be lower for a major chain than for a small independent bicycle shop) and the bicycle *becomes* more competitively priced. During these sales, the actual volume of bicycle sales can be staggering.

We always recommend buying your bicycle from a reputable bicycle shop, but we are aware of the many options that are available to the consumer. Accordingly, the remainder of this chapter is devoted to the assembly procedures necessary for a bicycle that is delivered "in a crate."

Before you buy your bicycle you must decide on the proper size. Typically, department stores will only carry bicycles in 19- and 23-inch frames. Most bicycle shops will carry the full range of sizes from 19 to 25 inches in 1-inch increments. If you are in between sizes, you should visit your local bicycle shop to see how the correct-size bicycle will feel. Chapter one details the procedure for determining the proper frame size.

Assuming you have determined the proper-size frame, have selected your new bicycle based on your riding needs, and have made the purchase, you are now faced with the job of assembling it.

Readers that have an assembled bicycle, might want to perform some of the checks to make sure that the person who assembled the bicycle did it properly.

Before you remove the bicycle from the carton, you will need some hand tools (see Appendix I) and a place to work. Most bicycle cartons, or crates, are made similarly; they hold the bicycle in place with the front wheel, saddle, handlebars, stem, and pedals removed. Since the front wheel is not on the bicycle, we would suggest that you take the time now to rig up a place to hang the bicycle while it is being worked on (figure II-1 in Appendix II). The time savings and reduced aggravation are well worth the effort.

Step 1

Remove the bicycle from the carton. Be very careful to watch out for loose parts to prevent them from scratching the frame as you pull it out of the box. Remove all of the packing materials and inventory the parts to make sure you have everything you need.

Step 2

Install the saddle and seat pillar so the bicycle can be hung for easy servicing.

Step 3

Remove the back wheel.

Step 4

Examine the frame and components for possible shipping damage. Some common problems are bent or twisted forks (since most bikes are shipped without front wheels), scratched paint on the frame, and flat spots or dents in the wheels caused by someone dropping the crate. A sure sign of trouble is when the carton has a hole in it. Make a close inspection now, before the bicycle is assembled. It is infuriating to put the bicycle completely together before noticing a problem that will require a complete exchange by the store!

Step 5

Check the wheels for trueness (see chapter eight). You should not attempt to true a wheel unless you have first removed the inner tube and tire. Many times the manufacturer will use spokes that are slightly too long and if you tighten the spoke, it may puncture the tube.

You should remove both tires and tubes (see chapter nine). This is the only way to insure that (1) the spokes are not too long, (2) there are no sharp edges on the rim, (3) the rim strip has been installed correctly, (4) the tube is not twisted inside the tire, and (5) the tire is properly seated on the rim. After the inspection, inflate the tires to the proper pressure (it's printed on the tire sidewall).
Check the cones in the wheel hubs to insure proper adjustment (see chapter eight). Correct as required.

Step 6

Install the handlebars and stem (see chapter three). This step will normally require the

hookup of the brake cables. You may route the cables, but do not attempt to adjust the brakes until later.

Step 7

Install the pedals (see chapter six). Remember: the right and left pedals have different threads. To install the pedals, turn the pedal axle toward the front of the bicycle to engage the threads. Install (but do not tighten) the toe clips and straps if the bicycle includes them. Check to see if the cranks rotate easily. All too often, bottom brackets are filled with dirt and miscellaneous pieces of excess weld that eventually work their way into the bearings. If you suspect any problems, disassemble, clean, grease, and reassemble the bottom bracket (see chapter five).
Note: This problem is not restricted to only inexpensive bikes; some expensive factory-made bikes have very dirty bottom brackets when new!

Step 8

Clean all areas of the frame and the major components. Now apply a coat of wax and buff. This wax will reduce rust and it will make future cleaning easier.
Caution: Do not wax the sides of the rim where the brake blocks rub.

Step 9

Install the wheels (see chapter eight).

Step 10

Position the brake lever, hook up the hand brakes, and tape the handlebars. Install handlebar plugs (see chapter three).

Step 11

Hook up the derailleurs and adjust (see chapter seven).

Step 12

Wipe off any grease on the chain. Apply oil to the chain and wipe off excess.

Step 13

Install miscellaneous equipment included with bicycle—pump, water bottle, rack, reflectors, and other accessories.

Step 14

Adjust the saddle and toe-clip position.

Step 15

Going from front to rear on the bicycle, tighten every nut or bolt. Remember, do not overtighten. It's easy to strip some of the small "hardware."

Step 16

The good part. Test-ride the bicycle to check on the operation of every component.

Now you see why the department stores are happy to let the customer assemble his or her own bicycle. You should remember to perform an overall adjustment again in approximately 30 days. You will find that brake and derailleur cables will stretch dramatically when new. Also, the spokes will loosen in the wheels during the first 200 to 300 miles of riding, and they will require retensioning. Both of these problems will be reduced after the initial break-in period. This stretching process is the reason why most bicycle shops offer a free 30-day checkup.

Now that you have the bicycle completely assembled and ready to go, what do you do next? That's right; you go out and ride it. But, before you go, you should review some of the simple techniques explained in the next chapter that will make your riding safer and more enjoyable.

CHAPTER FOURTEEN

BASIC RIDING PRACTICES

The art of cycling involves much more than learning to balance a two-wheeler. Whenever we mention the need for more qualified bicycle coaches, most nonriders laugh and think we are kidding. Their usual response is, "I've been riding a bicycle since I was a kid. What are you going to teach me?" Rather than waste a lot of time trying to explain advanced cycling theory, we usually respond with a simple, easy-to-understand analogy. Most beginning tennis players pay for the services of a tennis instructor. Yet how complex is a tennis racket compared to a bicycle? Like a practiced tennis swing, the proper techniques for cycling cannot be learned without some kind of coaching.

The lack of bicycle coaching in the United States is the primary reason for our poor performances in international bicycle races. We have the money to afford the best bicycle equipment in the world and we have some of the finest conditioned, healthiest bodies in the world, yet we haven't won an Olympic cycling event in over 50 years!

Worse than the lack of good coaches is the problem of the small amount of cycling information in print. Some of the so-called experts propose theories which are totally incorrect! How is the novice to learn?

The first place to start is with your local bicycle club. Most are small and often difficult to locate. The best way to find your local club is through a bicycle shop that specializes in high-quality lightweight bicycles.

Hopefully, some coaching will be available in your local club. Unfortunately, few coaches have enough time to devote to the casual, recreational rider. Their attention is usually directed to the development of the racer. Presuming that you aren't able to find a coach to provide guidance, we have prepared a general summary of riding techniques that are aimed at the novice.

Let's start with how to get on the bicycle. Many novices mount the bicycle as they did when they rode as children. That is, "pushing off" from one side and, after the

Photos 14–1A and 14–1B: **Mounting the Bicycle—Proper Method**. While standing still, raise one leg over the back of the bicycle (A) and swing the foot onto the pedal. Place the foot into the toe clip at the *top of the pedal stroke*. (B) Push down with that leg and insert the other foot into the toe clip as the bike rolls ahead.

Photo 14–2: **Mounting the Bicycle—Improper Method.** Do not mount the bicycle by scooting along with one foot on the pedal and raising the other leg over the saddle after the bicycle is moving. This method is very unstable with lightweight bicycles.

bicycle is moving, swinging the leg over the saddle to the opposite pedal, similar to mounting a horse.

This method of mounting is not used on the 10-speed bicycle for two reasons. First, most serious riders use toe clips and straps on the pedals to maximize the efficiency of the pedal stroke. Mounting from one side while moving increases the chance of a crash. Second, the lightweight bicycle is not as stable at slow speeds as the heavyweight children's bicycle.

You should mount the standard bicycle by first swinging your leg over the back of the bicycle and onto the pedal on the side of the bike that is opposite your body. Before pushing off, backpedal (rotate the pedal in a counterclockwise position until it is at approximately one o'clock. Now put your foot into the toe clip. After the foot is properly

positioned, push down on the pedal to get the bike moving and lift yourself onto the saddle. Stop pedaling with the foot that is already in the toe clip at approximately the six o'clock position. Now put the other foot in the toe clip. After you learn to mount the bicycle smoothly you can practice inserting your foot into the toe clip while the pedals are rotating. The task is easier than it sounds because most good pedals have little tabs on the back of the pedal that are designed to tip the pedal into position for easy entry by the foot.

Now that we have you on the bicycle, what are the optimum positions while riding? The three basic positions for your hands on the handlebars are illustrated in chapter one. Let's look at the benefits of each position.

Handlebar Positions

	Advantages	Disadvantages	Recommended Use
Position 1	Little weight on hands; relieves sore hands Most comfortable, upright position for the body Position permits freedom of movement for the rider's head	Most wind resistance Difficult to gain leverage for increased speed Difficult to reach hand brakes	Recreational riding/ touring where speed is of secondary importance to enjoying the ride
Position 2	Only slightly more pressure on hands than Position 1 Comfortable position for body that allows the benefits of increased leverage on the handlebars to assist in climbs or against head winds. Relatively free movement of head Reduced wind resistance Easy to reach hand brakes	Slightly more pressure on hands and increased bend in back contributes to more upper body fatigue	Recreational riding/ touring when increased speed is desired such as uphill or against head winds
Position 3	Minimum wind resistance Optimum position for quick acceleration Easy to reach hand brakes	Greatest fatigue for upper body Maximum weight on hands	High-speed riding and racing Preferred position against very strong head winds

Once the saddle is correctly adjusted, several positions may be comfortable under given circumstances. Sitting toward the narrow front of the saddle is *never* comfortable while riding slowly. That position is designed for the times when the rider is pedaling very hard. Strong pressure on the pedals concentrates the rider's weight on the feet, not the saddle. The advantage of the narrow front saddle section is the minimal interference with the inside of the cyclist's legs.

This is particularly important in the case of the well-developed leg muscles of the conditioned athlete.

During general recreational riding, you should sit toward the wide, rear section of the saddle. This position provides comfort. Obviously, you can slide around anywhere between the two extremes to provide a change in the pressure points that are created in each position.

RIDING POSITION

We have now reviewed the three basic positions of the rider's hands on the handlebars. Let's continue this analysis of position to include the proper use of the body while riding the bicycle.

Maintaining a relaxed position is one of the key elements in cycling. Many people ride with their hands gripping the handlebars as if someone were trying to wrench the bars from their grip. Although you must maintain a grip on the bars, remember that the bicycle is designed to travel in a straight line without any effort except pedaling. If the bicycle requires your attention to ride in a straight line, something is probably misaligned.

You should not be expending energy on the bicycle unless it benefits your pedaling. Imagine how tired you would become while sitting in your living room with a "death grip" on a pair of handlebars for two hours. Relax; *all* of your energy should be aimed at making the bicycle go faster. Don't allow your energy to "run out" through your handlebars.

When riding in any of the three handlebar positions (on the tops, behind the brake lever, and on the drops), the rider should concentrate on keeping his or her elbows bent slightly. One of the prime reasons that some riders find this uncomfortable is because their bicycle setup is incorrect. If you are experiencing difficulty when riding with your elbows bent (or you have specific neck or back pains when riding), review the portion of chapter one that details proper bicycle setup. There are several important advantages to riding with the elbows bent:

• Bent elbows provide a "safety buffer" in situations where a rider is bumped from the side by another rider. If a rider is riding with "locked" elbows and he or she is bumped, the possibility of a spill increases due to the reaction of the forks. If the elbows are relaxed, any sideward force will be absorbed by the elbow and arm, not the bicycle.

• The amount of bend in the elbow acts as a performance "multiplier." The position of the back determines, in part, which muscles are used during the pedal stroke. The large, powerful gluteus maximus muscles are not used unless the position of the back is below 45 degrees. The rider can increase the amount of bend in his or her elbows to adjust the angle of the back and bring these important muscles into play. Most recreational riders have mistakenly guessed that the racer uses the low position of the upper body simply because of improved aerodynamic efficiency.

PEDALING

Strictly speaking, intentional "ankling" is incorrect in spite of the many books and magazine articles that list its "benefits." None of the many coaches that we have spoken to advocate ankling. A review of the good European cycling books reveals that there is no mention of ankling as a benefit to cycling. The motion that has often been incorrectly described as ankling, is an exaggeration (or misunderstanding) of the motions used in walking. Let's review the motion of a person's foot taken during a single step before we cover proper pedaling technique.

1. As the foot is lifted, the heel naturally

precedes the toe in the upward motion of the leg. No one makes a conscious effort to raise the heel first. It moves first because the muscles controlling the foot are relaxed and the lifting motion of the leg is done by the muscles in the *upper* leg.

2. As the foot descends, the heel begins to lead the toe, in readiness to make contact with the ground; *the heel will touch the ground first, not the toe.*

3. The heel touches the ground first and, as the body moves forward, the person's weight is transferred to the ball of the foot and the motion continues.

If one is to believe the proponents of "ankling," the rider should move the toes down at the bottom of the pedal stroke. This is no more correct than it is to recommend the same motion when walking. Our muscles have functioned in a relatively fixed manner since we learned to walk. The most efficient pedal stroke utilizes the *natural motion* of the foot.

You can easily become misled when looking at the motions of a foot during the pedal stroke because, when a high rpm rate is maintained, the toe *will* precede the heel at the bottom of the stroke. The toe does not precede the heel because the rider consciously "pushes" the toe through first.

It occurs because the centrifugal force of the high rpm's does not allow a full drop of the heel. The opposite is true in the use of a high gear at low rpm's—the heel will often be as low as the toes.

There is one foolproof method to determine if a rider is ankling or if the lower leg is operating properly. Watch the calf muscles expand and contract during the pedal stroke. Watching from behind, check to see when the calf is under pressure (tight). It should occur only on the down portion of the stroke. If the calf is tight on the upward part of the

stroke, the rider is still pushing with the toes instead of concentrating on *pulling* his or her foot up. Muscles "rest" by receiving fresh supplies of oxygenated blood. Therefore, the rest period occurs during the relaxed position of the muscle. Obviously, a muscle that is under tension during twice as much of the stroke will tire faster than a muscle that is given more opportunity to "rest."

We hope that by providing these basic insights we can help you to understand the theory of efficient pedaling and that this better understanding will provide new outlooks and energy efficiencies.

Now that we have reviewed the majority of the theoretical aspects of pedaling and positioning, let's use real-life situations to illustrate the use of these techniques. To begin, let's assume that you have mounted the bicycle and you are riding on level ground at a comfortable pedaling speed of 70 rpm's.

After riding for a short distance, the inevitable happens; a hill is encountered. As you approach the hill, you should plan ahead so that your actions will be efficient and energy conserving. Maintain your pace at the bottom of the hill—don't be intimated by a hill. Soon you will notice that you must push harder and harder with each pedal stroke. Your pedal rpm's start to drop and your legs begin to tire.

If you are prepared, you will know which sprockets the chain is riding on and you will know how to best accomplish the reduction in gear ratios that is necessary. A couple of examples: You are riding with the chain on the large chainwheel in front and middle cog on the freewheel. If the hill is really steep, you will need to make a major reduction in the gear ratio in order to climb the hill comfortably. Probably, you would shift the front derailleur and use the small chainwheel. If on the other hand, the hill isn't too steep and only a small reduction in gear ratio is required, you might shift the rear derailleur to the next-largest cog to obtain lower ratios. Remember, only the very best derailleur will accommodate shifting under heavy pedal pressure. Plan ahead and ease up on the pedals when you shift. You must keep pedaling, but you can slightly reduce your pedaling effort to allow for a quick, smooth shift.

Presumably, you have reached the top of the hill and you now face the opposite situation. As you descend the other side, your speed increases with the assistance of gravity and your pedal rpm's increase rapidly. Depending on the grade of the descent, you should shift gears to appropriate ratios to maintain reasonable pedaling speed. Sometimes large hills will require more than one gear change on the ascent or descent.

After becoming familiar with your gear ratios, you will find it easy to maximize your efforts without becoming tired. The human body is very flexible and will adapt to widely varying conditions. It does operate best at certain levels, however; use the rule of thumb concerning leg versus lung fatigue to determine your optimum individual gear ratio.

As you become more familiar with your bicycle, you will notice that slightly different body positions will affect your cycling. Generally, you will find that you can spin your legs the fastest when you sit toward the front of the saddle. When climbing tough, steep hills, you may prefer to select a low gear and spin your legs while sitting fairly well back on the saddle or you may wish to select a high gear and sit relatively far forward on the saddle (thrusting at the pedals). These positions are primarily a matter of individual preference. One is not "better"

than the other. You should try each of them individually to determine your own preference.

BICYCLE HANDLING

Most riders are horrible "bike handlers" (a racing term that describes the rider's ability to control his or her bicycle) and it's not hard to understand why. Everyone must go through some type of normal training and evaluation to drive an automobile, yet there is no similar program for cyclists even though they both share the same highways! The problem is made worse since the 10-speed lightweight bicycle is far less forgiving of small errors than the automobile. Entering a corner with gravel usually has little effect on the automobile unless it is attempting to negotiate the corner at high speed. That same gravel at the corner means a crash unless the cyclist is very cautious.

Cornering

Riding a bicycle around a corner is no problem if you are going slowly. Many people have learned that it isn't quite so easy to control their lightweight 10-speed bike at the speeds that its performance permits. Safe and fast cornering requires proper "setup" which involves knowing the best "line" around the corner—negotiating the entrance, passing the "apex," and finally completing the "exit."

The proper "line" through a corner is usually the fastest and the safest way around a corner. It is the imaginary optimum path of travel around a corner. The theory behind cornering lines is simple. Cornering speed is

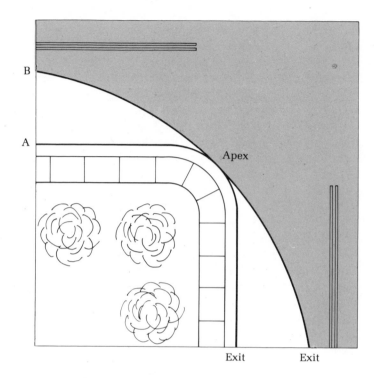

Figure 14–1: Two different lines through an identical corner.

maximized when the bicyclist "cuts" a corner with the least amount of actual turning. In the case of cornering, the shortest *actual* distance would be A in figure 14-1. In this case, the rider approaches on the inside of the road, and stays equally close to the edge of the road all the way around the corner. Although the distance in A is shorter than B, the cyclist riding on line A would be required to slow down considerably to negotiate the very tight radius that his or her "line" of travel necessitates. When cornering, the bicycle has a new energy acting on it —centrifugal force. That is, in addition to the force of gravity holding the bike to the road and the forward force caused by the rider pedaling, the cornering forces tend to push the bicycle *outward* on the curve. The tight radius of the rider's line requires turning the front wheels a great deal and any slippery road surface (gravel, sand, snow, or ice) will result in a crash since the bicycle will be forced out into the shadowed area. All of the forward force of the bicycle is concentrated in a corner with a very small radius, making the centrifugal forces greater and increasing the chances of a crash.

If line B is followed, the rider uses all of the road at his or her disposal. The corner is entered from the far side of the road. The rider's "line" goes from the outside of the road to the inside of the corner (called the apex) and out to the outside of the road for the exit. This results in a very large turn that creates smaller centrifugal forces which act against the bicycle. Theoretically, if the rate of speed is continually increased, the rider will eventually crash. Given the same speed, however, line B is a far safer line than line A on identical corners.

You can see that line B requires riding a slightly greater distance, yet it provides almost a straight line through the corner. The straight-line approach greatly limits risk of sliding or skidding. Every corner has a proper line which is easily determined by trying to minimize abrupt turning and maximizing the width of the road. This can be particularly important to the rider who is going too fast and encounters slippery conditions. Proper "lines" can make the difference between a crash or a safe ride.

Caution: When riding on public highways do not allow your "line" to cross into the path of oncoming traffic. On the street, your lines should attempt to straighten sharp corners within the boundaries of your lane.

Assuming you are able to determine the proper line through a corner, let's move on to the actual entrance and exit of the corner. If you are approaching a corner too fast, you will have to put on your brakes. Here is where many riders crash. Unlike a car where front and rear wheels are controlled by one pedal, the bicycle has separate brakes on each wheel. Improper balance between these two brakes can cause a spill.

The front brake does approximately 75 percent of the braking. This is caused by the "forward weight transfer" as the brakes are applied (notice how the front of a car dips as the brakes are applied hard). When applying the brakes hard while riding in a straight line, the only problem normally encountered is the reduction of weight on the back wheel caused by the forward weight transfer. Another example of this is the often reported, but rarely seen, phenomenon of the rider going over the handlebars if the front brake is applied too hard.

The back brake provides stability to the braking process. This is easily proven by a simple test. While riding at a safe speed, apply only the front brake. The back wheel will feel very light and you will sense that the seat of the bicycle is swinging back and forth out of control. Try the same test with the back brake used in conjunction with the front; the rear end will feel like it is following the front. To use the brakes properly, apply the back brake slightly *before* the front brake. Increase pressure on the front brake to control the degree of deceleration.

Since centrifugal force is pushing the bicycle outward from the corner, the real braking problem comes when riding around corners. If you apply the front brake too hard when leaning into a corner, the front wheel will slide out and you will crash. Conversely, if you apply the rear brake too hard, the rear end will slide out and you will *probably* crash. It is possible to correct a rear-wheel slide but it is virtually impossible to recover from a front-wheel slide. If the rear wheel starts to slide, remember, do *not* increase brake pressure. Accelerate instead. If you hold the handlebars firmly and accelerate smoothly, you may apply enough forward force to control the slide.

To reduce the possibility of a crash, brake as you *approach* the corner, ride past the apex, and accelerate smoothly out of the corner. In this way, the braking is done in a straight line while the bicycle is vertical. This provides maximum traction and stability.

In addition to mastering the careful application of the brakes and knowing what the best "line" is, there is another way to maximize cornering safety and speed— proper "body English" on the bicycle.

Since the bicycle is far lighter than its rider, it is easily affected by the rider's motions. This responsive handling can be used to increase the rider's speed through a corner. There are two accepted methods of cornering. The first involves pedaling through the corner and should be mastered before attempting the fastest method—coasting.

PEDALING THROUGH A CORNER

This method is important to master because it is necessary to achieve proper body position and rider confidence before attempting to learn the faster way around a corner. When pedaling around a righthand corner, the rider should attempt to keep the bicycle as upright as possible to reduce the possibility of hitting the pedal on the ground. To best accomplish this, the rider should bend the elbows slightly more than usual and move the upper body to the right until the rider's nose is approximately over the right hand.

On lefthand corners, the procedure is reversed. The body should lean to the left with the rider's nose over the left hand.

This method is effective until the rider leans far enough to hit the pedal on the ground and risks a spill. After you have learned to lean your bicycle to this point, you should learn to coast through the corner.

COASTING THROUGH A CORNER

To better understand why the correct body position used while coasting through a corner is effective, consider the primary factors that act on the bicycle when cornering at speed: the center of gravity of the bicycle and the traction of the tires.

When the weight of the rider is resting on the bicycle seat, the center of gravity is approximately three feet off the ground. The amount of weight on the seat decreases, of course, as the rider increases pressure on the pedals. Cornering power is increased as the center of gravity is lowered. Therefore, the rider should concentrate his or her weight on the pedals. The traction of the tires is influenced by tire construction, tire pressure, road surface, weight of the bicycle and rider, and the centrifugal force caused by going through the turn. Once the rider mounts the bicycle only one of these factors can be affected—centrifugal force (since it is related to the speed around the corner which can be varied). To increase cornering speed, the center of gravity of the bicycle must be lowered and traction must be maximized.

Specifically, a *righthand* turn should be accomplished as follows: The rider's nose is over the right hand. (This means that if a plumb line were dropped from your nose, it would fall just over the right hand.) The inside crank (right foot is in uppermost position) should be in the *up* position and the outside crank (left foot is in lowest position) should be in the *down* position.

The rider should concentrate his or her weight on the *outside* leg, effectively lowering the center of gravity as much as possible. In other words, the rider should stand on the outside pedal. With the outside crank in the down position, the center of gravity is very low and there is an additional benefit—the inside crank is up and will not scrape on the ground as the bicycle is leaned over.

A lefthand corner is negotiated similarly: Rider's nose is over the *left* hand. Inside crank should be *up*. Outside crank should be *down*. Weight on *outside* leg.

Some riders prefer to allow the *inside* knee to drop from its normal position near the top tube for improved balance; however, this is not required.

Fortunately, none of the material presented so far is nearly as difficult as it initially appears. It may take practice to perform the actions smoothly, but once the theory is understood, improvement comes quickly.

Another helpful hint: Whenever you encounter a large bump, chuckhole, or railroad crossing, you should let your bicycle escape the majority of the impact. This is easily accomplished by relaxing at the moment of impact. Do *not* push the bicycle into the point of impact. Instead, firmly grip the handlebars, flex your elbows, and concentrate your weight on the pedals, *not* on the saddle. The most stable position over bumps is found when the cranks are parallel to the ground. This position reduces the deadweight that causes bent rims and it lowers the center of gravity of the bicycle from saddle height. The bicycle will move freely under the rider with a minimum loss of control.

Riding with One Hand

Frequently, the rider is required to remove one hand from the handlebars whether it is to reach for a water bottle, signal for a turn, or shift gears. This can result in a potentially dangerous lack of bicycle control if not handled properly. The preferred method of one-handed riding can best be demonstrated by the riders in six-day bicycle races. When the rider pushes his teammate into the race, he always has his hand on top of the handlebar adjacent to the stem. With the hand near the center of the handlebars, the weight of the rider is as equally distributed on the handlebars as possible.

To prove the benefits of this position, perform the following test: Ride one-handed with your hand in Position 3 (at the bottom of the handlebars). Attempt a few swerves to the left and the right. Next, perform the same test with one hand in Position 2 on the handlebars. Finally, perform the swerve test with one hand in Position 1 on the handlebars. The difference in control between the three positions should be immediately obvious. Always put one hand near the center of the bars when riding one-handed.

Rules of Thumb

- Be careful when looking behind you while riding. Most riders will unconsciously swerve to the right when looking over their left shoulders. Similarly, the bicycle will swerve to the left when the rider looks over his or her right shoulder.

- More of the cyclist's power can be transmitted to the pedals if the rider's back is below 45 degrees. If you encounter a head wind or hill, *bend* your elbows slightly to lower your back which will allow greater use of the gluteus maximus muscles.

- Do not place your hands at the bottom of the handlebars (Position 3) when climbing a hill since this position causes too much constriction of the lungs. Ride uphill in handlebar Positions 1 or 2 to allow free breathing.

- Always apply the back brake slightly before the front brake to maximize stability.

- Try to pedal in "circles" rather than in an up-and-down motion. Since higher pedal rpm's are less fatiguing, you should concentrate on reducing the amount of weight on the pedals during the "up" part of the stroke. Normally, it is difficult to "pull" on the upstroke of the pedal because of the high rpm's. Simply reducing the amount of deadweight on the upstroke of the pedal will vastly improve cycling efficiency in all instances other than hill climbing.

- Adjust the position of your foot on the pedal according to your individual pedaling style and physique. The ball of your foot should be over the pedal axle as a starter. Position your foot farther into the toe clip if you are heavily muscled and you tend to be a "pusher" rather than a "spinner" (slow vs. fast pedal rpm's). Move your foot slightly out of the toe clip if you are lightly muscled and tend to pedal rapidly.

- Concentrate on relaxing as you ride and you will save energy that is lost by gripping the handlebars too tightly or by excessive movement of your upper body. Always ride with bent elbows, to allow shock absorption and improve bike control.

- Place your nose over your right hand when riding around righthand corners and place your nose over your left hand when riding around lefthand corners. This will shift your body position slightly and increase stability when cornering.

- Shift your weight to the pedals when crossing bumps, railroad tracks, or rough road. This action will lower your center of gravity and increase stability.

- If the gear you have selected is too high, your legs will fatigue before your lungs. If the selected gear is too low, your lungs will fatigue first.

- If you want to go faster or apply more force to the pedals, increase the amount of bend in your elbows.

- The wrist should be straight when using the "drops" of the handlebars.

RECOMMENDED TOOLS

FOR THE NOVICE

- Open-end wrench set
- 1 six-inch adjustable wrench
- 1 pair wire cutters
- 1 pair pliers
- 1 pair nine-inch slip-joint pliers
- 2 Phillips screwdrivers (size 1, small; size 2, medium)
- 2 standard screwdrivers (1 small, 1 medium)
- 1 can lightweight machine oil
- 1 tube of bearing grease
- 1 tire patch kit
- 1 small ball peen hammer
- 1 spoke wrench

FOR THE ADVANCED BEGINNER

All listed previously plus:

- Center punch
- 1 pair cone wrenches
- 1 pair needle-nose pliers
- 1 set miniature wrenches for brakes (8 to 11 mm.)
- 1 freewheel remover
- 1 third hand tool
- 1 chain tool
- Crank tools, as required
- 2 files (1 standard flat, 1 rat-tail)
- 1 plastic-tipped hammer
- 1 can Dri-Slide

FOR THE SERIOUS CYCLIST

All listed previously plus:

- Combination wrench set
- Pedal wrench
- Headset and bottom bracket cup tools
- Sprocket tool
- 1 set metric allen wrenches
- Wheel-truing jig
- Wheel-dishing tool, metric or standard, as appropriate
- Pedal dust cap wrench
- Additional screwdrivers, pliers, and other tools, as required

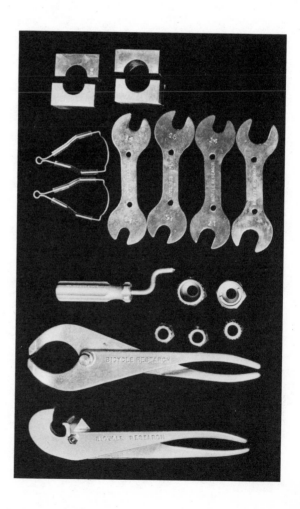

SHOP TIPS

For the cyclist who is interested in performing his or her own bicycle repairs, we have included basic repair information within each chapter for each specific component on the bicycle. Frequently, when the "mechanic" is unfamiliar with the equipment, minor adjustments cause more problems than they seem to correct. Hopefully, the technical information in the preceding chapters will eliminate any confusion over *how* to adjust or repair any standard bicycle component. To further reduce the possibilities of error, we will review the proper use of the hand tools necessary to adequately perform repairs. Although this sounds very basic, most minor cuts, abrasions, and bruises that plague the novice mechanic are due to lack of understanding of the basic hand tools.

If you intend to do a lot of work on your bicycle(s), you should devote a space in your garage or basement as a workshop. The shop does not need to be elaborate, but a few basic necessities can go a long way to making the repair work efficient and fun.

Most bike shops spend a lot of money for professional bicycle repair stands that are designed to hold the bicycle while it is being worked on. Do you need one? Yes! But, a perfectly adequate "holder" can be built with very little expense as illustrated in figure II-1.

In addition, you should have a place to store and protect your tools. Most people need a portable tool kit and choose to keep their tools in some kind of toolbox. Another alternative is to mount a sheet of pegboard on the wall and attach the tools to the board with hooks or brackets. Proper organization of your tools makes the work go faster and it tends to reduce substituting the use of an improper tool for the correct one simply because you can't locate the necessary tool.

Make sure you match each task with the

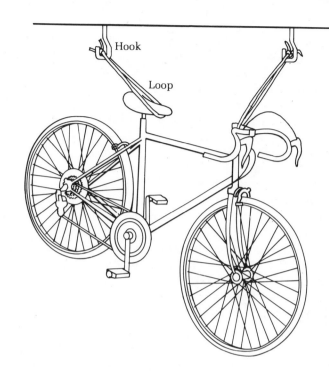

Figure II–1: To make your own "bicycle repair stand," attach two bicycle storage hooks to the ceiling approximately four feet apart. Tie a piece of rope in a loop and hang it from one of the hooks. The rope should be cut to the proper length to allow a convenient working height when the nose of the saddle is supported in the loop. The front of the bicycle is held by another longer loop. Loop the closed end of the rope under the handlebar stem and attach it to the bicycle hook. The rope should be long enough to insure that the front of the bicycle is lower than the rear or the rope holding the saddle will slide off.

right tool. To better understand good shop practices, let's review the design intention and use of specific hand tools.

WRENCHES

Using the benefits of leverage, wrenches multiply our strength. They are used to turn or hold nuts and/or bolts. There are several types of wrenches; each designed slightly differently.

The open-end wrench is open at each side of the handle. This type of wrench is very popular because each end is a different size and only a few separate wrenches are required to handle most common sizes of nuts and bolts. It is important to properly match the size of the wrench with the nut or bolt to be turned. If the wrench is too big, it may slip under pressure and could damage the nut or bolt and may result in a skinned knuckle. *Always* pull the wrench, do not push it. You are less likely to injure yourself when pulling the wrench.

The combination wrench is similar in design to the open-end wrench, except one end is closed. In addition, since both sides of the wrench are the same size, more are required to match all common nut sizes. The combination wrench is the same as an open-end wrench, except its closed end includes 12 miniature teeth to grip the nut. With only a 30-degree movement of the handle, the wrench will get a firm grip on the nut. This feature is particularly handy when a nut or bolt is in a tight place or when a large amount of pressure on the wrench could cause the wrench to slip. The box (or closed) end of the wrench will not slip as easily as the open end.

Variations of the above include box wrenches (both ends are closed), extra-short or extra-long combinations, and varying degrees of head offset for specific uses.

The adjustable wrench is the bicycle rider's first choice in an emergency tool kit. The opening of the jaws is adjustable and a six-inch adjustable wrench (named for the overall length of the tool rather than the jaw size) will fit every nut or bolt on the bicycle except the headset and bottom bracket. There are two very important rules in using the adjustable wrench: (1) Make sure the jaws have been adjusted tightly against the nut or bolt (if not, they can damage the bolt and make it difficult to remove), and (2) Always pull the wrench toward you, utilizing the fixed part of the jaw to do the pulling.

General Rules for Proper Use of Wrenches

• Always match the proper-size wrench with the nut or bolt to be turned.

• Do not hit the wrench with a hammer to "free up" a tight nut or bolt.

• Always pull the wrench toward you, do not push it.

PLIERS

Again, the principle of leverage is used to allow pliers to grip uneven surfaces with greater force than can be exerted by your fingers. There are several different types of pliers; each is designed to perform slightly different functions.

Vise-Grip pliers are unique from other pliers, since they lock and continue to hold in any set position even after you have removed your hand from the handle. Although they are very handy, extreme care must be exercised when using them, since their hardened jaws can mar the surface of whatever they are gripping. This tool is often used to hold a nut after the flats have been rounded as a result of using the wrong-size wrench.

Slip-joint pliers are very popular because the handle can be positioned in one of several grooves to vary the opening of the jaws. The primary advantage of this type of pliers is the large variation in jaw capacity. The unique shape of the jaws will hold almost any object firmly.

Combination pliers have two different jaw capacities because of their slip joint and, unlike the previously mentioned pliers, they include a built-in wire cutter.

Cutting pliers are not intended to grip. They are designed with hardened cutting surfaces and their sole purpose is to cut wire.

Although several other types of pliers are popular, we are not going to describe each one since they usually are a modification of one of the types previously mentioned.

General Rules for Proper Use of Pliers

• Do not use pliers in place of the proper wrench, since damage to the nut or bolt is likely.

• Do not use pliers as a hammer or pry bar. The alignment of the jaws will be affected.

• When using wire cutters, do not bend the wire back and forth against the cutting blades since the alignment of the cutters will be affected. The cutters should be of sufficient size to cut wire easily with normal hand pressure.

HAMMERS

Everyone thinks they know how to use a hammer properly but how many fingers have been bruised by improper use of the hammer? Hammers are available in several different configurations:

- The ball peen hammer is used when working with steel objects or punches since its striking head is flat (unlike the slightly curved head of the carpenter's claw hammer). Using a claw hammer for routine mechanical work will damage its head and make proper nailing difficult.
- The plastic-top or rubber hammer is used when hammering a soft surface (aluminum, for instance).
- Brass or aluminum hammers are used on surfaces that would be damaged if a steel hammer were used. The brass hammer is handy if a plastic hammer is unable to exert enough force. A brass or aluminum hammer is perfect for loosening stem expander bolts without scratching their surface.

General Rules for Proper Use of Hammers

- Always check to insure that the head of the hammer is tight on the handle before use.
- Never use the side of the hammer to strike an object.
- Take care to insure that the face of the hammer hits the object squarely to reduce the possibility of ricocheting blows.

SCREWDRIVERS

Although several different types of screwdrivers are manufactured to meet the demands of many different industries, only two types are required for bicycles.

- The standard screwdriver is available in varying sizes to match the size of the slot in the screw or bolt head.
- The Phillips screwdriver has two slots at right angles to one another. It is designed to permit easy leverage without the danger of blade slippage.

General Rules for Proper Use of Screwdrivers

- Do not use a screwdriver with a damaged blade—damage to the head of the bolt or screw will result.
- Always match the size of the tips of the screwdriver with the slot in the bolt or screw.
- Do not use a screwdriver as a punch or as a pry bar.
- Use the longest length screwdriver possible to maximize leverage.
- Extra leverage can be gained with screwdrivers that have flats near the handle. Use a wrench on the flats to gain twisting leverage only while applying force against the bolt or screw to minimize slippage.

Proper use of hand tools will insure minimum damage to your tools, your bicycle, and its components.

GEAR SELECTION
(27-inch wheels)

Number of Teeth on Sprocket	Number of Teeth on Chainring						
	36	38	40	42	44	45	46
12	81.0	85.5	90.0	94.5	99.0	101.2	103.5
13	74.7	78.9	83.1	87.2	91.4	93.4	95.5
14	69.4	73.3	77.1	81.0	84.8	86.7	88.7
15	64.8	68.4	72.0	75.6	79.2	80.9	82.8
16	60.8	64.1	67.5	70.9	74.2	76.0	77.6
17	57.2	60.3	63.5	66.7	69.9	71.5	73.0
18	54.0	57.0	60.0	63.0	66.0	67.5	69.0
19	51.2	54.0	56.8	59.7	62.5	64.0	65.4
20	48.6	51.3	54.0	56.7	59.4	60.8	62.1
21	46.3	48.9	51.4	54.0	56.6	57.9	59.1
22	44.2	46.6	49.1	51.5	54.0	55.2	56.4
23	42.3	44.6	47.0	49.3	51.6	52.8	54.0
24	40.5	42.7	45.0	47.2	49.5	50.7	51.7
25	38.9	41.1	43.2	45.4	47.5	48.6	49.7
26	37.4	39.5	41.5	43.6	45.7	46.7	47.8

47	48	49	50	51	52	54
105.0	108.0	110.3	112.5	114.7	117.0	121.5
97.6	99.7	101.8	103.8	105.9	108.0	112.1
90.6	92.6	94.5	96.4	98.3	100.3	104.1
84.6	86.4	88.2	90.0	91.8	93.6	97.2
79.3	81.0	82.7	84.4	86.1	87.7	91.1
74.6	76.2	77.8	79.4	81.0	82.6	85.7
70.5	72.0	73.5	75.0	76.5	78.0	81.0
66.8	68.2	69.6	71.0	72.5	73.9	76.7
63.4	64.8	66.1	67.5	68.8	70.2	72.9
60.4	61.7	63.0	64.3	65.5	66.8	69.4
57.7	58.9	60.1	61.4	62.6	63.8	66.2
55.2	56.3	57.5	58.7	59.9	61.0	63.4
52.9	54.0	55.1	56.2	57.3	58.5	60.7
50.8	51.8	52.9	54.0	55.1	56.2	58.3
48.8	49.8	50.9	51.9	53.7	54.0	56.1

Gear ratios not shown above may be calculated as follows:

$$\text{Gear} = \frac{\text{number of teeth on chainring}}{\text{number of teeth on sprocket}} \times \text{diameter of rear wheel in inches}$$

BIBLIOGRAPHY

Alth, Max. *All about Bikes and Bicycling: Care, Repair, and Safety.* New York: Hawthorn, 1972.

Ballantine, Richard. *Richard's Bicycle Book.* New York: Ballantine, 1974.

Belt, Forest H., and Mahoney, Richard. *Bicycle Maintenance & Repair: Brakes, Chains, Derailleurs.* Indianapolis, Ind.: T. Audel, 1975.

Bridge, Raymond. *Freewheeling: The Bicycle Camping Book.* Harrisburg, Pa.: Stackpole, 1974.

Browder, Sue. *The American Biking Atlas & Touring Guide.* New York: Workman, 1974.

Burstyn, Ben. *Bicycle Repair & Maintenance.* New York: Arco, 1974.

Central Sports School (C.O.N.I.) *Cycling.* Rome: F.I.A.C., 1972.

Cuthbertson, Tom. *Anybody's Bike Book: An Original Manual of Bicycle Repairs.* Berkeley, Calif.: Ten Speed Press, 1971.

Delong, Fred. *DeLong's Guide to Bicycles & Bicycling: The Art & Science.* Rev. ed. Radnor, Pa.: Chilton, 1978.

Humphrey, Clifford C. *Back to the Bike: How to Buy, Maintain, & Use the Bicycle as an Alternative Means of Transportation.* San Francisco: 101 Publications, 1972.

Bibliography

Kleeberg, Irene. *Bicycle Touring*. New York: Watts, 1975.

Kolin, Michael J., and de la Rosa, Denise M. *The Custom Bicycle: Buying, Setting Up, and Riding the Quality Bicycle*. Emmaus, Pa.: Rodale, 1979.

Leete, Harley M., ed. *The Best of Bicycling!* New York: Trident, 1970.

McCullagh, James C., ed. *American Bicycle Racing*. Emmaus, Pa.: Rodale, 1976.

Mohn, Peter. *Bicycle Touring*. Mankato, Minn.: Crestwood House, 1975.

Roth, Mark, and Walters, Sally. *Bicycling through England*. New York: H. Z. Walck, 1976.

Schad, Jerry, and Krupp, Don. *Fifty Southern California Bicycle Trips*. Beaverton, Ore.: Touchstone, 1976.

Sloane, Eugene D. *The Complete Book of Cycling*. New York: Trident, 1970.

Sutherland, Howard. *Sutherland's Handbook for Bicycle Mechanics*. Berkeley, Calif.: Sutherland, 1974.

Whiter, Robert. *The Bicycle Manual on Maintenance & Repairs*. Hollywood, Calif.: Laurida, 1972.

INDEX

E

D

F